MW00333095

Rethinking Pluralism

Ritual, Experience, and Ambiguity

ADAM B. SELIGMAN
ROBERT P. WELLER

OXFORD
UNIVERSITY PRESS

OXFORD
UNIVERSITY PRESS

Oxford University Press is a department of the University of Oxford.
It furthers the University's objective of excellence in research,
scholarship, and education by publishing worldwide.

Oxford   New York
Auckland   Cape Town   Dar es Salaam   Hong Kong   Karachi
Kuala Lumpur   Madrid   Melbourne   Mexico City   Nairobi
New Delhi   Shanghai   Taipei   Toronto

With offices in
Argentina   Austria   Brazil   Chile   Czech Republic   France   Greece
Guatemala   Hungary   Italy   Japan   Poland   Portugal   Singapore
South Korea   Switzerland   Thailand   Turkey   Ukraine   Vietnam

Oxford is a registered trademark of Oxford University Press in the UK and certain other countries.

Published in the United States of America by Oxford University Press
198 Madison Avenue, New York, NY 10016

Copyright © 2012 by Oxford University Press

All rights reserved. No part of this publication may be reproduced,
stored in a retrieval system, or transmitted, in any form or by any means, without
the prior permission in writing of Oxford University Press, or as expressly
permitted by law, by license, or under terms agreed with the appropriate
reproduction rights organization. Inquiries concerning reproduction outside the
scope of the above should be sent to the Rights Department, Oxford University Press,
at the address above.

You must not circulate this work in any other form and you must impose this same condition on any
acquirer.

Library of Congress Cataloging-in-Publication Data
Seligman, Adam B., 1954–
Rethinking pluralism : ritual, experience, and ambiguity / Adam B. Seligman, Robert P. Weller.
  pages cm.
Includes bibliographical references and index.
ISBN 978-0-19-991526-2 (hardcover : alk. paper) — ISBN 978-0-19-991528-6 (pbk. : alk. paper)
1. Pluralism. 2. Uncertainty. 3. Ritual. 4. Experience. I. Weller, Robert P. (Robert Paul), 1953–II. Title.
B830.S45   2012
390—dc23   2011046794

Printed in the United States of America
on acid-free paper

Marco Polo describes a bridge, stone by stone.

"But which is the stone that supports the bridge?" Kublai Khan asks.

"The bridge is not supported by one stone or another," Marco answers, "but by the line of the arch that they form."

Kublai Khan remains silent, reflecting. Then he adds: "Why do you speak of the stones? It is only the arch that matters to me."

Polo answers: 'Without stones there is no arch.'

Italo Calvino, Invisible Cities *(London: Picador, 1979), 66.*

This 'middle' means near the middle, for with respect to the exact middle, they have already said that no one knows the true central point except God alone.

Nachmanides, Commentary on Genesis, *ed. Charles B. Chavel (New York: Judaica Press, 2005), 71*

Contents

List of Figures

Acknowledgments

MANY FRIENDS AND colleagues—more than we can name—have given their time and lent an ear to us as we worked out the arguments in this book. We are grateful to all of them, as well as to the students in many iterations of our jointly taught class on ritual, which we have unscrupulously bent toward the aims of this book over the last few years.

We have also presented different aspects of these arguments, together and apart, in various venues. Especially helpful for us was our joint presentation at the Center for Myth and Ritual in American Life at Emory University, which helped us make the transition from heated discussions in our offices to committing ideas to paper. We are also grateful for the many helpful comments we have received from colleagues at various lectures: the Saler Lecture in the Department of Anthropology of Brandeis University; the Red House as well as the American Corner in Sofia, Bulgaria; the Law Faculty of the University of Hamburg; the Religare Meetings at the Belgium Senate; the Department of Ethnology at the Paissiy Hilendarski University of Plovdiv; the National University of Singapore; the Modern China Studies Seminar at Hong Kong University; and the Michaelsen Lecture at the Department of Religion in the University of California at Santa Barbara. Each of these served as a crucial testing ground for some of the ideas we develop here. The International Summer School on Religion and Public Life has provided a living laboratory, almost a crucible, where many of the insights that have been developed here were first apprehended. We are grateful for ten years of international staff, fellows, and local hosts at the school and the collective effort of which this is just a small icon.

We would also like to thank Bennett Simon and Steven Scully for reading and commenting on the Job/*Bacchae* interlude; Jonathan Klawans, Barry Mesch, and Nehemia Polen for their close reading and extremely helpful comments on the Red Heifer interlude; and Jay Berkovitz for generously sharing his knowledge of the development of Jewish law and Halachic reasoning in different periods. While we have not incorporated all of the comments (and often corrections) that we received, we have no doubt that it is a much better book for having been exposed to the critical comments of empathetic readers.

Introduction

ONE OF US had a friend in graduate school, Cathy, who was a very fine cook, but her grandmother was even better. Cathy would rave about her grandmother's wonderful cakes, with their perfect taste and texture every time—the best cakes in the world. Like a good modern cook, she asked her grandmother for the recipe. This turned out to be in vain, because her grandmother cooked in a different way. There had never been a recipe; the grandmother simply combined the ingredients by look, touch, sight, and smell. Thinking like the psychology graduate student she was, Cathy constructed a recipe by carefully observing her grandmother in the kitchen, measuring each ingredient before it went into the batter and writing down every action: this many cups of flour, that many tablespoons of butter. Armed with her newly notated knowledge, she returned to her own kitchen and baked the cake, only to be sadly disappointed. The cake was fine, but nothing like the original.

Thinking she had made an error, Cathy went back to her grandmother, carefully measuring, observing, and noting things once more. She did not find the simple notational error that she was looking for, however. Instead, every single ingredient measured out differently. She tried again with a third cake: different again, even though the result was as delicious as ever. The lesson she finally learned is that the perfect cake cannot be notated, but appears only in context. It is not the product of a recipe, but of unique interactions involving the cook's senses (how she packs her cup measure, how she stirs her batter), the temperature and humidity at the moment, the specific cooking utensils, and the particular histories of the ingredients (the fat content of the butter, how long the flour had been sitting on the shelf, and so on).

Cathy gave up on the recipe. Recipes let anyone bake a cake, but they let no one bake a perfect cake.

This is not a book about cooking, but it is about how we can deal with the intractable and untidy realities that make recipes and other instructive lists simultaneously so central to our lives and so inadequate to our needs. Much of human experience resembles those cake ingredients. It changes so constantly that even our bag of flour has different properties today from those it had yesterday. This is true of our understandings of ourselves, of the natural world, and of the social relations that surround us. All of these things are so complex and so variable that they force us to simplify, even just to see or think. Imagine, for example, those extreme close-up images of an unrecognizable terrain that we suddenly recognize as a human palm as the camera moves away. Only the simplification of distance and the loss of detail allow us to make sense out of the underlying complexity. Or recall the enormous burden of memory that Proust tastes in a cookie. Or think of the diplomatic impossibilities of dealing with a student who is also your waiter, your better in karate class, and the lover of a colleague. Out of all the infinite possible detail, which itself changes from moment to moment, what can we grasp on to? We must categorize, but every category pulls us away from the shifting and complex experience of reality. Every category thus leaves an ambiguous zone at its edges.

Ambiguity is built into our experiences and relationships, but we have to impose an order of some sort in order to live: this is the fundamental problem that we try to think through in this book. How can we create boundaries and transcend them at the same time? What grounds can we find to cross the lines that we must draw between categories of ideas, objects, and persons? How, to reduce this to a pressing social problem, can a genuine pluralism be possible, the ability both to accept and cross the boundary between "us "and "them"? Our first chapter is devoted to this problem of ambiguity, arguing that human existence and our need to interact with each other and the natural world force ambiguity upon us. The very production of categories to deal with those interactions, we argue, inevitably generates ambiguities and forces us to face the problem of how to deal with them.

Cake recipes are a subclass of one kind of solution to this problem. They reduce and simplify a shifting reality by giving us a checklist of rules to follow. We call this broad category "notation." It includes far more than cooking, of course. Any bookstore offers shelf after shelf of books with sets of rules for anything we want to do. There are all of the do-it-yourself manuals—the home shop equivalents of cookbooks. And just as Cathy found with her grandmother, those of us who try to learn plumbing or roof repair from a book quickly realize that it will never give us the skills of a veteran plumber or roofer whose extensive experience in many different contexts creates a kind of knowledge not captured in any list of instructions. There are also all the self-improvement books that offer us formulas to lose weight, cure addictions, get rich, appreciate fine wines, or win friends and influence people.

Then there are the social scientific attempts to distill ambiguities and complexities by elaborating new categories to name and simplify them. This book is no exception—all books are notations, and we have begun already by starting to limn the boundaries of terms like "ambiguity" and "notation." Classification remains a core piece of the scientific enterprise, as we try push further against the inadequacies of current categories to explain our data, and to develop new categories.

In contemporary societies, one of the most important forms of notation is the legal system. Sets of laws give us the rules that create one important basis for modern social life. They allow us, for example, to undertake a financial transaction with an utter stranger, or perhaps make a purchase over the Internet, and still feel confident that goods will be delivered. Laws are the way in which states notate social life. Lawyers are the people who best understand how to apply those rules as we draw up mortgages, wills, and deeds. But they are also the people who specialize in exploring the ambiguities at the edges of the law. Much of what happens in a courtroom, for instance, is not just the unearthing of facts in the style of Perry Mason. Usually all the facts are known to both sides before the trial starts. Instead, the lawyers work to clarify the ambiguities that always result when sets of rules run up against the complexities of real contexts. Arguments between prosecution and defense often center on exactly how the law applies in a given context. Every time a precedent is set through this process of interpretation, the legal system has attempted to reduce ambiguity a little bit more.

Chapter 2 carries this discussion much further, and it also makes the crucial point that notation can never fully resolve ambiguity. We cannot live without notation, but notation can never be complete. Just ask anyone who has never used a saw or a wrench before, but has tried to follow a home repair manual; or anyone who has never sewn to follow a dress pattern. We can return to cookbooks for an easy example. One of the most important cookbooks in the history of French cuisine is Auguste Escoffier's *Le guide culinaire*, first published in 1903. All of his recipes are short and direct, and quite impossible to follow without training. His recipe for a chicken fricassee with onions and mushrooms in a wine-cream sauce (*à l'Ancienne*), for example, is just 76 words long in the English edition. It begins: "Prepare the Fricassee in the usual manner as for veal" and says no more about cooking the chicken itself.[1] It gets no easier after that. These are sets of rules for someone who already knows a great deal.

The natural solution that most home cooks want is not, of course, the years of apprenticeship and bodily experience that Escoffier assumed. It is ever more detailed rules: rules that explain how to interpret the first set of rules. Supplying this was the genius of Julia Child and her co-authors in *Mastering the Art of French Cooking*. Their recipe for the exact same dish begins on page 258 of the first volume, and continues on through page 261.[2] This is not counting the two other recipes in the book (for the onions and the mushrooms) that this one requires. It is roughly ten times the length of Escoffier's version, even though it omits the "pale baked crescents of puff pastry" with which he decorates the plate, and which occupy about 20 percent of his recipe (just 15 words). The success of the book certainly indicates that more rules can help make things accessible. Nevertheless, instructions that tell us to cook the vegetables until they are "almost tender" are not very helpful to an inexperienced cook. A truly complete set of rules would be unreadably long if it were possible at all. And even then, the best we could hope for would be Cathy's perfectly adequate but far from perfect cake.

Endless notation, the attempt to conquer ambiguity by creating ever more categories and rules, is ultimately futile. It simply produces new ambiguities, as in the evolutionary biologists' joke that every time they discover a missing link it produces two new missing links. By saying this, we do not mean to argue that notation is unnecessary or undesirable. On the contrary, we do not see how human social life would be possible without it. Our claim is simply that notation cannot solve the problem of ambiguity, and that its primary mechanism of establishing new boundaries therefore causes as many problems as it solves. Pluralism and related problems will not be solved so much by notating new boundaries—new rules and categories—as by finding ways of working across them.

The remainder of this book is dedicated to two other general ways of dealing with ambiguity, not by trying to remove it through the creation of new boundaries but by learning to live with it in different ways. The first of these is ritual and the second is shared experience. There may well be other important mechanisms, but we have chosen to concentrate on these two because we think that they have important potentials as we struggle to live with ambiguity and difference. There has been a long tendency to look toward notation as the preeminent solution to problems like pluralism, measuring its objects in census categories, and legislating its problems away through constitutions and legal codes. This can take forms that vary—from the denial that there can be any significant public boundaries separating citizens or, at the other extreme, the ethnic cleansings that have haunted Europe's past. Ritual and shared experience offer alternatives to these notational strategies, and so deserve greater attention than they usually receive.

By "ritual," we mean primarily those acts that are formalized through social convention and are repeated over and over in ways that people recognize as somehow the same as before. We are less interested in phenomena like the personal rituals that psychiatrists sometimes discuss (which are repeated but not social), but we do mean to include a wide range of phenomena that are not limited to religion alone. As we will discuss in chapter 3, much of the anthropological literature on ritual has emphasized its notational capacities, its ability to define and create boundaries. This is certainly correct, but we emphasize that crossing boundaries is just as inherent to the ritual process.

Ritual crosses borders of all kinds: between humans and spirits, men and women, food and people. Like the potlatch, the Olympics, or Trobriand cricket, it can unite diverse peoples. As in purifications, initiations, or sacrifices, it can transform objects or people from one category to another. At the most fundamental level, it carries us across the very boundaries that it most clearly creates, the boundaries between everyday life and those moments of ritual life. This happens when people cross themselves when entering or leaving a Catholic church, when a judge bangs a gavel in a courtroom, or when professors march into or out of a room wearing mortarboard and gown for a graduation.

Émile Durkheim understood the sacred as the world that is "set apart" from the ordinary and profane. For him, the distinction between sacred and profane was the most fundamental category boundary of all, the beginning of all setting apart, and thus fundamental to society. In his sense, we usually think of ritual as dealing with the sacred world alone, but in fact the basic structure of every single ritual is to cross the boundary between sacred and profane, not simply to play in the world of the sacred. Unlike notation, which creates categories, ritual crosses over them, and it does this repeatedly. The repetitions themselves will form a crucial part of our argument on ritual, because they create a flow of time and thus the grounds for imagining a shared past and future. That is, the rhythms of ritual are one key to what may allow us to live together socially, even as we accept the differences that separate us.

A repeated crossing between sacred and profane has profoundly different social implications from a view that would leave us on just one side or the other of that boundary. We could think of secularism as the reduction of all categories to the profane. At the other extreme, the modern religious fundamentalisms attempt to reduce all categories to the sacred. Either alternative leaves no space for pluralism; boundaries are not crossed. It should probably not surprise us that both secularism and religious fundamentalism grew out of the Reformation, which itself was the beginning of a powerful attack on ritual that has in many ways continued to characterize attitudes in Europe and America and has had a strong influence around the world. Ritual, we hope to suggest, still has an important role to play in teaching us to live with differences and all their associated ambiguities.

The final response to ambiguity that we will discuss here (primarily in chapter 4) deals with boundaries and categories in a different way—it brackets those differences away for a period of time to allow us to work in the full complexity and idiosyncrasy of a particular context. On a temporary and ad hoc basis, this strategy lets us take practical action by eliding the problems of categories and the ambiguities they produce. Time flows here, too, but no longer in the predictable rhythms of ritual that allow us to imagine ourselves as a society. Instead, it is truly historical time that never repeats but instead constantly forces us into new configurations—configurations that can potentially challenge and remake our most fundamental understandings.

Let us indulge in one last food example. This is a story that one of us heard at a summer camp reunion, told by a camper recalling an event of the 1980s. This camp had a very strict rule that children could not eat sweets or junk food of any kind. Parents could send packages of food, but these were always opened in the office so that counselors could confiscate any contraband food. The office was tiny, though, and one day an enormous box arrived for one of the campers. There was no way to open it and pull out the contents in the office, so they agreed to open it in the child's cabin, closely supervised by counselors on guard against any possible junk food.

And indeed, mixed in among many other things, the box contained three packages of a greatly desired and utterly forbidden treat—Pringles. All the cabin's campers were standing right there, though, and a din of wheedling, pleading voices ensued. The counselors conferred for a minute and agreed to a compromise. The children could have all the Pringles they could grab in 30 seconds. Further negotiations ensued, for instance about whether opening the package counted (it did not). With the packages open and the Pringles in neat piles and rows, a counselor counted down: ready, set, GO!

Bedlam quickly followed as all the children grabbed the chips one at a time. One boy said to do it his way, and shoved as many as he could hold straight into his mouth. Soon everyone was doing the same. In 30 seconds, it was all over, except for the cleaning. There were Pringle shards everywhere—children had to be washed, bedding shaken out, floors swept, and so on. In the end, each child probably got little more than a mouthful of the forbidden food.

Rules must exist in order for us to share lives together. But we also have to understand when it is better to break them, when the social order is sturdy enough to allow a little shaking in exchange for some appropriate rewards. The counselors here did not follow the letter of the camp rules, but they were helping to strengthen the spirit of those rules, and many others besides: goods are collective and not individual, sharing is a key value, good fun is why everyone is at camp, and perhaps most importantly, decision making is a shared responsibility that includes campers as well as counselors.

The example is trivial, of course. We bring it up, however, because it illustrates the importance of the context, of the historical moment, and the way that it can work positively by bracketing away some of the usual rules, restrictions, and categories of life. The usual default in such a situation would be to enforce the letter of the law by confiscating the food, or perhaps a sort of passive rebellion in which campers manage to sneak some of the food away and eat it on the sly. Instead of either enforcing the law or actively rejecting it, the situation became an opportunity to work together, to reach a compromise that offered everyone more than just obedience or resistance would have.

These three modes for handling boundaries—notation, ritual, and shared experience—are not mutually exclusive. On the contrary, we argue that all three are necessary and important in all societies. They intermix in different ways, however, and the nature of that mix helps to construct alternative historicities and socialities. As we will discuss, each implies a very different notion of time and a very different conception of self and other. We devote one chapter to each mode, but also interweave a set of interludes to work through some examples—textual, historical, and ethnographic—with more sensitivity to their own contexts. In writing these interludes, we have allowed ourselves some room to wander, but most of our examples come from the Jewish and Chinese cases that we know best. These two long traditions lend themselves easily to our purposes because they provide many examples of the complex interactions among notation, ritual, and shared experience. Each has a long notational tradition, but each has also particularly emphasized ritualized ways of dealing with ambiguity and each has made room as well for the more contextualized uses of shared experience. We have thus chosen them not so much because they are representative but because they are illustrative of the full range of human possibilities that we want to explore.

From within the almost infinite possible range of human interactions, we are most concerned in this book with exploring the possibilities of empathy and living with difference that both ritual and shared experience evoke. Our contemporary world seems trapped in notational devices that absolutize our boundaries into binary divisions—increasingly impassable walls that separate without bridging, divide without uniting. Such powerful boundaries discourage us from exploring the unknown, from hosting strangers, from finding familiarity in the unfamiliar. We use our notational systems—our categories of knowledge—to isolate the worlds of security and danger, closely homologous to the known and the unknown. The grey shades of ambiguity get lost all too often, and with them the ability to widen the boundaries of ourselves through the creative illusions that the ambiguous space provides.

The increasing interconnections of our global world make the imperative of living together differently a central concern for everyone. This book suggests that such a genuine pluralism involves an approach to boundaries and their navigation that must make room for the ambiguous and poorly delineated just as much as for the clear conceptual distinctions on which our notational systems are based. Crossing boundaries without dissolving them, we will claim, forms the very heart of empathy and so of life with the other. Empathy grows out of hard, focused boundary work, which both ritual and shared experience demand.

While the chapters of this book work out the analytic armature of this argument, it is in the interludes that we contextualize concrete cases dealing with different ritual orders and frames of experience. For us, and we hope for our readers, these cases—from Greek myth, Jewish exegesis and law, Chinese politics, and Confucian thought—are first and foremost lessons in humility. They offer examples from former times and very different civilizational endeavors of the multiple ways in which ambiguity can be approached: valued, précised, and played with, without succumbing to the very present drive to disambiguate and so reduce experience to binary categories. It seems to us that there is much here to learn from.

Looked at from a different angle, we may well ask how we can order the world and still find a way to live with the problems that the resulting categories create. How can we deal with otherness in all its forms—the inevitable result of ordering—and still recognize how much we have in common with the other? In our contemporary world, notation and more notation seem to provide the default response to these issues. It is our hope here to enrich the possibilities by putting ritual and shared experience back on the table as equal partners as we all continue to search for solutions to the deep problems of a genuine pluralism.

1

The Importance of Being Ambiguous

AN EARLY DEATH knell for tonal music sounded in June 1865, with the opening notes at the first public performance of Richard Wagner's *Tristan und Isolde*. The initial chord—famous among musicologists as the Tristan chord—is dissonant, leading a listener with an ear accustomed to European music traditions to wait endlessly for a resolution into some more consonant chord. Consonance involves a perceived aural stability, a comfortable placement into one of the set of 24 basic harmonic patterns accepted in the tradition (such as A minor or B major). What we hear as dissonance are the notes that do not fit the pattern, the ones that have been borrowed from some other pattern. That is, dissonance presents itself to the ear as a tension that makes us yearn for a resolution. The ambiguity in the Tristan chord lies in the possibility of resolving it in several different ways. It seems to be in too many keys at once.

Wagner was, of course, hardly the first to use dissonance to add tension to his music. While exactly what people hear as dissonant has changed over time and varies culturally, the basic musical movement of dissonance to consonance, tension to balance, ambiguity to clarity, is both ancient and widespread. Even the particular notes of the Tristan chord had been used by earlier composers, who also played with its radical ambiguity.[1] Wagner's innovation was that he never let go of the chord. Every time it sounds as if it is about to resolve, he moves it into some new realm of ambiguity, androgynous and irresolvable. The result is a constant disquiet, a churning yearning that fits perfectly with the intertwined love/death at the heart of the story. Instead of relieving us of the ambiguity, Wagner makes us swim in it. The idea recurs several times throughout the opera, and he only allows a resolution at the end of the final act. The harmonic ambiguity of a chord whose tonal base was unclear meant that, at least for these long passages, the opera did not establish a key. It was the beginning of the end for the tonal system.

Except, of course, that reports of the death of tonality—common by the early twentieth century—turned out to be greatly premature. Tonality continues to predominate in all forms of popular music, and remains strong even within contemporary "classical" music. Listeners are now far more comfortable with atonality than during Wagner's day. Nevertheless, most music today continues the long tradition of using harmonic ambiguity as a device to produce tension, to toy with the boundaries of a stable tonal center, but then to return to a harmonic home. It is this productive tension between ambiguity and order that we hope to explore here.

A World of Categories

We bring up this musical experiment because it seems to predate some similar developments in social scientific thinking about ambiguity in a world of categories. Among the founding thinkers of modern social science, it was especially Durkheim who placed the problem of classification at the very center of our undertaking. Philosophically, Durkheim was very much a "constructivist" avant la lettre. That is to say, he refused to privilege any particular understanding or construction of the world as ontologically more "real" than any other. Instead, he understood the worlds we inhabit as constructed socially, together—a work of many minds, working with the tools of language and other symbol systems.[2] In Primitive Classification, he and his co-author Marcel Mauss argued that there is nothing natural about classification systems, but that they are a necessary and learned feature of human groups. While much that we experience is a fuzzy continuum, we need to classify things and concepts to survive, "to arrange them in groups which are distinct from each other, and are separated by clearly determined lines of demarcation."[3] In his later work, The Elementary Forms of Religious Life, Durkheim makes a case for the division between sacred and profane being the most fundamental classification of all, with the sacred's most important feature being its categorical clarity. Sacred things are utterly set apart and forbidden to the profane—the distinction is absolute in Durkheim, and there is no room for ambiguity.[4] At roughly the same time, Ferdinand de Saussure was also clarifying the notion of category in language, making the unambiguous contrast between categories into the fundamental building block of his analysis of language.

These insights shaped much of what came later, especially in anthropology, as it turned to fundamental classifications of things like space, time, and person. One of the important breakthroughs came with the structuralists, who drew heavily on both Durkheim and Saussure. A key insight grew out of the realization that if much of the world were really a continuum, then our arbitrary (i.e., culturally determined) imposition of categories would necessarily omit objects or experiences that did not fit neatly into any category. That is, while we cannot live without distinctions, we also never quite make our peace with them at either individual or social levels.

Claude Lévi-Strauss developed this, for instance, in his discussion of "mediators" in myths. While most of myth, for Lévi-Strauss, has a structure of underlying categories quite parallel to what Saussure saw for the grammar or phonology of a language, he also recognized certain features that stood between categories and could never be resolved. In *The Raw and the Cooked*, he discussed fish poison (an inedible food) and the opossum (combining life/motherhood and death/stench) as such permanent ambiguities. Both represent "a union of nature and culture which brings about their disjunction."[5] In a veiled reference back to the Tristan chord, he even wonders whether Isolde can be reduced to an "opossum function," and whether the mediation of the love philter/death philter in the opera relates to the essential ambiguity of its tonality.[6]

The British anthropologists Mary Douglas and Edmund Leach further developed the idea that the leftover bits that fall between are crucial to

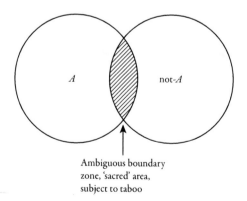

Ambiguous boundary
zone, 'sacred' area,
subject to taboo

FIGURE I.I Ambiguity in Leach

After Edmund Leach, *Culture and Communication: The Logic by Which Symbols Are Connected: An Introduction to the Use of Structuralist Analysis in Social Anthropology* (Cambridge: Cambridge University Press, 1976), 35.

clarifying the categories themselves. Leach would typically draw the idea with a simple diagram (see figure 1.1). Recalling Durkheim directly, Leach sometimes described the overlapping area that is both A and not-A as the arena of the sacred and hence subject to taboo. Defining the marginal zone as taboo clarifies the boundaries of the category itself. This is a key, for example, to his playful analysis of why certain animal categories count as verbal abuse ("pig") but not others ("ocelot").[7] More famously, Mary Douglas drew on much the same line of thinking when she argued that the prohibitions of Leviticus were really taboos on potential foods that fell between the cracks of the ancient Jewish classification system for living things, or that the heavy symbolic load of the pangolin among the central African Lele stemmed from the animal's anomalies: scaled like a reptile but bearing live young, an anteater that climbs trees, and so on.[8]

This understanding of the boundaries of our categories and of myriad ritually performed boundary-maintaining devices has especially shaped our thinking about pollution and the rules of ritual pollution. These rules "are unequivocal," as Douglas pointed out.[9] Pollution rules, as she analyzes them, supplement ambivalent and multidimensional moral dictates with hard and fast rules that brook no interpretive laxity. "Defilement" in Paul Ricoeur's telling phrase, "is itself a symbol of evil."[10] In these readings, pollution rules—which define certain acts as purifying or polluting—reinforce and clarify hard moral boundaries. They defend those boundaries from the compromises offered by the labile nature of a reality that is not so clearly demarcated. Without such demarcation, they imply, reality is ambiguous to its core. Interpretive differences and ambiguous understandings threaten all rules and categories.

Many of the anthropological insights into ambiguity recall what Donald Levine called the "flight from ambiguity." Levine argued that there has been a modern assault on ambiguity that has continued since the seventeenth century. In language, this meant a demeaning of its poetic character (a problem for thinkers from Saussure to Russell); in social science, it meant obscuring the ambiguities of actual experience in favor of the simplicities of rationalization or of status and role.[11] Levine argued that modernity as a form of social organization and as a philosophical, scientific, and ethical program rejects ambiguity and ambivalence. It positively values straight talk and clear thinking, unambiguous expressions and a linguistic practice modeled on mathematical precision. Direct communication rather than ambiguous circumlocutions are the hallmarks of Locke's philosophy as of Descartes'. They characterized the thought and writings of Condorcet and of Samuel Johnson. They lie at the core of modern science, of Protestant religiosity, and of social science.

Exploring Ambiguity

Nevertheless, the anthropological study of ambiguity did not stop with modernity's flight from it. One early classic example was Radcliffe-Brown's analysis of joking relationships around the world.[12] These are social ties in which disrespectful teasing between two people is positively valued; in some cases it is required. Such ties frequently occur between relatives by marriage, like a man talking to his wife's relatives. In some societies, they may also appear in ties between allied clans. For Radcliffe-Brown they resolve a form of ambiguity that arises between "consociates"— people who are members of groups that must be kept separate yet must also maintain friendly ties. A man's in-laws, for example, are clearly not members of his lineage, so pure solidarity is an inappropriate attitude. Yet he also must maintain good relations to them. They are both relatives and non-relatives, A and not-A. There is no way to resolve this status into one thing or the other; those people will never be lineage brothers but cannot be treated as strangers, either. The answer is the gentle disrespect of the joke.

Keith Basso's study of the Western Apache showed a different solution to a similar situation.[13] When social relationships are unclear for the Western Apache—strangers with whom one must interact, young men and women beginning to court, or children coming home after a very long absence, for instance—they simply sit in silence for long periods of time. As with Radcliffe-Brown's case, ambiguities in social position are met with verbal ambiguities, in this case the uninterpretability of silence.

The field's fascination with the things between the categories evolved further with the realization that taboo and verbal restriction are far from the only ways of dealing with such ambiguities. We will not delve far into Victor Turner's well-known writings on liminality, except to note that in his hands the area "betwixt and between" took on a new richness—a source of elation as well as terror, of learning as well as discipline.[14] Moments of transition often reveal the arbitrary, temporal, contingent and hence fragile nature of our world of distinctions. He showed this in fields that ranged from initiation rites to pilgrimage. Liminality was for him a deeply complex aspect of human life, not simply the dirt to sweep under the rug. These liminal moments make the whole skein of order visible, threatening to reveal that the emperor has no clothes after all. Our attitude toward order at these moments teeters with our increased realization of just how fragile are the categories and conceits upon which we construct our worlds of work and kinship, of play and politics, not to mention our religions, sexualities, diets, dislikes, and dementias.

Even Turner's work, however, continues to emphasize the clarity of the boundary between liminality and order. He describes "communitas," for example, as "essentially opposed to structure, as antimatter is hypothetically opposed to matter. Thus, even when communitas becomes normative its religious expressions become closely hedged about by rules and interdictions—which act like the lead container of a dangerous radioactive isotope."[15] The very focus on the "liminal" attempts to make a category out of what lies between, or of that which overlaps with more than one category (i.e., the ambiguous). Within much anthropological thinking, we have become used to understanding our categories—"liminality" included—as relatively clearly demarked units, symbolic structures with sharp edges, hard, impenetrable and sheer.[16] Even in Turner's complex and evocative version of the fuzziness, openness, and lability of the liminal space, we still find it well bounded, even as it is shunted off from the more properly ordered and categorized realms of social life.

When the force of ambiguity's intrusion makes the indistinct aspects of life impossible to ignore, they are recategorized as liminal, marginal, shut off by their own boundaries from the realms of social structure and social ordering. This maintains the idea of the inviolability of boundaries and preserves the coherency of our analytic models. The sheerness of the boundaries and hence of our categories remains, even if there is nothing sheer about the reality or thing that they define.

Embracing Ambiguity

Much of this book seeks alternative ways of understanding and relating to the labile, the fuzzy, the indistinct, and the ambiguous. We begin with the inevitability of the ambiguous, which is built into the core of our existence in the world. The world may well begin in chaos and be ordered through efforts human or divine, as so many origin tales relate. The very ordering of chaos, however, creates its own ambiguity. The generation of life entails death, just as purity implies impurity, and categories require margins. The generation of order thus generates ambiguity as well. The very process of categorizing always problema-tizes the area around the category. With cleanliness we get not only dirt, but endless debates (i.e., ambiguities) around what is clean, what is dirty, where the one ends and the other begins, and if it is water that purifies or our intentions.

At very roughly the same time that Turner, Douglas, and Leach were writing, some psychological and sociological studies began to explore just how central ambiguity was to modern life.[17] Robert Merton, together with Eleanor Barber, their followers, and critics, explored the concept of ambivalence and how a certain degree of ambiguity was embedded "in particular status and status-sets together with their associated roles."[18] The indeterminacy of social roles, the conflicting normative expectations of behavior and belief accorded to any one status or set of statuses, as well as "the incompatible normative expectations incorporated in a single role of a single social status" formed the root of what they termed "sociological ambivalence."[19] Ambiguity in this view is systemic, an aspect of the construction of society and not solely of the "feeling states of one or an-other type of personality." Roles came to be understood as containing both "major norms and minor counter-norms [that] alternatively govern role-behavior to produce ambivalence."[20] There was therefore no way around this systemic ambiguity. Social expectations had to be fulfilled, despite their ambiguity. Denying it was impossible.

Beyond these sociological insights, several studies showed that indi-vidual tolerance for ambiguity correlated directly with a strong sense of moral autonomy. In contrast, a low tolerance for ambiguity correlated with "crude stereotyping, rigid defenses and general lack of insight."[21] In the famous Frankfurt School study of the authoritarian personality, for instance, intolerance for ambiguity accompanied high scores for ethno-centrism and authoritarianism.[22]

While we do not usually associate either Turner or the Frankfurt School with post-structuralist theory, in retrospect both approaches share the insight that the categories of structural contrast can never tell a full story of human meaning—that the bits that lie between are critical to the human project.[23] More than Turner, post-structuralists like Derrida worked this through as part of a critique of the way in which language itself functions. One of the problems that they pointed to in the structuralist understanding of language as a set of clearly contrasting categories was that the cate-gories interacted with each other. If the sound "hat" means hat in part because of a phonological contrast with "mat" and "cat," and a semantic contrast with words like "shirt" or "fedora," then there is a sense in which all possible meanings are implied, at least as negations, by any utterance.

In addition, any sign must be repeatable to count as a sign; if we could only use it once, we wouldn't count it as a sign at all. We will return in a later chapter to the important problem of repetition, but here let us note only that no repetitions are ever exactly identical—and that meaning itself is thus unstable, never fully the same from one context to the next. With this sort of analysis, post-structuralists have been able to deconstruct any system of categories, to show that the sorts of ambiguities of meaning that we usually associate only with poetry in fact affect every utterance.[24]

And so, after a bit more than a century, the study of meaning also discovered a kind of Tristan chord in which ambiguity cannot be resolved. Yet just as tonality did not die from having its ambiguities unveiled, neither did systems of categories. Except for some of the more nihilistic practitioners of post-structuralism, there has been a general realization that recognizing the limits of linguistic categories draws us back to the ways that particular social contexts nevertheless allow shared interpretations through the works of social convention or of power.[25] We are left, as with music, with the constant interplay of ambiguity and order.

Ambiguities and Order

This interplay forms the heart of what we hope to explore here. One way to think about it is through the enormous plasticity of human social worlds. In the absence of social conventions, humans would face a world where anything is possible at any time—perhaps not entirely in the world of nature, but certainly in the world of men and women. We need food and shelter, of course, and it still (usually) takes two genders to reproduce. Yet there are no biological or other "natural" determinants to chart out which woman will conceive with which man. In stark terms, there is nothing preventing incest, other than social convention.

Incest, the one universal taboo, has long generated scholarly interest as a marker of the differentiation that makes all other distinctions possible. It is a hard-won crease in the permanent flow of the world; it breaks the boundlessness—and hence chaos—of nature. It imposes on the flow of experience the beginnings of those human categories that allow us to think and ultimately to act upon the world. Differentiations and distinctions are the primary tools of human order, hard won and hard preserved. This was a key insight of both Durkheim and Freud, in their very different ways, early in the twentieth century. Civilization is the process of categorization, of distinguishing and separating.[26]

With the primary human activities of distinction and differentiation, we immediately encounter the problem of boundaries. Differentiation presupposes limits; horizons and margins mark off all discrete entities. The concepts of distinction and those of boundaries are inconceivable without each other.

Boundaries, however, beget ambiguities. They do this in two ways. First, boundaries both connect and divide. They unite and separate. This is because the act of distinguishing between one entity and another always brings them in relation to one another. The work of D. W. Winnicott on child development is perhaps the paradigm statement in human relations of how it takes a prior separation for two entities to connect and to be in relation with one another.[27] For him, culture develops out of our contestation with the differentiation and distinction necessary for life. The first and most difficult of such distinctions, as he describes it, is our recognition of the mother as standing apart from the self. How does a child come to perceive the mother as a separate entity, and thus develop its own category of self? He argued that this happened through the imposition of a "third space"—a mediation of transitional objects like teddy bears—that could occupy the space that was both A (child) and not-A (mother), as in figure 1.1. This allows our psychic recognition of the autonomy of each (on a good day). Boundaries thus point both outward as well as inward. They signify the world beyond, as well as what is contained within.

Boundaries are ambiguous in another way as well, for boundaries both constrain and are constrained by the power of the center, that organizing force or principle whose margins they define. As limits or margins, boundaries share in the defining traits and characteristics of whatever field of meaning they circumscribe. Yet whatever lies beyond the field of such meaning impinges upon them. Hence their dangerous nature. The structuring of human cognitive fields mandates boundaries, but at the same time they always threaten those fields. Perhaps this is just another way of saying that differentiation is never secure. The propensity toward some form of de-differentiation always exists, and the threat comes from the boundaries themselves—the very entity upon which differentiation itself stands.

The two of us often teach a course together, and we usually have one session in which we empty our pockets and bags into a miscellaneous heap on the desk, making sure that there are plenty of different types of coins, keys, paper clips, rubber bands, lint, assorted small bits of rock or glass or whatever. We ask a student to order the objects into categories and then to explain her thinking. And then we ask another student to do the same exercise differently. It is not difficult for them to observe that the ordering involves: (a) division, the distinction, and separation of our pockets' contents into different groups; (b) the imposition of categories and boundaries; and (c) the possibility of vastly different possible organizing principles for this division (all forms of money together, or all forms of metal, or all items with writing on them, or all round objects, or brown ones, etc.).

Any choice of categories brings along its inherent ambiguities. Should the penny be classified as an item of money, one with writing on it, a round object, or a brown one? There is no one "right" answer, and yet the order established (i.e., what will be separated and what united, where are the boundaries drawn) varies enormously in each case. Ordering brings ambiguity: the penny could go in so many vastly different spaces. Still, this sort of ambiguity about where to place the penny already differs greatly from the absolute chaos that reigned when everything was mushed together in a jumble. Chaos has given way to ambiguity through the imposition of distinctions between different units. And while these distinctions are ambiguous, especially at their margins, we are still a far cry from the senseless world occasioned by purely undifferentiated existence.

Any creation of order, any imposition of boundaries and categories, brings ambiguities. Note also that the very idea of ambiguity implies the existence of difference. If there were no differences (or differentiation), there would be no ambiguity. Plurality—otherness—rests on difference, with all its boundaries and all its ambiguities. In contrast, the absolute has no boundaries and no differentiation (the chaotic jumble of our pockets). It is not ambiguous; it just is. It has no margins, no distinguishing characteristics. It is not ordered by categories that include A and exclude not-A, and that always leave other cases ambiguous. Ambiguity, which is the price we pay for our need to make distinctions, is a feature of order, not chaos. A true pluralism, we hope to argue, requires categories and boundaries, and thus also an ability to accept ambiguity.

Ambiguity and Possibility

Just as the Tristan chord could resolve into multiple keys, our categories of thought and relationship carry ambiguity because they speak to more than one possibility of distinction. That is, we recognize ambiguity when, as with sorting pennies from shoelaces on the classroom desk, we realize that there are alternative principles of order. This is a potential that exists in all human relations. (The penny went with the dollar bill and the nickels, but maybe it would have been better with the brown shoelace and the crumbs from the brownies.) The ambiguous is ambiguous because different possibilities exist. The existence of alternatives poses a constant threat to our conceptions of order, but it also begins to let us regulate this threat.

Recognizing a realm that exists outside our categories thus implies understanding the limits of those categories. Boundaries do not just limit us but also force us into awareness of the possibilities that lie beyond them—a duality if not a multiplicity of existences that cannot be absolute. Later we will address attempts to deny this multiplicity, to see one possible order as the only Order. Here we want to make the point that boundaries are the point of distinction as well as that place from which any and every distinction can be questioned. The categories that they create underlie human cognition, but boundaries also give us the vantage point from which to question any set of categories and conceptions. They are dangerous spaces because they define space itself.

Ambiguity, as the work of anthropologists like Douglas and Turner has taught us, threatens the whole conceptual system with collapse. Moreover, as we have seen, there are really two kind of ambiguity (for which we may need different words). One is the undifferentiated whole: the chaos before the (social) world was formed, which is not so different from the imagined nirvana beyond any social world. This is the space where anything at all is possible and nothing is possible, the space of utopia and disaster, the absolute continuum. The other is the ambiguity built into any system of boundaries—hence also a space of potential, of creativity and danger. This space coexists with order, and it can be accepted and controlled (unlike the continuum, in which human life is impossible). Because humanity requires categories and categories create ambiguity, human life requires us to accept an ambiguity that is always with us.

In the field of human relations it was Freud, rather than the anthropologists, who gave us the strongest handle on ambiguity's dangers, with his concept of the "narcissism of small difference"—the threat posed to us by the near (rather than the far) other.[28] Someone who resembles us in so many ways and differs from us in but one characteristic threatens us much more than the totally other or alien. That distant other's strangeness may pose a physical danger, but no threat to self-conceptions and cognitive worlds. The very difference of the "near other," however, poses a continual question to our own sense of self in the familiarity and sameness of our shared traits.

Ambiguity is always present. It does not appear solely in the presence of the "near other." It exists in the endless possibilities that all moments present and in the particular choices that we make: it lies at the interstices of these choices, of doing x rather than y and their endless possible correlates. The infinite structuring of possibility thus contains an equally infinite quotient of ambiguity. The problem of boundaries and their inherent ambiguity is therefore not restricted to rites of passage or those bits of information that do not easily fit into our conceptual categories (sea creatures without fins or scales, in the case of Jewish dietary laws). Instead, these problems are with us, potentially, at all times, a somber or perhaps carnivalesque shadow play going on behind and before every act and every thought.

It may seem as if ambiguity could be reduced through a more thorough search for knowledge. Sometimes we believe that we can eliminate it entirely, but this is false because, as we have noted, in the realm of human relations ambiguity is inherent to the process of categorization, without which we can neither think nor act. Ambiguity is not a function of some lack of information, but—to use a religious term—of the free will of men and women, whose biological template is open in certain very fundamental ways that preclude too great a reliance on the "laws" or "regularities" of social life. It is a function of the endless horizon of action and, as such, dogs our every step. This ambiguity—tied to the boundaries that make up our cognitive universe—provides the focus of this book.

How do human societies reduce ambiguity to a level we can live with? How can we manage in a world where the laws of regularity too often fail to work, where alternate schemes of categorization confound our conventions, and we are left with a totally open field of possibilities in our relations to one another? One crucial technique to reduce ambiguity in social life is the simple act of repetition. The structuring of infinite possibilities, which begins in infancy and ties to role expectations, is the primary mode through which we build some sense of regularity in our social relations. Toilet training was the classic Freudian example, but it is by no means the only one. Learning to use the toilet entails the social construction of a biological need according to set cues (here spatial rather than temporal, though in some cultures, temporal as well). The spatially agreed-upon place where one can evacuate one's bowels is a form of regularity. Norbert Elias's work on the development and spread of forms of *civilité* and *politesse* in Western European cultures points to similar phenomena.[29]

Of course, the matter goes far beyond using forks and spoons or learning where it is appropriate to urinate. It goes to the basic forms of address between humans, to formal and informal modes of speech, to learning that you cannot talk to Grand Aunt Sally in the same tone and with the same words that you use when playing stickball with Billy in the street. What sociologists used to call "role expectations" is the gradual accrual of shared expectations between role-set members who learn to expect a set of behaviors, who adjust their expectations to what have become regularities of intercourse—both of the spoken word and the actual act.

Regularity is central to our imposition of order and cohesion on a world of human interaction that is, in principle, open to infinite permutations. Those familiar with the debates of recent decades in the social sciences will realize that disputes have tended to focus on the basis for these regularities.[30] Do we share regularities of space and time (repetitions) because of mutual interests given to rational calculation (social choice theory), or shared values (Durkheim), or the coercion of hegemonic power structures (post-Marxist or Foucauldian), and so on? This is not a debate we wish to enter into. At the moment, we emphasize simply that for the regularities to take effect they must contain an important element of repetition. Repetition is the key to regularity. It ties intimately to the issues of boundary and distinction that we have been discussing. If there were no distinction, there could be no repetition. There could only be one, total, primal (or final, it does not really matter) act. Repetition is possible because the existence of something beyond order makes it both possible and necessary.

Note that repetition does not "solve" the problem of ambiguity. The same problems that adhere to the issue of ensuring the larger social or cognitive orders also affect the small orders of repetition. Repetition allows us to live with ambiguity, not to remove it. This book explores the dialectic between ambiguity and order in which repetition plays an important role, in the hopes of revealing ways of living together socially, even as ambiguous others.

Social and Cognitive Ambiguities

These are some of the definitions of "ambiguity" in the *Oxford English Dictionary*:

1. Doubtful, questionable, indistinct, obscure, not clearly defined;
2. Of words or other significant indications: admitting more than one interpretation or explanation, of double meaning or of several possible meanings: equivocal;
3. Of doubtful position or classification, as partaking of two characters or being on the boundary line between.[31]

Whatever else, then, there would seem to be an indeterminate quality about the ambiguous. It continually questions the conceits of our usage and of our thought. Though it may be inseparable from categories through which we think the world, it also exists as their shadow. Perhaps a bit like Peter Pan's shadow, these shadows at times lead lives of their own, in need of a Wendy to reconnect them.

As we know from the creation myths of many peoples—from Genesis as well as from such sagas as the *Enima Elish*—the world originates in chaos. The process of differentiation (which is the creation of categories) is only won with much pain and suffering and is never fully guaranteed. These founding cultural texts typically recognized the continual threat of backsliding into a de-differentiated existence. Chronos eating his children, the biblical stories of the flood, the Tower of Babel, or Noah's naked exposure to Ham—all of these tales register the continual possibility of slipping back into a world of chaos, where order and divisions and categories and hence meanings are uprooted and all is again one.

If Sigmund Freud is to be believed, each of us repeats this process ontogenetically as we painfully learn the restrictions (and hence distinctions) of civilization, even as we continually yearn for a more unrestricted world of fulfillment (which paradoxically leads to our own dissolution in the "oneness" of all being). The endless and immensely effort-consuming process of sublimating the drives of sexuality and aggression mark, at the end of the day, our acceptance of those primary distinctions through which we come to be social (and socialized) beings.

To refer back to the language of Victor Turner's anthropology, the liminal is not restricted in space and time. It is instead continually present, the shadow of the deed, an option always available. The rituals that Turner analyzed so cogently bound only the social representations of these shadows. We should not, however, confuse the representation for the thing, which cannot so easily be captured. We may celebrate anniversaries only once a year, but that does not keep us from being married the other 364 days. And while that social fact may not always be at the very forefront of consciousness for all the days of the year, it certainly plays an important role at more than the odd moment and well beyond the one demarked day. Similarly, while rites of transition may represent the liminal ambiguity of reality, the ambiguity is not restricted just to those moments. Its nominal registration (and attempted circumscription) in ritual is but acknowledgment of a reality that is ever present.

Generating categories of what is permitted and prohibited, desirable or abhorred, preferable or ignored is perhaps the most important notational knowledge that we produce. Knowledge of these categories also entails knowledge of their limits, their margins, and the endless ambiguities that attend to them. Ultimately it is social convention that defines the limits to these margins. But recourse to social authority happens only *in extremis*. In daily life we traverse these limits—or are at least faced with them— every day. We can hardly enter any interaction without myriad possibilities that potentially challenge and perhaps also scuttle our plans, hopes, and desires. Social roles and role expectations are not genetically programmed, and aunts have been known to become sexual partners at least as often as paupers have become princes.

Actionable Knowledge and Uncertainty

John Dewey, the father of American pragmatism, argues in *The Quest for Certainty: A Study of the Relation of Knowledge and Action* for the need to come to terms with the ambiguity and uncertainty that characterize all practical deeds. He eschews the philosophical tendency to seek any sort of pure Being, any "disclosure of the Real in itself, of Being in and of itself."[32] "The quest for certainty," he exhorts, seeks "a peace which is assured, an object which is unqualified by risk and the shadow of fear which action casts."[33] Unfortunately, practical activities "take effect in an uncertain future, and involve peril, the risk of misadventure, frustration and failure."[34] Embedded in a world of particularities and change, of probabilities and contingencies, the world of real life decisions is inherently uncertain. Actionable knowledge, rather than theoretical speculation, requires recognizing the necessarily ambiguous nature of the world, as well as of our very categories for knowing it.

With Dewey, we recognize two critical aspects of our social knowledge, the knowledge of the world that we share with other human beings. First, it is practical knowledge, knowledge that is important to action. And second, it is profoundly uncertain. As a social construct, its concepts and categories are open to change and transformation. Its boundaries are fuzzy and not given to precise delineation (especially over time). The world of human action, which those boundaries seek to enclose, remains protean, in spite of all our attempts. It is thus not surprising that the tools we use to grasp that world are likewise malleable.

Important research into this malleability, if restricted to the domain of literature, appears in William Empson's *Seven Types of Ambiguity*, first published in 1930. Empson defined ambiguity as "an indecision as to what you mean, an intention to mean several things, a probability that one or other or both of two things has been meant, and the fact that a statement has several meanings."[35] Not only is ambiguity the heart and soul of poetry, but Empson also saw it occurring "when the author is discovering his idea in the act of writing, or not holding it all in his mind at once, so that, for instance, there is a simile which applies to nothing exactly, but lies half-way between two things when the author is moving from one to the other."[36] He argued that ambiguity of word and world is often part and parcel of our cognitive capacities (and his examples are from the very greatest poets and texts of the English language).

A similar intuition ran through Owen Barfield's strictures on language and the metaphorical meaning inherent to words themselves—that is, from the fundamental unit that creates meaning:

> It will, I think, appear that th[e] "soul" latent in words, and waiting only to be discovered, is for the most part a kind of buried survival of the old "given" meaning under later accretions; or, if not of the "given" meaning itself, then of an old "created" meaning which has been buried in the same way. For created meanings, once published, are as much subjected, of course, to the binding, astringent action of the rational principle as the original given meanings. Like sleeping beauties, they lie there prone and rigid in the walls of Castle Logic, waiting only for the kiss of Metaphor to awaken them to fresh life. That words lose their freshness through habit is a more humdrum way of saying the same thing; and it will do well enough,

as long as we remember that "habit" is itself only a familiar name of the repetition of the identical.[37]

Metaphor, he suggested, enacted the ambiguous in language, and is the only way (however much mediated) to get to the "real" meaning of words beneath the accrual of habitual usage and the loss of the particular in the abstract forms that have attached themselves over time to original meanings. Repetition of the identical, for Barfield, results in the loss of the concrete, what the phenomenologist Husserl called "the things themselves" as direct objects of intuition and experience. Abstract universality, which enters consciousness with symbolization (and hence language itself), entails the loss of particular, concrete meanings. That is, the very work of categorization and symbolic representation pulls us away from the full complexities and uncertainties of particular experiences. Yet this work also permits the institutionalization that is the sine qua non of social life and language itself—of civilization in Freud's terms.

As we know from Freud, the costs of this are always high, in both repression and the loss of meaning. Only metaphor, according to these authors, can bring us back, in however mediated a manner. Metaphor, in its very artifice, thus becomes a way of traversing the boundary between the thing and its meaning, the sign and the signified, between world and mankind. Barfield noted that a similar process is at work in the development of language. As he writes, the "single meanings" of words are:

> split up into contrasted pairs—the abstract and the concrete, particular and general, objective and subjective. And the poesy felt by us to reside in ancient language consists just of this, that, out of our later, analytic, "subjective" consciousness, a consciousness which has been brought about along with and partly because of this splitting up of meaning, we are led back to experience the original unity.[38]

Now none of this should be surprising if we take into account the central role of metaphor in both cognition and in producing the categories of social organization. Lakoff and Johnson, for example, held that "metaphor is pervasive in everyday life, not just in language but in thought and action. Our ordinary conceptual system, in terms of which we both think and act, is fundamentally metaphorical in nature."[39] We can think about this further through the posthumously published work of the anthropologist Roy Rappaport.[40]

Orders of Meaning

Rappaport suggested that three different patterns of order—three ways of positing boundaries—characterize all systems of meaning, symbolic as well as social, ideal as well as material. The first he called "low-order meaning." This is grounded in distinctions between entities—exactly those distinctions around which the division of labor and social order are organized. This is also the usual level referred to in the structural analysis of language, where meaning lies in contrasting categories. Thus in the expression "the cat is on the mat," meaning lies in the distinction between cats and mats. These are also, to a great extent, the ordering of meaning in the economic realm, where the value difference between entities becomes the logic of exchange.

Rappaport's second form of meaning, "middle-order meaning" is characterized by analogies or similarities between the kinds of objects distinguished through low-order meaning: "my love is like a red, red rose." Allegory and metaphor are the residents of this level. This is the type of meaning that Empson was concerned with and which we, in this book, have set ourselves the task of unpacking further. Here, boundaries do not just divide, but are crossed and blurred. The boundaries between entities and meanings still exist, but are not absolute as in low-level meaning. Nor are they totally eradicated as in the third level of meaning.

The third or "high-order meaning" brings absolute unity, grounded in the oneness, the radical and total identification of self and others. This is easily seen in such religious statements as *La ilaha illa Allah* (there is no God but God), or *Shema Yisrael adoshem eloheinu, adoshem echad* (Hear O Israel, the Lord our God, the Lord is One). This level erases all boundaries, as noted by Cassirer in his remarks on "the One Being [which] eludes cognition. The more its metaphysical unity as a 'thing in itself' is asserted the more it evades all possibility of knowledge until at last it is relegated entirely to the sphere of the unknowable and becomes merely an X."[41]

Importantly, these three sets of meanings characterize not only signs and symbols—as pointed out a hundred years ago by the American philosopher Peirce—but also social order. Rappaport's point was that social order consists of distinction and reaggregation, differentiation and reintegration. Many aspects of social interaction, especially those not defined solely by economic exchange or the division of labor, can best be understood at the level of middle-order meaning. Social empathy and trust work by crossing boundaries, much like metaphors. Just as we can draw verbal analogies ("my love is like a red, red rose"), so we cross the boundaries of affect—his pain may be like my pain. For Aristotle this is the role of tragedy; it generates empathy and expands the boundaries of the self.

Beyond this lies the ultimate level of unity, which is sought in some religious rituals or gatherings in houses of worship across the world. Social life continually vacillates between orders of differentiation and orders of reaggregation or reintegration and unity. When Claude Lévi-Strauss discussed the "conjoining" effects of ritual, he explicitly referred to this phenomenon of reintegration. Once again, we see the metaphysical unity, the "thing in itself" that Cassirer identified as lying beyond distinctions.

In the main, however, the social world—the world of quotidian affairs, of families and friends, of citizenship and community, of petty rivalries and dramatic jealousies, of gossip by the water cooler and baseball with friends, of Christmas dinners and college jaunts—belongs in no small measure to the world of empathy as it is realized, extended, and circumscribed in specific contexts. The world where we meet and share our everyday triumphs and failures, hopes and disappointments belongs to that second, middle level of meaning. This is the level of metaphor, of my ability to reach across the boundary between self and other, to apprehend your feelings, at least in part, through the imaginative leap from my own. Empathy rests on some elision of self. It requires some renunciation of ego's central place in its own symbolic universe (however momentarily). It rests on some blurring of boundaries and our capacity for metaphor. Recall, moreover, that what we are calling "renunciation of self" has a dual character. First, it renounces the self's limiting and defining conditions by requiring a willingness to play with the boundaries of the self. Second, it renounces immediate gratification by accepting social rules of order, which also transcend the self even as they constitute it.[42] This is what Freud and some his followers, such as Heinz Hartmann, understood as the acceptance of reality or the reality principle: a willingness to defer immediate gratification.[43] This means, in essence, to accept the ambiguous nature of reality by both recognizing and deferring the satisfaction of desire.

Empathy and proper ego-functioning—that is, recognition of the world as it stands outside the self—seem to go hand in hand. Both involve recognizing limits, but also the capacity to transcend them (if sometimes only in the imagination). They both fuse the edges but do not confuse the boundaries of objective and subjective realities. They define our abilities to empathize with others but also to recognize objective reality outside ourselves. Order's constraints and boundaries, its rules and regulations, bind the ego and circumscribe its action; this can induce pain and modify pleasure, and must be born with Freudian stoicism. Yet, however paradoxically, these constraints are necessary if either social order or empathy is to exist. The contemporary post-modern embrace of ambiguity often loses sight of this dynamic, of the need for the conventional rules and regulations that constitute the boundaries that separate but also connect our shared world. Boundaries may always be blurred or ambiguous, but societies can neither renounce nor absolutize them. Empathy and metaphor rest on the ability to play the edges, retaining some sense of separation and distinction between entities or selves, and yet not creating rigid boundaries that forever keep subject and object, world and feeling (and fantasy) apart and inviolate.

When Marion Milner discussed the ability of ego to perceive the other as external object, she came back again and again to the fusion of ego and object. She saw the loss of boundaries between ego and object as one necessary stage in the development of such apperception. The "confounding of one thing with another, this not discriminating, is also the basis of generalization" she says. Quoting Wordsworth, she sees it as the key to the poet's ability to find "the familiar in the unfamiliar."[44] Symbols are critical to this process, acting as mediums, intervening substances, transitional objects (that is, poorly defined and with no clear provenance). In blurring boundaries between ego and object, such symbols enable the eventual possibility to perceive objects outside the ego. Symbols, as transitional objects, are the critical link that allows us to perceive the other through a process of not quite incorporating the other within our internal space.

Symbols for Milner allow both the blurring of boundaries and their reconstitution—analogous to the workings of ritual, and not all that distant from what Winnicott claimed for transitional objects and for all acts of creative play. Generalization—a necessary component of empathy—rests on a prior failure to discriminate, a prior tendency to note identity in differences, as Ernst Jones pointed out.[45] Here, too, we see boundaries blurred and ambiguated, and then reconstituted in an ever shifting perception of reality. Moreover, as Milner wrote, the ability "to find the familiar in the unfamiliar, require[s] an ability to tolerate a temporary loss of sense of self, a temporary giving up of the discriminating ego which stands apart and tries to see things objectively and rationally."[46] Again, we find ambiguity as something central to the core human propensity to connect and establish empathy with an other. Ambiguity thus plays an important role in our education toward empathy, resting as it does on a decentered self, and on an ability to generalize beyond one's own experiences. For this to take place, boundaries must in some sense be fuzzy and less than strict and fully discriminating.

If the preceding argument is correct, empathy must rest on the dialectic between boundaries and their dissolution that we are identifying with the sense of the ambiguous. Empathy lies in achieving this balance, rather than in the denial of boundaries and a concomitant ideal free of limits and constraints, a totalizing vision of self, other and society. But neither does the balance come by absolutizing boundaries, by denying the creative need to reframe. It needs the creation and recreation of boundaries, but not their abrogation. Chaos is overcome, but never univocally.

Conclusion

Most academic work on ambiguity tends to be carried out by philosophers and logicians, semioticians and literary critics, linguists and psycholinguists. In fact, under the rubric of the *sorites* paradox, the problem of ambiguity was addressed in ancient Athens by the Stoics and other philosophers. The *sorites* paradox (from the Greek word *soros*, meaning "heap") was the problem of determining how many grains of sand could be removed from a heap of sand before it ceased being a "heap": one, two, three, 30,000, 300,000, and so on. The problem hinged on the boundaries of our definitions and hence of our categories.

While the problem is cognitive, the nature of language lies at its core, as it does in so many inquiries into ambiguity. Scholars such as Roman Jakobson (who dissected polysemy) and Roland Barthes (whose book *S/Z* analyzed different meanings of a single text) come to mind as exemplars of this type of scholarly engagement.[47] Generations of linguistic analysis and distinction have explored the inherent ambiguity in statements like "the fat major's wife was fond of macaroni" or "the bill is large." The first exemplar can be parsed in a way that removes its ambiguity, while the second shows a deeper structural ambiguity that can never be clarified without an extra-grammatical context to clarify its sense.[48]

While ambiguity is rooted in the nature of language itself, we have also been arguing that it is just as much an inherent part of interpersonal relations, from the most micro level of individual behavior to the legal codes and injunctions that are the most abstract and formalized modes of regulating such behavior. Ambiguity characterizes intra-psychic as well as inter-psychic activities, defining social roles in societies at all levels of differentiation.[49] Further, as the writings of John Dewey explicate, ambiguity is at the core of our relation to the physical world around us. "The distinctive characteristic of practical activity, one which is so inherent that it cannot be eliminated, is the uncertainty that attends it."[50] Dewey reminds us that "all activity involves change" and hence "judgment and belief regarding actions performed can never attain more than a precarious probability."[51] Note the past tense of "actions performed." He is arguing that we can never have complete, unambiguous knowledge, even of what we have done. Ambiguity is an aspect of our relation to all of our surrounding worlds, both the sentient and non-sentient.

Much of our focus will be on ambiguity as a necessary and irreducible context for all of our framing and meaning-giving endeavors. By attending so single-mindedly to shared meanings and causal links, the intricacies of organizational grids and institutional functions, or the rules of reciprocity and exchange, our fields have sometimes lost sight of the reality that makes all of this necessary. It is as if we shy away from the ground (or perhaps morass) that inevitably accompanies the human construction of social categories, legal rules, role expectations, kinship taboos, and terms of commensality. Like Lot, we dare not look back, afraid (quite rightly, perhaps) of being turned into a pillar of salt. The consequence of this, however, is that we tend to be blind to the effect of all the codes, rules, and expectations on the manner in which we approach those free-flowing, undocumented, uncategorized bits of reality that always exist at the margins and in the interstices of our meaning-giving grids.

Most social scientists take this undifferentiated and uncategorized reality for granted and leave its articulation and expression to the arts. Others, like Victor Turner, have attempted to frame it through a new type of category, what he termed the "liminal." We have tried to argue, however, that in some sense this defeats the purpose of approaching the ambiguous on its own terms. Only a few have concerned themselves with the ambiguous in its own right, or with the boundary between the analytically clear and the hopelessly ambiguous. Even fewer try to apprehend the effect of our systems of analysis and notation (hence of classification and categorization) on what cannot be classified and categorized.

One of the important exceptions, of course, is Gregory Bateson (who, we are pleased to say, seems to be discovered anew by each generation of social scientists). Bateson's groundbreaking work on frames and meta-communication clarified how every communication carries with it not only a message, but a message about the message, a nod at the frame within which the message makes sense. Some of his best work showed the hopeless muddles we all get into when we are unclear about the relevant frames of communication, about what refers to the message itself and what to the frame. His use of Russell's theory of logical types and Korzybski's insights in semantics has become famous through his question: "When is a bite not a bite?" What allows a dog to interpret another dog's bite as an act of play rather than one of violence and aggression? The answer, of course, is when its tail is wagging—an act of metacommunicative framing.

Both of us, however, have had dogs that never quite figured this out. Most of us know unfortunate people with similar framing problems, and all of us can remember such situations in our own lives as well. It is all too easy to confound frame with content or one frame with another. Regardless of the degree of abstract notation, communication is prone to misunderstanding and ambiguous renderings because one can never be absolutely certain at what level the communication is pitched. The psychiatrist Edgar Levenson warned that "the illusion of clarity increases with the level of abstraction."[52] The more intricate the symbol system, the more abstract the process of categorization, the more developed, universal, and generalized the system of notation—the more we fool ourselves into believing that we have attained clarity. Alfred Korzybski and John Dewey, in their very different ways, also warned us against such thinking. Mindful of these warnings, we explore three different ways of parsing ambiguity and their implications for social ordering and interpersonal behavior, starting in the next chapter with the problem of notation.

Before engaging in this analysis, however, we offer as our first interlude an excursus on two texts—Euripides' play *The Bacchae* and the book of Job in the Bible. Both address the problem of ambiguity and the categories of knowledge head on. Both approach the problem of meaning and the consequences of an insufficient awareness of the limits to our understanding. Both Pentheus in *The Bacchae* and Job in the Bible presume to knowledge of what is clearly beyond human apprehension. The one demands order (Pentheus) and the other, justice (Job). Both are met by very different types of furies, the madness of the Agaves in the Bacchae and of God, emerging out of the whirlwind, in Job. Both end with very different forms of resolution.

Our purpose in bringing them here, however, is to show just how seriously some ancient civilizations took the limits of knowledge and the problem of its boundaries. Indeed, the issue of boundaries emerges again and again in both texts. Both recognize the necessity of boundaries, but they insist that tragedy awaits any human actor incapable of bridging them and playing their edges. Much more than in our own highly notated world, these texts remind us that ambiguity lies at the heart of all order, and of the disaster that awaits if we ignore it.

Interlude: Ambiguity, Order, and Deity

PAST TIMES AND traditions clearly recognized the pervasiveness of ambiguity. The modern conceit, however, seems to be that we can excise the ambiguities from the ethical, political, and legal spheres and replace them with a morally precise and unitary vision. Less modernist readings of society, whether in China, among the Dinka, in ancient Israel, or in Periclean Athens, recognized the inherent ambiguity of the world and its created orders. The Greek concern with excess, with hubris, is a study in the interconnectedness of entities and the lack of sharp boundaries distinguishing "daring and passion from excess and transgression."[1] The Greeks understood power, for example, as necessary for the workings of an ordered city, but also as transgressive and dangerous when it breached its limits. The close connection of the sacred with the profane, purity with pollution, healing medicine with deadly poison (both meanings of the Greek word *pharmakon*) all point to a deep recognition of an inescapable ambiguity. In the words of Oudemans and Lardinois, this is the uniquely tragic and cosmic ambiguity that inhered to Greek culture. Both the *Orestia* and *Antigone* have become icons of this understanding for us.

Many cultures recognize that ambiguity inheres in all things—in their constitutive nature, their boundaries, limits, and defining characteristics. In this interlude, we will examine this ambiguity through ancient Greek and Hebrew notions of ritual purity and pollution. Certainly among both groups, the rituals of purity tied intimately to infinite attempts at reconstituting boundaries that had been abrogated and hence polluted. We need to recognize that this polluting infringement of boundaries was an almost quotidian affair, even if one did not sleep with one's mother or murder one's father on a daily basis. Daily life meant being in touch with the powerful generative but also destructive force of nature—something to be dealt with rather than denied. The final Mishnaic tractate *Tohoroth* (Purities) minutely parses all possible conditions and modes of impurity that make up daily life: coming in contact with the dead, or with creepy crawly things or scale disease; even earthenware pots in an oven could transmit pollution. The Hebrews and Greeks, like many other peoples, saw pollution as an everyday affair to be dealt with accordingly. Each day brought breaches of boundaries through the simple experiences of living a human life. Perhaps it was most felt when coming in contact with the dead—where, as we shall see, the very ambiguity of purity and pollution constituted the rites of purification themselves.

Death is always with us, along with its pollutions. We experience power, too, on a daily basis—the power of order, but also the power and threat of order's dissolution, which is always but a step away. As Oudemans and Lardinois write about the Greeks:

> Power confronts us with a blend of paradox and ambiguity. Stressing the aspects of paradox means emphasis on the ineluctable fissions which run through human life and the cosmos, the broken links between opposing categories. Stressing the aspect of ambiguity means emphasis on the fusion of opposites which is the counterpart of paradox: the "impossible" blending of categories. Power is responsible for both fusion and fission, for both generation and destruction.[2]

We ourselves daily encounter comparable ambiguities in law, even though we may not recognize them as such. They show in our debates over legal pluralism, sexuality and gender, justice and mercy, or truth and trust. In the following we take up some ancient texts to help us appreciate just how much certain other civilizations understood and accepted ambiguity, and to study the lessons of such recognition.

Order and the Ambiguous

Jon Levinson deftly addressed the ambiguity of the biblical narrative of creation in his important book, *Creation and the Persistence of Evil*. There, Levinson shows just how pervasive the fear of a slip into chaos is. How fragile is the triumph of creation and the order upon which it rests and how undaunted are the forces of chaos, most often represented as their aquatic monster—the Leviathan. As Levinson argues: "the Flood is not the great deluge of Noah's time, but rather the assault of chaos upon order in

the form of the sea monster's bellicose challenge to the pantheon."[3] This
challenge is never fully put to rest. In periods of national crises its threat
was to be met in specific ritual and liturgical practices, reenacting the
story of creation. He continues:

> Both the flood and passages such as Psalm 74:12–17 (and perhaps
> Isaiah 51:9–11) attest to a view of creation in which God's ordering of
> reality is irresistible, but not constant or inevitable. The conclusion
> of the Flood story includes a divine pledge to maintain creation, but
> the story itself manifests a profound anxiety about the given-ness of
> creation, a keen sense of its precariousness and how bound up it is
> with its own dissolution. On the one hand, God vows to maintain
> the created order. On the other hand, he does so only after having
> ended a state of chaos that began with his announcing that he
> regretted having ever authored Creation in the first place.[4]

This awareness of chaos as a part of creation is common to many civilizations. The *Enima Elish* story points to such ever present dangers, as does
Hesiod in the *Theogony*, where order and the boundaries of order are only
the final, hard-won, and precarious result of bloody and violent conflict.[5]

Here we will explore the biblical book of Job and Euripides' play *The
Bacchae*, both of which show the ambiguities that adhere to the generative
force of order.[6] Both stories were composed (or redacted) in about the
same period (5th to 4th century B.C.E.).[7] Both distill earlier stories and
myths.[8] Job has its counterpart in many stories of the Near Eastern
Wisdom literature, like the Egyptian *Complaint of the Peasant* and the similar *Dialogue about Human Misery* (also known as *Complaint of a Sage over
the Injustice of the World*), or the Babylonian *Pessimistic Dialogue of a Master
and a Slave*.[9] Both Job and *The Bacchae* have been written about exten-
sively; however, as far as we know, they have never been compared or
explored from this perspective.[10] Both go beyond reflection to critique and
both were incorporated into the major traditions of Western civilizational
thought and meaning.

The story of Job is much the better known of the two. It tells how Satan
dares God to test Job's faithfulness and how God sends down afflictions
upon Job: the loss of his crops and his wealth, the death of his children,
and finally a plague. Through it all, Job does not lose his faith in God,
though he does demand that God account for unjust sufferings. Job's
three friends appear and argue with him. If he is suffering so, they reason,

God is punishing him for offences that he committed, whether he admits them or not. God eventually appears "out of the whirlwind" and justifies His actions by pointing out how Job has no understanding of the cosmic order or the orders of creation and world-maintenance and so cannot presume to judge the Supreme Judge. Job is, finally, reconciled with God and His ways. Job's fortunes are restored, new children are born, and his friends must make amends to God and to Job for their false words. This, in brief, is the well-known story, as recounted in the Bible.

The Bacchae was Euripides' last play, and it was performed only after his death. Its themes are madness, illusion, and the failure of recognition. Pentheus, the young King of Thebes, refuses to recognize Dionysus (his cousin) but is fascinated by the activities of the Maenads (the female followers of Dionysus) outside the city walls. He ends up spying on them—dressed as a woman by Dionysus. The wild Maenads, led by Pentheus's mother, Agave, apprehend him, however, and tear him limb from limb. Dionysus, the son of Zeus and Agave's sister, Semele, brings confusion to Thebes by replacing existing traditions with the mad frenzy of his followers. In their actions and cultic rites, they represent the blurring of all categories, the confusion of all norms, the conflation of all boundaries and their replacement by an order where, in essence, all is one. The rather straight-laced Pentheus refuses to countenance this, leading directly to his tragedy and the ultimate fall of the house of Cadmus.

Both texts go beyond merely telling a story, because they relate to some form of practice, that is, to ritual action. The Bacchae concerns the cult of Dionysus, which arrived from Thrace and Asia at an unknown time in Greek history.[11] It is unclear if the play is to be taken as a condemnation or acceptance of order's dissolution and ecstatic religion, or perhaps both. The conflicting forces in The Bacchae have, as Charles Segal claimed, "no resolution." He goes on to note that the play's "concern with the dissolution of order and boundaries—the boundaries between divinity and bestiality in man, reality and imagination, reason and madness, self and other, art and life—makes it unusually accessible and particularly important."[12] It is especially important, we would add, as an example of the ambiguity that inheres to those boundaries themselves.

Segal makes a critical connection between the *sparagmos* (the dismemberment of Pentheus) and the *omophagia* (the eating of his raw flesh) undertaken by the ecstatic Bacchae Maenads in the play. These moments draw attention to the continual re-creation out of destruction within Dionysian ritual. "Within the Dionysian cult and its Orphic adaptation the sparagmos of the victim leads ultimately to a symbolic rebirth of the god. Torn apart in the form of a beast and eaten by his worshippers in a symbolical reenactment of his sparagmos by the Titans, the Orphic Dionysus is renewed from the portions which remain uneaten and the ashes."[13]

The mysteries of the cult, according to Walter Burkett, continued to be performed into the fourth century c.e.[14] In fact, they continued via representations "to adorn various kinds of funeral monuments, aediculae, stelae and altars down to its last flowering in the art of sarcophagi." They presented a "response to the blatant senselessness of death," as Burkett says.[15] Of course, and in contrast to the Orphic rite, which ends in a purified state, the play results in a terrible state of impurity—in what Segal calls "sterility."[16] The play ends, we recall, with Pentheus's dismemberment, and with Cadmus and Agave going off into harsh exile in the face of the total and utter destruction of life and any regenerative possibilities (the end of the house of Cadmus as prophesied by Zeus). This contrasts interestingly with the ending of the book of Job, which reasserts regeneration and the continuity of the kinship line.

As with the story of Dionysus, the problem of Job has been analyzed and commented on over the course of the past two millennia within Jewish, Christian, and Islamic societies. Retold in the Qur'an and addressed by major thinkers in all three religious traditions, it provided a focus for Islamic *tafsir* literature (exegesis on the Qur'an) and has been explored by such Islamic thinkers as Al-Zamakhsari, al-Tabari, Ibn Kathir, Jalal al Din Mahalli, Jalal al Din al Suyuti, Ibn Asakir, al-Kisa'i, and al-Maqdisi.[17] Major Jewish philosophers who grappled with the text include Maimonides (who devotes two chapters to it in the *Guide to the Perplexed*), Saadiah Gaon (who devoted a whole book of commentary to Job), and Gersonides.[18] Maimonides, in fact, notes the Islamic traditions of the Mutzaila and Ash'ariyya in his study of Job.[19] Christian thinkers include John Chrysostom, Jerome, Gregory the Great, Theodore Beza, Luther, Calvin, William Blake, Herder, Kierkegaard, John Henry Newman, and Thomas Carlyle, as well as Reinhardt Neibur and the contemporary founder of Liberation Theology, Gustavo Gutierrez.[20]

Interestingly, Job is the only book of the Hebrew Bible that a mourner may read during the seven days of mourning. Jewish traditional practice thus relates the problems of theodicy and divine justice in the text to the problem of meaning that death poses for us. The connection, we suggest, is that both death and the problem of theodicy make us face the deeply ambiguous nature of meaning, which puts it beyond our understanding.

Both threaten to betray creation through the threat of cosmic dissolution. This is made clear, for example, when Maimonides explicitly and approvingly quotes the Babylonian Talmud (Baba Batra 16a): "Rabbi Simon ben Laqish said: Satan [who, recall, put God up to Job's afflictions], the evil inclination, and the angel of death are one and the same."[21]

The medieval Jewish commentators Rashi, Ibn Ezra, R. Joseph Karo, and R. Nissim Gaon all identified the day of Satan's accusation of Job with the Jewish New Year day (Rosh Hashanah), that is, the day on which the world and all its inhabitants are judged. Their positioning of the Job story within this context questions the working of divine justice and points to its continuing ambiguities. Just as Satan's dare moved God to afflict Job, it may be that even on the Day of Judgment the terms of His decrees are no less arbitrary.

Job and *The Bacchae* both delineate the complex relation between order and chaos, creation and death, generation and dissolution. That is to say, both recognize that chaos is very much part of order, not something that exists beyond it. The complex intertwining of order and its opposite, however, differs greatly in the Hebrew and the Greek texts. In Job, it is God who is beyond order. The "beyond" is the realm of the transcendent. This transcendence posits order as theodicy, which means as well that the failures of order, its lacunae, are either sin or injustice. The discussions between Job and his friends turn on this. The friends argue for the transparent justice of the theodic order, which must mean that somehow Job has sinned, or else he would not be suffering so. This is theodicy as taught in Sunday schools. Job insists on his rectitude and so that God's world must not be just—that, given his sufferings, there must be no (moral) order. God's famous response is that there is a (moral) order on the cosmic scale, but Job and mankind are incapable of accessing it. God is maintaining that, given the limited nature of human understanding, the order can only appear to humans as ambiguity, even disorder. Had mankind the acuity to understand the cosmic scale of distributive justice, then they would affirm the greatness of God and so the existence of a transcendent order. What appears as the lack of a moral order (the existence of evil and injustice) is simply the result of our own limited vision and understanding.

The Bacchae, on the other hand, does not posit order in terms of transcendent justice or morality. Proper order instead entails recognition of the world as it is, the world *für sich*. Yet this recognition also entails accepting the essentially unordered, uncontrolled, and uncontrollable elements in the world, together with its more ordered capacities. This comes up early in the play, in the actions of the Bacchants as reported to Pentheus:

Some of the women held in their arms a roe
or wild wolf cubs, and gave them white milk—
those who had newly given birth, whose breasts were still swollen,
and who had left behind their babies. On their heads they put garlands
of ivy and oak and flowering bryony.
Someone grasped a thyrsus and struck it into a rock
from which a dewy stream of water leapt out;
another struck her rod on the ground
and for her the god sent up a spring of wine;
and those who had a desire for the white drink
scraped the ground with their finger tips
and had jets of milk and from out of the ivied
thyrsi, sweet streams of honey dripped.[22]
So we took to our heels and escaped
being torn to pieces by the baccants; but they attacked the grazing
heifers, with hand that bore no steel.
And one you could have seen holding asunder in her hands
a tight-uddered, young, bellowing heifer;
while others were tearing full-grown cows to pieces.
You could have seen ribs, or a cloven hoof,
being hurled to and fro; and these hung
dripping under the fir trees, all mixed with blood.
Bulls that were arrogant before, with rage
in their horns, stumbled to the ground,
borne down by the countless hands of girls.
The garments of flesh were drawn apart more quickly
than you could close the lids over your royal eyes . . .
They snatched children from their homes;
and whatever they set on their shoulders stuck there
without being tied . . .
They carried fire and it did not burn them. The villagers, in a rage
at being plundered by the bacchants, rushed to arms.
The sight that followed was strange to see, lord;
for the men's pointed spears drew no blood,
but the women, discharging thyrsi from their hands,
wounded the men and made them turn their back in flight:
women did this to men—some god must have helped them![23]

Here, Euripides pairs an image of natural bounty with one of mothers abandoning their children, of women suckling wild animals and of women defeating men in battle. The murderous acts of Agave, the *sparagmos* of Pentheus (as well as his own transformation into a woman under the god's direction) mark boundaries transgressed and hence the disruption of order. They appear, nevertheless, together with the spontaneous formation of chorus and dance by the worshippers (an image of order, par excellence). Thus, with the dissolution of all boundaries of differentiation between man and animal, animate and inanimate, all become one in a new, undifferentiated order (and hence one not accessible to our understanding).

Dionysus and his followers represent just this inherently ambiguous understanding of entwined order/disorder. Indeed, there is the strong impression that if only Pentheus could step outside his propriety and rather straight-laced sense of order, if only he could recognize the existence of chaos (or madness) as itself part of order, then the order of the City could have been maintained. He cannot, and the result is tragedy for the City and his household. As in Job, the human propensity to impose clear-cut categories and our failure to appreciate the essential ambiguity of the world propel the drama.

Both texts recognize the coexistence of order and its negation—in other words, the deep ambiguity at the heart of life—though, of course, the tension differs in each. Job posits this ambiguity in the moral terms of transcendent justice, while *The Bacchae* does it by recognizing the balance of order and its dissolution that is human existence. Both texts recognize that the negation of order—whether in sin and injustice or in madness and a world turned upside down—is part and parcel of order. Both address the deeply discordant needs and circumstances that tear at human life and existence. Both attempt to address the dilemmas that result. The introduction of Satan at the beginning of Job already hints at the problems of identifying all order with God, including the discordant side of order. In Euripides, the god is identified with the negation of human order, with the dissolution of its boundaries and with madness. An important consequence of this different rendering of the problem is that in the Hebrew text, the protagonist Job finally arrives at an understanding of his situation, indeed an understanding of what he previously had not understood: the partial nature of his own vision and understanding. This never happens in *The Bacchae*. Neither Pentheus nor Cadmus nor even Agave ever understands or reconciles with the problematic nature of order, which combines both ordered codes and their negation. They are simply punished.

Justice, which is about right measure, is also about boundaries. Boundaries delineate an entity, defining it, giving it a place from which we can assess its relation to other entities. We cannot measure or balance anything, let alone justice, without boundaries. Thus it is no surprise that in the Greek play, Pentheus represents boundaries while the god is the one who abrogates boundaries, transgresses their limits and blurs all categories. Again, this nods to that ambiguity which is beyond human comprehension—or at least that of Pentheus. Pentheus is destroyed by his inability to accept these blurred boundaries, and by the extreme hubris with which he defends the boundaries of his conception of order. We infer from the play that human order must recognize also what appears to it as chaos, because both the order and the chaos are divine. The failure of this recognition leads to horrific consequences.

The book of Job parses the problem somewhat differently. The deity remains the source of order, of justice, and of boundaries (though to be sure, he appears "out of the whirlwind"). The apparent abrogation of boundaries—those of justice, right measure, reward and punishment—was only appearance. God explained to Job how the eternal, constitutive boundaries of the world and its rules of distributive justice and resource distribution do exist, even if they are not comprehensible to mankind. Job falsely understood the problem of the world's boundaries—of order and its abrogation—as one of morality and not of epistemology. The voice of God from the whirlwind, which reasserted the existence of boundaries and order, also reaffirmed the problem as epistemological. Job's problem was his ontological incapacity to understand creation. As God explains to him:

> *Where were you when I laid the foundations of the earth?*
> *Tell Me, if you have any understanding.*
> *Who marked out its measure, if you know it.*
> *Who stretched the plumb line upon it?*
> *Upon what were the earth's pillars sunk;*
> *Who laid down its cornerstone,*
> *When the morning stars sang together*
> *And all the sons of God shouted for joy?*
> *Who shut in the Sea with doors*
> *When it broke forth from its womb whence it came,*
> *And I made the clouds its garment,*
> *And dark clouds its swaddling clothes,*
> *Prescribing my limit for the Sea,*
> *And setting for it bolts and doors,*

Saying, Thus far shall you come, and no farther,
And here shall your proud waves be stayed?[24]

As any reader of the book knows, God goes on and on, questioning Job as one would a school boy to show, in a manner that can brook no questions, just how circumscribed are the limits of human knowledge:

Have you ever commanded the morning,
Or assigned its place to the dawn . . .
What is the way to the home of light;
And darkness, where is its dwelling place . . .
Have you ever entered the storehouses of snow,
Have you seen the storehouses of hail, . . .
Do you know the laws of the heavens;
Can you establish order on the earth?[25]

According to Maimonides, had Job been wise, he would not have had to be subjected to this lesson in human humility. In it, as we see especially in the final quoted question, chaos (as injustice) is but an appearance, an illusion, brought on by human ignorance. Entities are not fungible, God is not arbitrary, and justice is not lacking, even if we cannot comprehend its terms. What appears to us as chaos and the lack of a moral order actually reflects the deep ambiguity of the created world.

Primal Bonds and Particular Entities

While their resolutions are markedly different, both Job and *The Bacchae* question any neat and binary conception of order, justice, and meaning. They question as well the social mechanism through which primal human bonds are generalized. This is most clear in the relation of Job to his friends, who, as representatives of society, fail him and do not keep faith with him. *The Bacchae* questions the very constitutive position of the city and its order. The city shakes, Dionysus escapes the prison, and the order of civic life is rent asunder again and again throughout the play.

Given the ambiguity of the generative principle itself, this should not surprise us. Indeed, this questioning appears in the elemental, almost biological microsociology of the mother-child bond. This is most clear in *The Bacchae* and in Agave's murder of her son Pentheus, but the book of Job equally questions this bond in the metaphor of the ostrich:

The wing of the ostrich beats joyously
But is her pinion like that of the stork or vulture?
For she leaves her eggs on the earth
And lets them be armed on the ground,
Forgetting that a foot may crush them
Or a wild beast trample them.
Her young ones grow tough without her;
That her labor may be in vain gives her no concern,
Because God forgot her when He allocated wisdom,
And He gave her no share in understanding.
Now she soars aloft
And laughs at the horse and his rider.[26]

Everything appears to be fungible, open to change, redirection, redefinition and the loss of meaning and commitment. This is the chasm that opens at one's feet in both texts. They undo our preconceived ideas of order at the most elemental, constitutive, and primal level. What is more unthinkable than the disruption of this bond between mother and child? What is more threatening to any fundamental sense of well-being and of life in the world? Yet, as we know, at least since Sigmund Freud, these primal bonds are ambiguous at the core, stubbornly resisting all univocal readings.

We may do well to remember that while *The Bacchae* engages with the power and importance of women (and the failed attempt to control them and keep them in what Pentheus believes is their place), Job has no real engagement with the feminine. Indeed, Job declares:

It was You who poured me out like milk,
And like cheese You curdled me.
You clothed me in skin and flesh
And knitted me together with bones and sinews.[27]

Here God replaces the mother's very womb as the origin of life and so as refuge from its chaos.

Both texts question human ties through the bonds of the collective, as well as that most primordial bond between mother and child (which is to be sure more the case in *The Bacchae* than in Job). In Job, it is most evident in his friends—his community and by extension society in general—who represent and indeed present the law and the common, taken-for-granted understanding of theodicy (that if Job is suffering, he must be at fault). The story juxtaposes the friends, as society, against the individual, who has been subjected to God's arbitrariness. The community cannot accommodate such a reading of God's actions and so must interpret them through traditional theodic understandings. The friends represent the workings of culture, law, or *nomos*. They are the generalization of the primal bond, which is as frayed here as it is in *The Bacchae*.

The rabbinic midrashic commentary notes that Job was the most pious of all the Gentiles.[28] His provenance, however, is unknown.[29] Maimonides did not believe that he ever existed and notes how some believe that Job was a contemporary of Abraham, some believe he was contemporaneous with Moses, others with David or with the return from the Babylonian exile.[30] This question of provenance brings us to the role of the Gentile, the other, standing at the margins of order. With the partial exception of King David— who was a forerunner of the Messiah (but also a descendent of Ruth the convert)—all figures listed are central symbols of Jewish belief, but are also deeply evocative of the world beyond Judaism. Abraham, the first Jew, cannot but evoke the world of family and idolatry that he rejected. Moses' ambivalent provenance (recalling the two sets of parents characteristic of so many cultural heroes, from Oedipus to Cyrus) goes without saying, and his marriage to a non-Israelite sharpens the point further.[31] The Babylonian exile was marked by intermarriage and a great deal of interpenetration between Jews and Gentiles, with later attempts at eradication as Ezra and Nehemia led the return from exile. Job, who is a sign of the good and whose book can be read in the face of death, thus marks not only the ambiguity of order, but also of communal boundaries and their limits.

It should not surprise us that *The Bacchae* shows a similar engagement with both destruction and creation, death and regeneration, exile and return, inside and outside: the boundaries of order. Walter Burkett noted that tragedy itself is tied to the goat (*tragos*) sacrificed at the same altar (*thumele*) that was central to all Dionysian performances.[32] "The rites of sacrifice touch the roots of human existence. In the ambivalence of the intoxication of blood and the horror of killing, in the twofold aspect of life and death, they hold something fundamentally uncanny, we might almost say, tragic."[33] This uncanniness is tied to the figure of Dionysus, who bridges the power of creation and the horrors of death. The very origins of this tragedy in the slaying of the he-goat (*tragos*), symbol of procreative power, every five years at the Dionysian altar recalls both the creation and destruction of boundaries.

Tragedy, seeped in the horrors and fascination of death and destruction, in the blood of sacrificed animals and human undoing, provides us with the wellsprings of empathy. We understand empathy as a cognate of pity, in Aristotle's famous definition of tragedy as "the imitation of an action that is serious and also, as having magnitude, complete in itself; in language with pleasurable accessories, each kind brought in separately in the parts of the work; in a dramatic and not narrative form, with incidents arousing pity and fear, wherewith to accomplish its catharsis of such emotions."[34] Turning to the other involves turning away from oneself, accepting and recognizing what is beyond our own ordered microcosm of the universe. Moving beyond the familiar—that is, beyond what we have ordered—is the critical mechanism for empathy. It moves into the subjunctive—which is precisely how Aristotle describes tragedy as "a kind of thing that might be."[35] Tragedy decenters the self as a precondition for empathy. It forces us to move beyond the boundaries of our own order and to recognize what we cannot control. In these terms Pentheus fails the test of recognition and is destroyed. Job rises to its heights and is justified.

Both responses entail empathy, but on very different levels. In Job, the text itself engenders the empathy. In *The Bacchae* it occurs in the audience. The book of Job ends not only with Job having achieved a vision of God, having all his property doubled, and new sons and daughters born, but with his friends Eliphaz, Bildad, and Zophar commanded by God to offer up sacrifices. These sacrifices are accepted and the friends forgiven only because Job intercedes in their behalf.

Job himself experiences catharsis and empathy within the text itself, although readers may also identify with his struggle with meaning and meaninglessness. *The Bacchae* offers no such collective resolution or broadening of empathy within the text. Agave goes off into exile alone and still polluted by the murder of her son. Cadmus bids her goodbye and the chorus reminds us of the inexplicable ways of the gods. Job ends with a scene of social harmony and the restitution of human (not only material) relations. *The Bacchae* ends in dissolution, so that empathy lies with the audience and is not internal to text. Perhaps it is the play's evocation of unresolved pain that engenders empathy in the spectator, while the reality of harmony in Job precludes such empathetic catharsis.

Both Job and *The Bacchae* bring us face to face with the contradictions at the heart of all order. In Job, these are resolved in God's majesty—which is, however, beyond anything that humans can comprehend. In contrast, *The Bacchae*'s god is as capricious and hubristic as his human counterpart (who is, after all, his cousin). Pentheus never grasps the meaning of the Dionysian rites of the Maenads and continually attributes a lewd sexual meaning to them. He is continually drawn to what he believes is the sexual nature of their activity outside the city. Seeing only excess—when in fact it is god-work—he himself becomes a man of excess, overstepping the boundaries of order in his display of power, his madness, and his transvestite disguise. In such excess, he unleashes forces of violence (fire and earthquake), finally to be cut down in the most violent manner imaginable.

Both Job and *The Bacchae* bring us to an encounter with that undifferentiated, deeply ambiguous symbolic reality that stands beneath all order. Job and *The Bacchae* force us to come to grips with both the dissolution of boundaries and their affirmation, with both chaos and the act of creation—with the transcendence of all order in that which is beyond its limits. As we have seen, each text frames the poles of chaos and creation, of boundaries and their dissolution, in a different way and with a different resolution. Yet both teach us that we can escape neither pole.

Finally, we would do well to recall God's final defense in the face of Job's accusations: God claims that Job may have some knowledge of what is just, but he has no authoritative knowledge of the world, nor does he have any responsibility (hence no practical knowledge) for ordering the world. Hence, in the end, he really knows very little. There is an important point hidden here. God is claiming that because Job has no notion of the real world, that is, of the real material circumstances of feeding the world, he can have no truly authoritative knowledge. Authoritative knowledge is, in the final analysis, practical knowledge, knowledge of particulars. Job's knowledge is only of abstract categories.

God's claim is that the only real, authoritative knowledge is practical knowledge of everything. Humans, the story teaches us, can only have a very limited degree of practical knowledge. Our knowledge of the practical and of the concrete is severely circumscribed; it is always limited because it is only our own experience in space and in time. Yet we clearly make claims to knowledge—to universal knowledge that transcends our empirical experience. We do so in all realms, and certainly in the realms of morality. Nevertheless these claims, so we learn from Job, precisely because they are abstract and general, do not accord us real authoritative knowledge.

In the most radical of terms, we may say that God valorizes the particular—every particular—as particular. In contrast, humankind can only relativize the particular in the universal. Our knowledge and so the ground of our action is thus always only partial, incomplete, frail, and wanting. Moreover, because of this relativization, language has only a limited and partial ability to express what is, to express the real. Language always, by necessity, loses the particular entity in the universality of linguistic categories. The particular quiddity of this unique *brick* is lost in the general category of "brick."[36]

The consequences of this are dramatic. It means that some element of deceit, if only the deceit of language, is built into social life. Job's friends are no more than human, representing the partial and structurally mandated deceit or falseness of social life. They say what can be said, and only what can be said. In contrast, as we learned from Job's encounter with God, what truly is, cannot be said.

The tension between the particular and the general is central to the whole problem of boundaries and of order, of how we reflect on order, of the encounter with chaos and with the other—that is, with the themes of this book. Chaos is, in human terms, the plethora of particulars. The truly limitless number of particulars requires us to generalize, to abstract; this is the only way we have available to grasp them. The price we pay for this is the loss of the particular and with it of real knowledge. Only God, it seems, can apprehend the infinite set of particulars without it becoming chaos. Our own circumscribed vision and partial knowledge leave us forever on the brink of chaos. This is salvaged in Job only by faith in an entity that transcends such chaos; *The Bacchae* leaves us to reflect on our fate.

2

Notation and Its Limits

NEAR THE BEGINNING of Herodotus's *History*, he tells us the story of the Lydian King Candaules and his bodyguard Gyges. Candaules was so enamored of his wife and her beauty that he arranged for Gyges to see her naked. Though Gyges remonstrated and begged his master to spare him this unlawful sight, Candaules was adamant that Gyges had nothing to fear and that the wife would never know of his presence. Candaules contrived for Gyges to be hidden in their bedroom as the queen was removing her clothes and placing them on the chair near the bed. Gyges did indeed see her nakedness, but when he slipped out behind the door to exit the room, the queen saw him and understood what Candaules had orchestrated.

The following day, the queen brought together all of her most loyal retinue and called for Gyges. She confronted him with his act and gave him the choice of dying on the spot or of killing King Candaules, reigning in his stead and, of course, taking the queen for his wife. "For," in her words, "either he that contrived this must die or you, who have viewed me naked and done what is not lawful." Gyges tried to talk the queen out of this awful choice, but did not succeed and, forced with necessity, chose his own survival. He killed the king and, in Herodotus's words, "had the wife and the kingship of Lydia."[1]

Like so many of the stories recounted by Herodotus, this is rich and multilayered. It touches on many critical issues, from the danger of loving one's wife too much to the fatal weakness of needing another man to validate the beauty of one's own wife. As one woman friend judged Candaules when recounted this story: "He is not a man." Our interest lies in the excluded middle. Or, in slightly different terms, with the erasure and dismantling of an ambiguous situation. To be seen naked by a man who is not one's husband and, on the other hand, to see the queen naked when one is not the king are both impossibilities—yet, they are impossibilities that clearly occurred, and only could occur through the contrivance of the king. Hence the king must die to restore order. "Barbarians" like the Lydians considered viewing a woman naked to be a severe breach of the normative order, leading to a situation best understood in sociological terms as "anomic" (taken from the Greek *anomos*).[2] A-nomic, a-nomous, a-nonymous: all point to what is beyond the normative frame, outside the named, exceeding anything that society can configure. Gyges clearly could not see the queen naked. Yet he did. The situation was impossible and thus required a resolution. One of the men had to die, and in so doing the ambiguous and anomic were reintegrated into the normative order: kings and only kings see their wives' nakedness.

Lest this story seem too distant, too fictitious, and much too politically incorrect, allow us to complement it with the following tale, told by Rahel Wasserfall, a visiting French anthropologist who spent time as a Fulbright exchange scholar at a left of center American university campus. We quote from her account of that period: "I was meeting a male anthropologist who was about my age and we were on our way to have lunch. Almost immediately he said something about going with his wife to Washington over the weekend. I myself found a way to answer a few sentences later that 'I will be going to visit my partner in LA next month.' After this (in my view strange) dialogue, we went on talking about anthropology and his interests."[3] Wasserfall was struck by how, in this country, people hardly tolerated ambiguity in gender relations and how the professional American academic environment did not countenance the type of flirtation and "letting things happen" that she was familiar with in other cultures. Rather, at the very beginning of any interaction, even the most innocuous and professional, her interlocutors (regardless of their own gender) felt it imperative to establish almost immediately the boundaries, possibilities, and restrictions of the incipient interaction. She soon learned that—again, as opposed to other cultures and climes—men and women both were very concerned to know "not my class, my kin, my religious or political beliefs, or the origin of my family, but my marital situation."[4] That was the boundary that could not be crossed.

While clearly not as sanguine as the Lydians, here, too, we find a high level of intolerance for ambiguity in gender relations and the need to preclude the emergence of any ambiguity in the interaction (perhaps because the options for resolution open to Candaules's wife are less available among the professoriate). We bring up these stories to illustrate one way in which ambiguity has been dealt with over the ages and across cultures.

This is simply to do away with it: a policy of "zero tolerance." In certain matters, people do not tolerate ambiguity and so immediately resolve it into a more binary structure of preexisting categories. Hence, only kings see their queens naked, and a profanation of this rule must be righted by its reinstantiation. It does not really matter who will be the king (either Candaules or Gyges), but the point is that the status quo of kings and only kings seeing queens naked had to be reestablished, and so it was.

Though Foucault's *History of Sexuality* is devoted to precisely this theme—that is, the increasing categorization of sexuality and the resolution of the amorphous and ambiguous into the socially scripted and sanctioned—the realm of sexuality is far from the only one in which people deny and erase the ambiguous. We need only reflect on the phenomenon of exile to see, again, the banishment of the a-nomic out beyond the realms of society's categories. Examples include Cain's murder of his brother Abel, which forced him into a life of wandering, as well as to the cities of refuge commanded in the Bible—where the perpetrators of manslaughter (but not murder) could find safety from avenging kin. The exiles had to stay there, however, until the death of the high priest. This was a common solution to the ambiguity occasioned by the spilling of blood and consequent upset of cosmic harmony. Exile, however, is not purely a category of the ancients. A very interesting study by the Dutch social psychologist Wilma Vollebergh found exile to be an operative concept among youth presented with the task of constructing, from scratch, their own ideal island society.[5]

Vollebergh conducted her studies to rethink the old Frankfurt School theories of the authoritarian personality, and she thus divided her subjects into groups of "non-authoritarian" and "authoritarian" types (according to rather well-established categories that do not interest us here). Interestingly, and perhaps counterintuitively, she found that the "authoritarian" subjects, who had an array of punishments at their beck and call for all manner of law breakers on their imaginary island and who saw law as backed by the coercive powers of the majority, had no need for exile in their array of responses to deviant, non-normative behavior. On the other hand, the "non-authoritarian" group had liberal politics based on ideals of governance by direct democracy, with the island governed by internal and voluntary submission to universally shared moral rules. Consequently, they had no place for any form of punishment on their island, but they also had no place for those who chose not to submit to the moral authority of the group. Those people had to be exiled and thrown off the island.[6]

Exile thus remained a cognitive option among Dutch youth at the end of the twentieth century. Even more interestingly, it existed among Vollebergh's liberal and "non-authoritarian" subjects, those who sought to do without any explicit set of laws and regulations, but wished to order society purely on the basis of an internal and voluntary acceptance of the moral order. Vollebergh's study warns us to question any easy identification of intolerance with the explicit avowal of principled rules, categorical imperatives, and adherence to ritualized modes of behavior. The subject is much more complicated than any easy identification of tolerance with liberal and liberal-individualistic notions of self and society, at least if we maintain the minimal definition of tolerance as living with what you disapprove of. Exile in such cases would not, one would think, be in the cards.

At present, however, our concern is with the type of response to ambiguity that exile (and the status of Lydian kings) personifies—and that is to eradicate it, to remove it because the ambiguous is impure, something the social fabric cannot entirely incorporate. Exile and similar responses attempt to maintain the existing categories of order as if there were no ambiguity. Until now, we have been discussing social practices: killing kings, exiling deviants, sequestering killers, and so on. We must also consider the cognitive correlates of these deeds, which attempt to abstract reality into a reified understanding of moral or social categories as somehow pure, through censoring out the problematic and ambiguous "middle."

Humor provides a very good illustration of this. At least since the writings of Freud on *Jokes and Their Relation to the Unconscious*, we know how bound up ambiguity is with the very structure of the humorous. The mechanisms of condensation, double meaning, and the multiple use of the same material in jokes rely on the ambiguity of language and context to make humor, in the form of jokes, possible. Playing between frames is, after all, what makes so many jokes humorous. To take a short example offered by Freud of a humorous simile: "A wife is like an umbrella—sooner or later one takes a cab."[7] The humor revolves around implicit meanings. Just as an umbrella does not protect one from a downpour and so one ends up taking a cab, so a wife does not fulfill all of a man's sexual urgings and he ends up maintaining illicit sexual relations (with the public nature of the cab comparable to "public women," i.e., prostitutes). When spelled out, the humor is lost and it becomes a crass statement of dubious worth. The humor is in the play of signifier and signified, in the move between meanings that allows the release of certain sexual tensions and repressed desires. In Freud's own words, "What these jokes whisper may be said aloud: that the wishes and desires of men have a right to make themselves acceptable alongside of exacting and ruthless morality."[8]

On first sight, then, humor and the comic have an apparently "emancipatory" role—allowing the expression of the repressed. In truth, though, Freud was not one to accept such a reading. Rather, he clearly indicated that desires must remain unsatisfied (rather than illegitimately fulfilled) "because only the continuance of so many unfulfilled demands can develop the power to change the order of society."[9] Real emancipation and challenge to social mores and categories could not come through jokes, which only sublimate the unfulfilled desires, rather than challenging the categories and frames that channel them.

The semiotician Umberto Eco expanded this relatively undeveloped insight of Freud in his essay on "The Frames of Comic Freedom."[10] There Eco presents an important distinction for our concern with ambiguity and its erasure. He compares the tragic and the comic to show that both have to do with violation of a rule and the consequences of this violation. The difference between tragedy and comedy is that in tragedy the rule violated is a major one (do not kill one's father, say), while in comedy it tends to be minor (e.g., do not sneeze on people). Similarly, we identify with the violator of the rule in tragedy; he elicits our sympathy even as we share in his remorse. In comedy, on the other hand, the character generally appears repulsive, inferior, ignoble and animal-like. Consequently we do not identify with him or her, but feel superior. We can share in the pleasure of the broken rule as well as its reassertion with the wrongdoer getting his comeuppance. The comic, says Eco, "is always racist: only the others, the Barbarians, are supposed to pay."[11] He is pointing out that both the tragic and the comic register the perennial and unalterable existence of rules and obligations.

Comedy disrupts order no more than tragedy. In both, order triumphs over the ambiguities that it creates and reasserts its own categories—albeit with very different emotional responses by the viewer in each case. Whether in tears or in laughter, the possibility of being ambiguous is lost. Neither form allows us to exist between more than one normative order, whether these are the contradictory demands of civic justice and personal morality or the conflicting obligations to kin and polis, piety and vengeance. The comic, like the tragic, registers the breaking of an unspoken, yet easily recognized and accepted law—just as Freud's umbrella joke works on the basis of an infringement of an unstated moral injunction.

The end in all cases is to reassert those very laws and injunctions that have been profaned. No place remains for unregulated sexuality, unframed morality, or unrestricted filial obligations.

At the end of the essay, Eco interestingly contrasts the tropes of the comic to what he sometimes calls irony and sometimes humor. Here he tells us: "The laughter, mixed with pity, without fear, becomes a smile."[12] We no longer laugh at the characters, but at the contrast between the characters' desires and the frame of their actions. Don Quixote is humorous but not comic—precisely because Cervantes shows us his ambiguous position in relation to the frames in which he acts. This humor, he writes, "does not promise us liberation: on the contrary, it warns us about the impossibility of global liberation, reminding us of the presence of a law that we no longer have reason to obey. In doing so it undermines the law. It makes us feel the uneasiness of living under a law—any law."[13] Here, then, we no longer find the eradication of the ambiguous, but a form of its instantiation or notation. This, as we shall discuss, provides a powerful alternative to exile and censorship as a way of dealing with ambiguity's inevitable presence in our lives.

Unlike the ironic, comedy for Eco does not gently undermine our structure of categories by letting us stand outside them for a moment in a world where the demarcations of order are not so clear. Instead, just like exile or the murder of King Candaules, it insists on the uncrossable categories of order, keeping the other as Other. These techniques deal with ambiguity by isolating, ridiculing, and destroying it.

Projects to Resolve Ambiguity

As Eco's discussion of irony implied, there are other important techniques to minimize the threat of ambiguity. Here we will discuss the project to disambiguate by constructing ever more precise and detailed categories. This process resembles a photographer trying to remove fuzziness by achieving ever greater resolutions. Think of color terms, for example. The permutations of hue, saturation, and brightness lead to a vast number of perceivable colors. Most languages, however, have fewer than a dozen basic color terms.[14] This can easily lead to confusion ("Do you want the blue shirt or the other color of blue shirt?"), which we answer by creating new ad hoc categories ("the blue of your eyes") or with a multiplication of specialized terms ("cerulean," "azure," and so on). Color virtuosos—fashion designers, for instance—may have a huge professional vocabulary, although not even they can cover the entire range of sensory possibilities.

Loosely following in the path of John Henry Newman, we call this process of constant clarification "notation." By this, we mean the process of intellectual abstraction from real experience or apprehension to general category and rule: "creations of the mind" in Newman's terms, rather than of direct apprehension.[15] Notation is not simply a matter of new words. We do it, for example, when we follow the inevitable child-rearing advice that we should define clear boundaries for our children. A simple rule that everyone should eat dinner at the same time might soon find itself vastly elaborated as a teenaged child pushes on its edges and parents try to clarify the boundaries over and over again. There is just too much homework, and she has to eat at the computer. She had a big snack and is not hungry. Forced to sit at the table anyway, she brings a textbook (pushing on yet another rule), or demands to leave far earlier than everyone else. New rules (leaving early is allowed, but only if there is a lot of homework) are met by new challenges (it is always a lot of homework). Smaller children test limits just as constantly, and clarifying the limit just leads to a new test. The process may be crucial for growing up and establishing understandings of both self and how to deal with a social community. Yet it also illustrates the constant push to notate as well as the inevitable limitations on the possibility of notation.

In quite a different context, something similar goes on with lawyers in a courtroom, who often argue less about the facts of a case than about their conflicting understandings of how the law applies in this unique case. Passing a new law will move the arguments onto new turf, but it can never get rid of the gap between the complexity of any specific (i.e., particular and unique) situation and notation, which is always general and hence leaves an opening for different interpretations—for ambiguity. There is a paradox of thought here: every increase in notation, in the detail of description or prescription, takes us further from the unique context because it entails greater use of abstraction. The more we "understand," "think," or "represent," the further from the thing we get. We gain clarity of vision at the expense of the fullness of experience. By increasing notation, we have, among other things, increased abstraction and hence the ambiguity of the experience itself.

Every human notational act is to some extent caught in this paradox. We cannot speak without categories, and even societies without legal systems still have rules of some sort, always at one remove from experience.

There are important differences, though, in how far different societies push this paradox or try to resolve it. At one extreme, we have mystical traditions that suggest the rejection of all categories, and thus a deep suspicion of language. The *Daode Jing*, for example, warns us that "When all in the world know beauty as beauty, ugliness arises; when all know good as good, evil arises . . . therefore the sage teaches without words."[16] Words only work through difference, and each thus carries its own opposite; better to avoid language completely. Or consider the great Sufi poet Rumi: "This is how it always is when I finish a poem. A great silence overcomes me, and I wonder why I ever thought to use language."[17]

At the other extreme, we have attempts to remove ambiguity forever by finding the right words for everything through an ideal language, and defining rules to cover every possible contingency. While this can never be more than an aspiration, it has been a vitally important project at some historical times, perhaps never more than in the period that began with the Enlightenment and continues in many ways today. Stephen Toulmin, for example, has argued that Enlightenment philosophers devoted themselves to the twin goals of abstraction and notation: "From 1600 on . . . there is a shift from a style of philosophy that keeps equally in view issues of local, timebound practice, and universal, timeless theory, to one that accepts matters of universal, timeless theory as being entitled to an exclusive place on the agenda of 'philosophy.'"[18] In part, he sees this as a move away from the art of rhetoric to the rigor of logic, from the oral to the written. As Toulmin describes the change, it is a self-conscious attempt to wipe out ambiguity. Somewhere between 1590 and 1640, he argues, a skeptical tolerance of ambiguity and uncertainty lost its intellectual respectability.[19]

Alain Besançon makes a similar claim about the French Enlightenment as a key step that led first to French Revolutionary radicalism and then, when added to German idealism of the nineteenth century, to Leninism. Describing early eighteenth-century thinkers in France, he says that "the whole of the real—which is all matter—can be justified in terms of scientific knowledge. We do not know everything, but everything can be known. . . . So a whole sequence of secondary philosophers exhausted themselves searching for the equivalent of universal gravity in the psychological, the physiological and, soon, in the political arenas."[20]

The French Revolution showed particular concern with resolving all ambiguities. In many cases, this took the form of clarifying the non-linguistic world by trying to turn it into a system of symbols like words. In clothing, for example, even as old sumptuary conventions were rejected, everything else was suddenly being decoded: silk or wool, long jackets or short, and so on. The effort to encode fully something as variable as dress, however, was doomed. The answer seemed to be uniforms: a national civil uniform was designed but not implemented, and there were endless arguments about official uniforms.[21] Art needed just as much disambiguation, sometimes through direct notation. When the artist and Deputy Jacques Louis David designed a colossal Hercules statue, he planned for explanatory words to be engraved on its body parts so that viewers would properly understand the allegory; the people would know how to recognize themselves.

> On his brow would be inscribed "light" (a rather weak reference to intelligence); "nature" and "truth" were to appear on his chest; "force" and "courage" on his arms; and "work" on his hands. Hercules brings light and truth to the world in David's vision, not through his intellect or cleverness, but through his strength, courage, and "labor."[22]

This attempt to disambiguate by naming continues through the modern period. As Besançon argued, we can see it especially clearly in the Communist states of the twentieth century. As an example, Mao Zedong described the features of good literature in his 1942 "Talks at the Yenan Forum on Literature and Art," which laid out the principles that would define Chinese policies on literature for the entire Maoist period. One of the problems he took on was that of "dark" and "bright" characters. Was it good to dwell on the dark side of society, as much of the most influential Chinese literature of the 1930s had? How about half-and-half characters— mixed and troubled souls? Mao answered that we indeed required both dark and bright, but they had to be distinguished absolutely from each other. The purpose of the dark was to throw the bright into even greater illumination.[23] Shades of grey had been ruled out.

A similar attitude toward ambiguity occurs with instrumental music, where the ambiguities are far deeper than in any form of literature because there are no words. The Baroque "doctrine of the affections" attempted a solution somewhat like David's writing key words on his Hercules. The idea was that forms of affect could be clearly described and rationalized (as Descartes had attempted) and that particular harmonic and melodic patterns directly translated into those affective responses.[24] Rapidly rising thirds created euphoria, for instance. Further, a piece of music should strive for only one main affect, otherwise there would be confusion. While composers lost interest in this approach after the eighteenth century, the idea that musical meanings had to be clarified remained important through the "program music" of the nineteenth century, in which a written program told the audience what the music described—a way of adding words back into instrumental music, again reminiscent of David labeling his statue. The Communist states, too, found the ambiguities of instrumental music deeply troubling, as we can see most clearly in the endless Soviet arguments about what Shostakovich's music actually meant. In every case, the non-linguistic world of possibilities is reduced to a notation, an ideal type.

We have so far been discussing two primary ways of trying to abolish or minimize ambiguity: the attempt to censor or forbid the ambiguous through erasure and the attempt to disambiguate it through ever clearer categorization. While both try to steer clear of the uncertainties of ambiguity by drawing clear boundaries, they do this through different means that may come into conflict with each other.

We can see this, for instance, in contemporary American arguments over gender identity. On the one hand, we can continue to see a strong argument for the reduction of sexuality to a simple binary with nothing between. There are men and there are women, and sexuality requires one of each. We see this in the frequent attempts by American voters in some states to pass laws defining marriage as the union of a man and a woman only. The ban on homosexuality in the United States armed forces is similar, and the "don't ask, don't tell" policy adopted in 1993 was simply a promise to allow claims of ignorance while leaving intact the basic prohibition on acts that penetrated the category boundaries. Attempts to redefine sexual identity through drastic surgical and hormonal intervention also renounce any kind of position between in favor of creating a singular "man" or "woman."

On the other hand, there has been another trend to deal with the fuzzy world of love, sex, and identity as actually experienced: new categories are constantly being created in the attempt to grant them some legitimacy. Legalizing homosexuality was a first step in many places, as with the states that have defined marriage to include relations between two people of the same gender. We also now have categories of people who are cisgendered and transgendered. Then there are people of neutral gender, bigender, and intersexual gender. Paralleling this has been increased academic interest in gender categorization outside the West, like the South Asian *hijra* or the "third gender" role, often called *berdache*, in many Native American groups.

These two approaches to gender identity are engaged in a strong argument, but both similarly reduce the flux of behavior, feeling, and experience to named identity. Both "notate" gender in an attempt to avoid ambiguity and to legitimize identities (many of them or just two of them). Such notations are an inescapable part of human life because they are fundamental to the way in which language works. Yet they do little to help us to accept ambiguity and indeterminacy or to teach us how to move between our categories.

Problems with Categories

Language is arguably the most fundamental human way of dealing with the ambiguities inherent to experience. All language abstracts away from the infinite richness of our experience in the world; all of it reduces flow to categories. As many have pointed out, every word is both too general and too specific: too general because it loses the precision and detail of actual objects and experiences, and too specific because it bounds those objects within the clear borders of some class. The problem of categories thus remains rooted in the very ambiguity of language. To paraphrase Bateson again, one problem is that every communication is both a message and a message about a message.[25] It is both descriptive and, in a sense, normative—a claim about the world-as-it-is and a claim about the nature of claims. The interstices of the two kinds of messages are always ambiguous, as the orientations of these respective messages pertain to very different realms.

Alfred Korzybski went further in a 1931 lecture when he attacked the rooting of language in Aristotelian logic. This logic, as he described it, rests on three assumptions, each of which bans ambiguity:

1. *The law of identity*: whatever is, is.
2. *The law of contradiction*: nothing can both be and not be.
3. *The law of the excluded middle*: everything must either be or not be, never both at once.[26]

He then demolishes each of these. The identity relationship, he says, should be abandoned because it is always false when applied to "objective, unspeakable levels . . . Whatever we might *say* a happening 'is', *it is not.*"[27] Exactly because every word is already abstracted, even a simple statement like "this object is a book" is already false in an important way. This reasoning applies equally to the other two logical principles. His rejection of the law of the excluded middle is especially important for our purposes. By insisting that the middle must be included, that things can be both A and not-A, he embraces ambiguity.

Korzybski sums much of this up in his famous dictum that "the map *is not* the territory,"[28] Gregory Bateson expanded on this in an important essay in which he asks what in the territory actually makes it onto the map.[29] His answer is that maps pull out the differences in the territory. If there were no differences, there would be nothing to put on the map except the boundary—and that is itself a difference, of course. He pushes hard on this idea of the prioritization of certain differences over others because the actual differences that we could choose to map are infinite. Mapping (or speaking) requires choosing the differences that matter, at least for some people, and some times, and in some contexts.

Given that middles cannot be excluded, identities are never identical, and differences are infinite, no system of bounded categories can be sustained. No wonder, then, that the *Daode Jing*, Rumi, and other mystics from many traditions have been so suspicious of language. Yet even mystics have nothing but language with which to express their thoughts. While scientists still argue about exactly how language differentiates us from the great apes (ambiguities even here!), no one doubts that language is a necessary component of what makes us human. Language does not just offer the ability to abstract, but it requires abstraction and categorization in every sentence that we utter. Every utterance creates difference and thus opens up alternatives (as beauty requires ugliness and orthodoxy requires heterodoxy).

The previous sections of this chapter discussed attempts to resolve these problems of language with more language or with less. We get more language when we spin out ever more categories. If a word is too general, we can coin a more specific one (azure, not just blue). If the opposite confounds our meaning, we can try a new and more detailed classification. Like the sorcerer's apprentice, we can keep making mops until they threaten to overwhelm us. On the other hand, if someone threatens our categories, we can also attempt a solution through less language—censorship.

It should be clear by now, however, that neither attempt can fully succeed. Indeterminacy creeps back into any system of categories. This is a discouraging thought about any search for truth or the ultimate comforts of certainty. Yet it also lets us see the potential for change in any system because the intractable spaces between the categories can ultimately spawn new structures. Earlier in the chapter, we discussed exile and censorship as examples of ways to excise ambiguities and solidify categories, but ultimately inherent ambiguities can undermine strategies of exile and regimes of censorship.

Exile can, of course, silence offending voices. In the process, however, it can also free the exiles—as much from the social conventions and relationships that had shaped their thought as from the political constraints under which they had been operating. The most famous case in China was Qu Yuan, a scholar and minister to the king of Chu in the third century B.C.E. Chu was one of several Chinese states at war with each other for control at the time. Qu Yuan recommended alliance with a neighboring state against the aggressive Qin, but other, less upright ministers stymied him. Their slander led to his exile among the "barbarians" to the south. As a result, the Qin were able to defeat each of the other states in turn, finally uniting China. During Qu Yuan's years of exile, he composed some of the most loved poetry in Chinese history, apparently combinations of local folk odes and his own feelings of longing, loss, and frustrated patriotism. When news of the fall of Chu reached Qu Yuan, he composed a final lament and then drowned himself.[30]

Exile certainly saved those other ministers from having to deal with Qu Yuan, leaving them to define the situation without challenge. But it also allowed Qu Yuan an artistic and political achievement that far outreached anything they did—and almost surely outreached anything Qu himself could have accomplished had he stayed home. Not even death silenced him: his suicide is still commemorated every year in the Dragon Boat Festival. The Tang dynasty poet Du Fu is another whose long exile led to an artistic outpouring that might otherwise never have happened. Exile has had political consequences as much as poetic ones. One need only think of Dante and Machiavelli, not to mention the long-term consequences of the ideas worked out in the exiles of Marx and then Lenin.

Exile attempts to excise the threat to the categories of order by removing the voice of doubt, while censorship attempts the same thing internally. To take a rather intimate example, European and American concert halls in the nineteenth century began to expect a regime of audience silence during performances.[31] Before that, performers had to earn the attention of what could be a raucous and unruly audience. As a consequence, modern performers in classical venues look out over a sea of dimly seen and silent bodies, each the same as the others in every important way. The only order will be that of the composer and the performers, unsullied by input from the crowd. From the points of view of audience members, however, things look quite different. Minds are free to wander in the silence, and thoughts are free to move with the music but also to move far away into the inner concerns and ideas of each individual. By silencing the audience, performers no longer know what people are thinking.

The same can also be true of more literal censorship and related forms of control, where the imposition of absolute and unquestionable categories and orders allows no public alternatives and no open exploration of gray zones. Truly successful crushing of all speech outside the boundaries of acceptability is a recipe for disaster. It may be only a minor problem when a musician does not know what people in the audience are thinking, but for a state it can be highly destructive. Take the case of the Great Leap Forward in China, during which the government imposed new categories of control that ranged from the sudden and total transition to state planning from market mechanisms for moving goods around the society, to new forms of sociality (communal dining and child care, for instance, or marching to the fields in military formation), to specific goals for production. Local officials who wanted to preserve their careers reported total success. It is not just that policy narratives critical of the Great Leap were censored and their proponents purged. Much more seriously, the only possible language was declaration of success. In several years of terrible weather for agriculture, with the earlier structures for running the economy dismantled, local officials continuously reported that their targets had been met or exceeded. They turned over their full quotas of grain, based on wildly optimistic plans, even if it meant losing food that they needed to eat and to use for seed for the next year. With the categories not open to discussion—not even such flimsy ones as projected grain yields—the state had no way of responding to disaster. Millions starved. A similar situation held for the American intervention in Vietnam, where intelligence operatives understood that their superiors would hear only stories of success. This logic went all the way up to the U.S. National Security Council. The consequences for American policy are well-known.[32]

As the examples above show, the unavoidable ambiguities of social orderings and categories preclude simple erasure through power. Foucault's work on sexuality, for example, does not argue that there was a simple censorship of talk about sex from the seventeenth century on. On the contrary, he sees the silencing of sexuality in arenas like the home or school as having been matched by a huge outpouring of sex talk in other realms.[33] In a similar way, White House efforts to control discourse on Vietnam could not prevent massive demonstrations that insisted on speaking truth to power. Judith Butler generalizes the argument even further. She points out that every linguistic category, even (or especially) a simple "I," is an act of censorship—in our terms, a banning of the ambiguities at the edges of the concept. Yet this very process of censorship also creates the possibility for oppositional speech.[34] Categories, in other words, can never be absolute.

Notation, Legalization, and Trust

Creating categories is an example of what is perhaps the most common strategy of dealing with ambiguity—notation. Notation solidifies and refines boundaries. It works through the contrast of categories, through the creation of clearly defined alternatives. It attempts to disambiguate for all times (and climes) rather than to understand its categories as indexed to a particular people or place. It therefore tends toward the abstract and general rather than the local and particular, more toward what Basil Bernstein called an "elaborated code" rather than a "restricted" one.[35]

There are many forms of notation as a means to disambiguate, and they have appeared in myriad realms of human endeavor. We may think, for example, of sumptuary codes over the ages, from the conical hat that Jews were made to wear in thirteenth-century Christian Europe, to the revolutionary costumes noted above, to the grand balls of the French bourgeoisie in the days of the Second Empire. High fashion and the cult of the couturier during that period were exercises in notation through design. They created a canon of costume around the figure of the Empress Eugenie that was as well structured, imbued with discrete meanings, and bounded as any other well-defined field.[36]

Didacticism in art, which has a pedigree back at least as far as Luther, is yet another example of notation as a means to dispel ambiguity rather than play with it.[37] No fan of images for their own sake, Luther justified artistic production only if it served a pedagogic practice—in a manner not unlike Bertolt Brecht or, for that matter, much of twentieth-century artistic production. Form, as in the canon of modernist architecture, increasingly follows function. Boundaries grow sheer and rigid (in Le Corbusier as in *Mother Courage*) and the modernist descendants of the Reformation abjure the play of ambiguity in favor of nominative statements. The examples offered above of J. L. David are thus not simply revolutionary enthusiasms, but a chapter in a much longer tale.

Perhaps the most important field defining the idea of notation, however, is law (*nomos*). The very term "category" comes from the Greek *kategor*, that is, "prosecutor." Laws and categories are interwoven. Both attempt to disambiguate in the most critical realm we inhabit, that of human relations. They have been doing this, moreover, for millennia—even before the invention of written codes of law (such as the code of Justinian), which merely added to and fortified this tendency. The decidedly early and culturally widespread practice of blood brotherhood provides a wonderful example of this "legalization" and hence structuring of ambiguous fields. From pre-Homeric Greece to contemporary Africa, we are familiar with this phenomenon of ritualized friendship. Blood brotherhood and similar forms of ritualized personal relationships define or include a relationship with an unrelated other, which—given a cognitive grid based on kin classifications—simply cannot exist.[38] Yet, like the fatal blunder in the story of Candaules, it clearly does. Such ritualized friendships permit the existence of relationships that the logic of the existing system cannot otherwise encompass—a system based on ascriptive categories nevertheless accepts non-ascriptive ties into the system. The interstitial or ambiguous points in the system (i.e., its inability to accommodate non-ascriptive ties) are negated through the creation of what is essentially a legal fiction (*avant la lettre*).

Friendship (like love) is, after all, a very ambiguous thing. From Confucian sages to modern anthropologists like Evans-Pritchard, people concerned with human relations have been struggling to understand just how this rather unstructured, loosely bounded, poorly defined, very labile, and often conflicting web of affective ties relates to more structured, institutionalized, bounded, and defined (i.e., notated) roles and expectations.[39] Love, after all, was seen in the Christian middle ages as the "dark passion," constantly threatening social stability, order, and the always only tenuous regulation of sexuality within marriage.[40] Certain societies considered friendship as no less dangerous. Just as sexuality—in all societies—has to be disambiguated in agreed-upon roles and expectations, so friendship too had to be formalized, bounded, and woven into a web of preexisting and socially accepted expectations of reciprocity and responsibility.

Thus Evans-Pritchard notes in his classic study of blood brotherhood among the Zande: "a man could not enter into a pact solely on his own initiative, since its clauses bound also his kin, who became subject to its sanctions. He would therefore first consult his father and uncles and would only carry out the rite of blood brotherhood after he had obtained their consent."[41] The ambiguities of friendship were thus severely circumscribed within a set of clearly defined expectations and obligations that were themselves enmeshed within existing kinship obligations. Of course, this also set up the very real potential that the fictitious blood relations would foster a competing and conflicting system of obligations to that of existing kinship rights: the stuff of Greek tragedy. As we pointed out above, this is to be expected, and there is no ultimate retreat from ambiguity and contradiction—only a temporary ad hoc refuge.

Over 150 years ago, Henry Sumner Maine explicitly recognized the role of legal fictions in providing such temporary refuge, or, in terms somewhat closer to his own, of providing a bridge between the normative order (the Law) and the exigencies (what we would term the ambiguities) of history.[42] Maine rooted his analysis of legal fictions in the Roman legal concept of *fictio*, which was a device to permit jurisdiction in a case involving a foreigner. He showed how it continued to be used as a means to maintain the fiction that the law has not changed, is as it ever was, while the fact was that it had "wholly changed." Interestingly, he cited the "Fiction of Adoption," that is, the creation of artificial family ties, as critical to the very growth of civilization.[43] Such legal fictions occur in all legal codes, of all peoples. Our quibble with H. S. Maine would only be that he saw these overcome by the mechanisms of legislation and equity, while we argue that while such development may well have characterized Western jurisprudence, it does not characterize all judicial systems.

The real problem, however, is that regardless of the mechanism invoked (certainly including notation), there is simply no way to shun ambiguity. Today, for example, legal decisors face the major challenge of legal pluralism: the coexistence within distinct nation-states (as well as supranational entities such as the EU) of vastly different interpretations and understandings of what once appeared as unified and coherent frames of worldviews, desiderata, and normative orders. This is a problem for state actors who have to wrestle with the ability and willingness of its legal orders to accommodate alternative, sometimes conflicting modes of legal ordering. It is even more problematic for legal traditions of non-state actors who must accommodate themselves to the laws and demands of the state.

There are no clear answers here, especially because we are not dealing with ambiguities within one system, but with the coexistence of diverse systems in a single juridical space. Many global places face colliding fields of nomos. It is impossible to arrive at a point of arbitration, as there is no common or shared system of notation that can mediate. Many ancient states finessed similar situations through agreement that the gods of different peoples would each guarantee the contract—a form perhaps of overlapping consensus.[44] Lacking such gods today, we seem bereft of a solution. Wherever the solution lies, more notation seems unlikely to help—something that an invocation of gods would seem, implicitly, to recognize. Later in this book, we will return to the possibility of a more practical, even pragmatist appreciation of the inevitability of overlapping jurisdictions, the ambiguities of communal life, and the need for accommodating more than one consensus.

We speak of canons of art, architecture, music, or literature to indicate systems of well-defined, self-referential meaning, often symbolic in nature. Law is paradigmatic of such systems of canons because it represents the multitude of human relations. Such relations are not just multitudinous, but infinite, and that problem is a basic limit of law. One way to explore this problem further is to distinguish between the concepts of confidence and of trust. Confidence, as we are using the term, means knowing what to expect in a situation of social interaction; trust, in contrast, is what allows us to maintain interaction even in the absence of confidence.[45]

Confidence—along with the necessary knowledge—can stem from many different things. It can come from the ability to impose sanctions and the knowledge that one's partner to an interaction also knows that sanctions will be imposed if he or she fails to live up to the terms of an agreement. Sanctions may be formal or informal; they may be based on an intricate web of kinship obligations or on the verities of contract law. They may be immediate or inter-generational, symbolic or material. In all cases, confidence rests on knowledge that our interactions exist within a context, within a well-notated—though not necessarily written—normative system that will impose sanctions in the case of an abrogation of agreements. Hence it is not quite correct to say that I "trust" the doctor. Rather, I have confidence in her abilities, in the system that awarded her the degree on the wall, as well as in the epistemological assumptions of American medicine. Of course, I may also lack such confidence and take my daughter to Lourdes instead. Or I can trust—have faith in—the Lord if, for instance, I am a Christian Scientist.

Similarly, when the philosopher Annette Baier says that she "trusts the plumber to do a non-subversive job of plumbing," that is also not quite true.[46] She knows that if he does a "subversive" job, she will not only not hire him again, and tell her neighbors not to hire him, but she will also complain to the local Better Business Bureau. She may even refuse to pay him. In short, she can impose sanctions, formal and informal. She knows this and he knows this; she knows that he knows this and he knows that she knows that he knows this, and so on. Again, all parties to the interaction share a system of meaning and notation. They interact through mutual interest and maintain the relationship through mutual confidence in this system within which their exchange takes place. Now if she were to rush off to meet a colleague and leave her baby with the plumber until her husband came home, that would be a very different story, one involving both parties in a relationship of trust.

Confidence, to reiterate, requires knowledge of what will be. And this knowledge may in turn be based on the ability to impose sanctions. It may also be based on what we may term familiarity, or what we can call "stickball." Because John played stickball on East 13th Street as a boy, we share certain codes of conduct, certain moral evaluations, certain ways of being and acting that allow for mutual confidence. We are alike, the same, and hence his actions are predictable. Confidence and prediction here stem not from sanctions but from sameness or familiarity. Of course, the relevant other may not be "the same" at all, but we will often draw certain conclusions (true or false) from modes of dress, speech, school background, neighborhood, religion, and so on that allow us to construct a narrative of sameness that will allow us to have confidence.

As in the case of sanctions, confidence too rests on some system of shared notation, of encoded similarities or differences (such as could be noted by sumptuary codes, for example). We often combine as many bases of notational confidence as possible before entering an interaction: formal sanctions may be costly and involve too great a transaction cost. Thus we like to know that we can impose informal sanctions as well. This is why our conversations turn so often to places of origin, school background, family, or even sports. These are all icons, symbols—at the end of the day, nothing but notational devices—of familiarity, of ways to demonstrate some underlying sameness to the other as well as to ourselves. We do this all the time, every day, in situations involving no more than choosing whom to sit next to on the bus or what architect to employ in redesigning our house. Such talk and judgment weaves through much of our public life.

Trust, we are claiming, is much more ambiguous. Trust must emerge in an interaction if we have no basis for confidence, no shared notational system—thus in situations where behavior and outcomes cannot be easily predicted. We need trust to interact with strangers. We need it if the other is unknowable. And the other is unknowable when we cannot impute or predict behavior because there is no shared notational system and hence either (a) there is no system within which sanctions can be imposed, or (b) there is no underlying sense of familiarity or sameness that would allow such prediction.[47] Unlike the Roman *fides* which carried very clear sets of obligations and terms of reciprocity, trust is essentially an open relationship, not given to legal notation. Its very essence thus remains ambiguous.[48] For just that reason, however, it is the arena in which we can talk of empathy and of the type of creative play with boundaries of self and other, broached earlier.

Relations between members of all societies, to greater or lesser extent, are predicated on one or another of these forms. Some forms of social organization leave more room for the ambiguous, others less. We have already noted the tendency in many kinship-organized groups to circumscribe the ambiguity of personal friendship within the notationally recognized arena of ritualized kinship. The modern form of universalistic, achieved, and *gesselschaftlich* social organization, however, generally accommodates the ambiguous no better, though the terms of what is understood as ambiguous are perhaps different. The contemporary, seemingly endless and exponential growth of bureaucratic regulation of just about everything equally attempts to circumscribe the ambiguousness of human relations within notational systems. And while moderns do not understand friendship to be so circumscribed (perhaps at our peril), we certainly do circumscribe trust. Such endless notation returns us to the map/territory conundrum. We eventually lose sight of the difference. If many non-state societies seem to want to reduce everything to territory and context, more contemporary societies seem to try to turn everything into map and rule.

Problems with Boundaries

The inability to remove ambiguity from our speech and from our categories leaves us with a strong critique of any attempt to impose a pure or rigid view of boundaries and of the orders that they delineate. A pure category implies rigid boundaries, while in reality we have but temporary, fungible, and fragile categories that are always only *good enough* to present a holding ground for the development of action and understanding. As the psychiatrist Edgar Levenson pointed out, any interpersonal experience is always the product of two kinds of communicative systems, one verbal and one embodied, which he terms "the language of speech and the language of action." Both, he argues, are "harmonic variations" or "transforms" of one another.[49] They are not identical, and they comprise different communicative systems. Levenson thus also concludes that ambiguity resides at the very core of shared social action, because all interaction relies on two forms of communication that have very different semiotic rules. Successful interaction thus requires us to "play," to shift and to dance with the ambiguity rather than fix it in one or another non-fungible grid of identities and meanings. Play, as Winnicott reminds us, rests on trust, and trust is, of course, precisely this ability to accept change and the changeable nature of categories, prescriptions, and realities without demanding the guarantee of the immutable.[50] Living in time requires us to play—to substitute word for thing, wine for blood, ram for beloved son, liturgy for spectacle, icon for idea, symbol for reality.

We suggest that this "playing" with the shifting nature of boundaries—but never totally dissolving them—forms the root of social empathy as well. Empathy rests on some elision of self, on some renunciation of ego's central place in its own symbolic universe. Only this allows us, following Wordsworth, to find "the familiar in the unfamiliar"—in what is, in the end, an act of creative play.[51] The workings of social empathy and trust illustrate mid-level meaning—that of analogy—as we described in chapter 1. We can draw analogies in social affect as much as in poetry. We are suggesting that an ability to move between self and world, inside and outside, the boundary and its field, renunciation and expectation, is critical to the possibility of social communication. Such moves educate us toward empathy, because they rest on a decentered self, and on an ability to generalize beyond one's own experiences. For this to take place, boundaries must be less than strict and must be fully discriminative.

Iterated activity may provide an important learning tool for negotiating boundaries and their fields, and thus for empathy. Empathy occurs through learned patterns or rhythms of behavior. It does not involve the denial of boundaries or any ideal of freedom from limits or constraints. Instead, it suggests a move across boundaries and the creative possibility of reframing them. All of this implies that a simple, dichotomizing idea of the boundary is inadequate. We need, in addition, to realize the benefits (and challenges) of a highly fractal, complex, porous—even ornamented—idea of boundaries.

We take boundaries to be "given" in any situation, to be authoritative. The given defines the field of our vision, including our innovative and revolutionary visions, that is to say, our visions of change. Boundaries, the origins of our categories, always come to us from the past. The ground of our existence is thus the assumed reality that provides the boundaries in and through which we experience the world; language is an obvious example. This historical characteristic of boundaries makes memory central to the continual symbolic differentiation of reality.

Existence in time implies the new as well as the old, the future as well as the past. Yet the future can bring new frames, just as the stranger can. It can also reorder the contents or patterns of the frames. It can, in Gregory Bateson's terms, turn existing frames into muddles. The future carries a risk. This is the risk of love as well. The future represents the possibility for creativity, for change, and for adaptation, as well as the risk of disaster. Either way involves breaking apart and reordering what is already framed in one particular pattern or set of patterns. The very openness of the future thus carries the potential to question existing categories and the boundaries through which we construct them. Though given, boundaries are never completely uncontested and the inherent open-ended nature of this contestation makes boundary work an endless project, part of the continuing human enterprise.

To some extent, the integration of existing boundaries with future possibilities is the boundary work of each generation, even if sometimes accomplished with a good deal of tragedy, pain, and suffering. In a sense, it is also the work of each and every individual. This work filters the dialectic of past and future through two contradictory impulses: on the one hand, the impulse to absolutize existing boundaries; and on the other, to overcome the constraints of all boundaries. The first impulse grows most often from an orientation to the past; the second most often comes with a more future-directed orientation (sometimes expressed in revolutionary or, among the religious, millennial, messianic, or eschatological thought). Trying to integrate past and future without the risk of boundary work requires some process of absolutization, of freezing existing boundaries, or of denying them completely. Yet this dissolves boundaries into absolute totalities or absolute negations. Both overcome and so deny their very quality as boundaries.

This presents us with a conundrum. Boundaries, which make possible our cognitive capacity and fundamental processes of ordering, must also have some degree of porousness, some lability, in order to continue to exist and fulfill that constitutive role in a future that will inevitably challenge them. How to do this without either erasing the ambiguous or disambiguating by the endless creation of new categories (a truly Sisyphean task) is a continual challenge. Notation is not enough.

Living with Ambiguity

Thus far, we have been arguing that the anxious dialectic between notation and ambiguity characterizes all human thought and social life. Modern state bureaucracies have developed notation to a truly astonishing degree, but the process of category definition is fundamental to being human. At the same time, we have tried to show that no system of categories can ever be adequate to the complexities and ambiguities of actual experience.

Notation, however, is not the only way in which we can deal with the problem of how to set boundaries on a flow that has no firm boundaries of its own. We began with notation because it seems so dominant at first glance. Notation, after all, is not merely the stuff of bureaucrats and lawyers, but has become the preeminent model through which we construct knowledge. It shapes, for example, the process of professionalization in fields ranging from urban planning to medicine. In each of these cases, practitioners have the job of coming up with solutions to problems that are unique to one particular context and one particular time (an ailing body, a design for a new highway). They attempt to do this, however, through the application of abstracted rules and principles. As Donald Schön has shown, the attempt to notate fields like this has been riddled with problems.[52]

No one is more wed to the processes and goals of notation than academics like us. Notation is the means and the end of much social science. We clarify and define terms, classify and correlate behaviors, and identify underlying rules. We look for generalizations that work regardless of context. We write for a living: we notate. While we have argued that no humans can avoid notation, we also live in a world that values this particular form of boundary construction to an extraordinary degree.

The process that we have called notation works by clarifying boundaries and separating categories. In this mode, the inevitable ambiguities, as we have argued, can only be dealt with through taboos and censorship or through creating ever more categories. Boundaries, however, need not always work as impermeable containers around categories, like the lead shield around uranium to prevent radioactive pollution or the Great Wall of China to keep the barbarians out. Boundaries of some sort are inevitable, but they can work in very different ways.

In the remainder of this book, we will explore two primary mechanisms beyond notation. In each case, we are interested in ways of conceptualizing boundaries that allow more freedom of interaction with the underlying ambiguities, that insist less on excluding the middle, and that reject the uncrossable absolutes of notational boundaries. In spite of the obvious ironies of offering alternatives to notational thought in such a highly notated form, we present a very brief summary of some of the forms of action we have in mind in table 2.1.

The first line on the table refers to the processes of notation that we have been discussing and that have so dominated the ways that we have thought about knowledge since the Enlightenment. The key point, as we see it, is the impenetrability of such boundaries, which attempts to keep categories pure without having to cede any ground to ambiguity. The only feature of table 2.1 that we have not discussed for notation is "form of rhythm." What we mean, in brief, is how each way of parsing boundaries relates to the flow of experience—to time. The reason that we have not yet had much to say about this is that notation tends to nullify time. From the "self-evident" truths of the American Declaration of Independence to the laws of physics, notated knowledge generally exists outside the flux of time. The process of abstraction itself dehistoricizes; it is atemporal and trans-historical.

We will develop these points about time and rhythm, however, much more in the chapters that follow. Those chapters extend the ideas suggested by the rest of table 2.1. Chapter 3 takes up what we are calling the "ritual" mode. A great deal of the literature on ritual emphasizes its

Table 2.1 Three Approaches to Boundaries and Ambiguity

Way of Parsing Ambiguity	Quality of Boundary	Example of Action	Form of Rhythm
notation	impermeable	law	none
ritual	crossed	ritual/rhetoric	meter
shared experience	mosaic, fuzzy	negotiation	pulse

creation of boundaries. We agree, but also draw attention to the way in which ritual always crosses boundaries at the same time. Rituals create a kind of subjunctive and temporary world in a way not so different from theater. The ritual worlds of the Roman Catholic Mass, Muslim daily prayer, or the Chinese offering of incense are examples of such subjunctives.[53] These worlds must always be entered and exited, that is, the boundaries of the ritual event itself must always be crossed. If we consider notation to be something like standard locutionary acts, like statements of fact, then ritual is more like metaphor, which always crosses between categories.

Ritual also relates to time quite differently from notation. Rituals repeat. Many do this rhythmically, that is, their repetition is predictable in time—birthdays, annual holidays, weekly services. One could even say that they create time in the sense of defining a shared social convention to understand its flows. In so doing, they also create a sense of shared pasts and futures, which is so critical to feelings of community. This conventionalized structuring of time is what we mean by meter. Time flows in an alteration of ritual moments and non-ritual moments, one kind of subjunctive universe and another.

The final row of table 2.1 points to yet another way of dealing with ambiguity, through pragmatic negotiation across boundaries. Here we mean deeply contextual understandings where the rationalization of boundaries fades to unimportance and the edge between A and not-A can be fuzzy, fractal, or mosaic. Differences here are not the stuff of clear boundaries, or even the crossed boundaries of ritual, but rather something that can be negotiated ad hoc at each meeting. There is still repetition, still a structuring of time, but it grows more organically from people interacting with each other—the variable pulse of beating hearts or breaking waves rather than the conventional one of the clock.

The chapters that follow work through this quick and elliptical summary in much more concrete detail, but it is worth recalling that much more is at stake than our own notation of a classification scheme. In the end, we hope to understand what allows us to live together in spite of the differences that separate every one of us. How we create empathy or trust between one individual and the next is ultimately a story of how we create and negotiate across boundaries. Understanding the possibility of boundary negotiation between parents and children is just as difficult and important as that between utter strangers. This problem of empathy also underlies the pressing issues of how to live in a truly plural society, one that accepts differences and lives with them. In places where Christians, Jews, and Muslims live together, for example, we can often see all three ways of dealing with boundaries. Sometimes people notate the legal rights of each group, as in Lebanon's carefully titrated system of religious representation in government. Sometimes rituals allow boundaries to be crossed in various ways, for instance by sharing in each other's rituals. This was true, for instance, in parts of the Hellenistic world, in Crete between Orthodox Christians and Muslims before the demise of the Ottoman Empire, and between Jews and Muslims in North Africa who worshipped at the same saints' tombs until the middle of the twentieth century. Sometimes, instead, we see new ritual forms, like national days created by the modern nation-state. And sometimes people just build a hospital together, because they need it. They interact, at least at that time, just as people and not as identities.

These thoughts on the limits to notation lead to our second interlude, which explores the duality of boundaries as illustrated in ancient Israelite texts on ritual purity and in Chinese understandings of the power of the center and its margins. Both examples show how two old civilizations—not surprisingly, both with strong ritualist orientations—viewed boundaries. Ritual, as we shall argue in chapter 3, plays with boundaries in myriad creative ways. Rather than construct impermeable boundaries along the lines of pure notation, it recognizes both the existence of boundaries and the fact that they can be crossed. Its boundaries are empowered no less than its center. The margins point both outward and inward, toward the power of the center, but also to the outlying fields of meaning beyond its purview.

In the following interlude, however, our main concern is to use the example of the ancient Israelites and the imperial-era Chinese to elaborate our claims so far: first, that boundary creation is vital and unavoidable as we deal with the inherent ambiguities of human life; and second, that any set of boundaries is inherently problematic. No boundaries, no matter how elaborate, can eliminate ambiguity. Ambiguity remains with us, no matter how hard we try to define it out of the system, whether through the rules of ritual purity or of power's purview.

Interlude: The Israelite Red Heifer and the Edge of Power in China

MUCH ANTHROPOLOGICAL THEORY has claimed that systems of ritual purity are unequivocal modes of maintaining the moral boundaries of community.[1] Both our cases illustrate the importance of this process, but they also show just how impossible any purely binary or totalizing reading of boundaries will be. The ancient Israelite ritual of the Red Heifer (whose ashes purified those contaminated by contact with the dead during the Temple period) deals with the contagion of death, the pollution occasioned by contact with dead bodies. In spite of its crucial role in marking the apparently clear and culturally vital binary distinction between pure and impure, the Red Heifer as expressed in the Biblical description of the ritual, as well as in later Rabbinic writings, nevertheless shows how boundaries are multivocal and labile, with a good deal of passage between center and periphery, purity and impurity, knowledge and the unknown, ordered meaning and the chaos of death. The Chinese case deals with a very different realm of boundary creation, that of the physical and cognitive structure of the empire itself, maintained through a system of clearly demarcated and hierarchically organized units that achieves expression through the flow of power from the emperor and his officials in politics, but also in many other realms, from temples to food. Yet even this system, refined and elaborated through more than two millennia of imperial rule, gave way at the edges of its categories to a fundamentally different image of a power that rose instead from the boundaries of the system.

While the idea may be counterintuitive to modern geometrical sensibilities, we see the duality of boundaries to be found in both cases as neither an oversight nor a failure of rationalization, but instead as a recognition of some fundamental limits and lacunae in the art of ordering itself,

The Red Heifer

The entire Rabbinic system of commandments or obligations involves a dualism that clarifies the place of ambiguity in the rite of the Red Heifer. The Jewish tradition recognizes a bifurcation of its theoretical and experiential aspects and has, from the earliest Rabbinic writings, posited both the rational and the irrational (or more closely to the emic formulation, the "knowable" and the "unknowable") as equally valid sources and components of Jewish practice. This dualism is best represented in the concepts of *mishpatim* and *chukim*—laws and ordinances. Both are God's word, yet only the first are given to rational conceptualization, akin perhaps to natural law in the transparency of their rationale. The second set of commandments, the *chukim*, is not accessible to our understanding. Jews are equally commanded to obey both forms, regardless of whether they are amenable to the workings of human reason.

Within Rabbinic literature, the example par excellence of a commandment that cannot be understood rationally is the law of the Red Heifer, the Parah Adumah. The ritual of the Red Heifer, whose burned ashes, when mixed with water and fragrant woods and spices, would purify those contaminated by contact with the dead, is thus understood as the paradigm of all of God's commandments whose reasoning escapes us. Even King Solomon, whose wisdom was greater than all other humans, could not fathom the meaning of the Red Heifer.

In the Babylonian Talmud, Tractate Yoma (67b) lists those *chukim* not given to ratiocination, and then rhetorically asks if these are therefore acts of absurdity (*tohu*), of formlessness, and so devoid of all meaning. The answer is that God enacted them, and so they cannot be questioned. While Kierkegaard would no doubt have been pleased, we cannot help but note the authorial or editorial distress which sees the abyss that opens when meaning is absent and the limits of human reason reached. Nothing can be done, however: the system of human reason offers no way to understand these *chukim*. Only the Divine has such understanding, and it lies beyond all systems of order and reasoning open to mankind.

This suspension of meaning, even of the search for meaning, resonates with what we saw in the story of Job above. It raises interesting issues from the paradoxes of negative theology to the more emically Jewish discussions of *ta'ame hamitzvot* (the reasons for commandments—a pursuit alternatively prohibited or encouraged by different voices within the Jewish tradition). Our interest here, however, is in the way this projection of meaning to what is beyond human reason(s) leaves us with an ambiguous reading of categories and their boundaries. We begin here with the textual basis for the ritual of Parah Adumah, laid out in Numbers 19:1–13.

> The Lord spoke to Moses and Aaron, saying: This is the ritual law that the Lord has commanded: Instruct the Israelite people to bring you a red cow without blemish, in which there is no defect and on which no yoke has been laid. You shall give it to Eleazar the priest. It shall be taken outside the camp and slaughtered in his presence. Eleazar the priest shall take some of its blood with his finger and sprinkle it seven times towards the front of the Tent of Meeting. The cow shall be burned in his sight—its hide, flesh and blood shall be burned, its dung included—and the priest shall take cedar wood, hyssop, and crimson stuff, and throw them into the fire consuming the cow. The priest shall wash his garments and bathe his body in water, after that the priest may reenter the camp, but he shall be unclean until evening. He who performed the burning shall also wash his garments in water, bathe his body in water and be unclean until evening. A man who is clean shall gather up the ashes of the cow and deposit them outside the camp in a clean place, to be kept for water of lustration for the Israelite community. It is for cleansing. He who gathers up the ashes of the cow shall also wash his clothes and be unclean until evening.
>
> This shall be a permanent law for the Israelites and for the strangers who reside among you.
>
> He who touches the corpse of any human being shall be unclean for seven days. He shall cleanse himself with it on the third day and on the seventh day, and then be clean; if he fails to cleanse himself on the third and seventh days, he shall not be clean. Whoever touches a corpse, the body of a person who has died, and does not cleanse himself, defiles the Lord's Tabernacle; that person shall be cut off from Israel. Since the water of lustration was not dashed on him, he remains unclean, his uncleanness is still upon him.[2]

Jewish tradition recounts the preparation of nine Red Heifers from the time of Moses until the destruction of the Temple (the tenth will be prepared in the time of Messiah) and the rules and regulations surrounding the preparation of a Red Heifer are treated in the Talmud, Tractate Para.[3]

A preliminary understanding of this rite would be to see the sprinkling of the blood in the direction of the Sanctuary as a dedicatory act. Death, as chaos, threatens to undermine order and structure. The Sanctuary and the entire wilderness encampment construct an order in the face of looming chaos: they represent a return to Creation, to Eden. The ashes of the cow have been aligned with the sanctity of the Holy of Holies, the place where the glory of God—the source of life—is to be found. The *hazayah* (sprinkling) in the direction of the Sanctuary thus preempts the threat of death by generating a substance with the restorative powers of the source, the Holy of Holies. The ashes are forever charged with the powers of renewal and restoration. Yet, they are stored outside the encampment, so that the person who has brushed with death and its threat of looming chaos may still have secure access to the restorative powers of the core without himself endangering the system by bringing death into direct contact with the Holy of Holies. When the time comes and death disrupts order, the restorative substance has already been prepared and is available.[4]

The rite of the Red Heifer preempts the threat temporarily, by being prepared prior to, and in anticipation of, any actual death. It preempts death spatially, by being prepared outside the camp, yet in a way that orients it and links it with the core, the Holy of Holies. And it preempts it also by being prepared by the high priest's representative—in the biblical account, by Eleazar, the son of Aaron. Aaron the high priest cannot leave the Tabernacle precincts (Lev.), so his son performs the rite for him. The ritual tames death's threat—the breakdown of order and eruption of chaos—by acknowledging it, anticipating it, and preparing for it ahead of time. It establishes an apparently clear mechanism to separate the pure from the impure, the living from the dead, in spite of death's threat to those very boundaries.

Note, however, a series of paradoxes that characterize the ritual of the Red Heifer. The most obvious one is that while the burned ashes of the Red Heifer bestow purity, the actual engagement in preparing them renders one impure. This has been the subject of both Rabbinic and scholarly debate and will not immediately concern us.[5] This duality, however, seems related to the unique understanding of death in Jewish ritual law: while physical contact with the dead renders one impure, the dead themselves are—at least in one midrashic understanding—not impure![6] Purity and impurity apparently matter only among the living. Meaning-giving categories hold power only in the conditions of life. This paradox suggests that death is so devoid of meaning that the categories of meaning—including those of purity and impurity—hold no sway. What lies beyond the system of purity and impurity—death—is not their negation, but only something totally other to it.

The second paradox of the Red Heifer is that it is clearly an act of sanctification, as expressed in the sprinkling of the blood toward the Temple, even though the animal is slaughtered and burned outside the Temple precincts. In all other sacrifices, the blood of the sacrificial animal is sprinkled on the altar. Sacrifice in Judaism always takes place within the Temple precincts, yet here the slaughter of the Red Heifer is beyond the Temple perimeter. On one level, then, it appears not to be a sacrifice. Nevertheless, the very act of sprinkling and the purification involved, the very nomenclature used—"a purification from sin"—do create some relation to the class of offerings that we know as sacrifices. It both is and is not a sacrifice.

Connected to this paradoxical state, the Red Heifer, including its ashes, is subject to *me'ilah* (sacrilege), a category that would not apply to the ashes of a regular sin offering.[7] In spite of the resemblance to sin offerings, this rite does not take place inside the Temple and, critically, does not need the type of verbalized intentionality (of designating a specific sacrificial victim) that sin offerings require. Here again, the Parah Adumah seems to be a liminal substance par excellence—it purifies but renders impure; it is burned outside the Temple and hence cannot really be a sacrifice, but its blood is sprinkled in the direction of the Temple in an act of sanctification; it is subject to *me'ilah* as a sacrifice, yet it does not call for the intentionality of sacrificial rites. All this is not surprising, given the purpose of the Parah Adumah to purify from death, from contact with that which is beyond all order, from that which threatens existence and its ordered categories. Death ultimately challenges our categories of order, and confutes all our plans and reasons. It questions human existence—indeed, challenges existence itself. Perhaps we should not be surprised that paradoxes crop up as this rite attempts to move between the forces of death and life—to reintegrate those who have brought the realm of the dead into quotidian social existence through physical contact. Recall the Jewish understanding noted above, that death is so far beyond the living categories of order that the dead themselves are not impure, even though death renders those who come into contact with a corpse impure. The dead are simply beyond. The boundary between life and death, seemingly as stark and absolute as any boundary can be, here looks complex and contradictory.

The Powers of Center and Edge in China

The ambiguity that inheres to our concepts of order holds even for such fundamental categories as space or self. We always realize that something else lies beyond—both an absence of whatever constitutes the category and a presence of something beyond. Beyond purity lies impurity, but beyond both purity and impurity lies the abyss. The boundaries of the first generate ambiguity, and the boundaries of the second generate chaos. While it might be possible to argue for many conceptions of space and power in Chinese history, we highlight here one dominant understanding of place-based power and the challenge that it constantly faced from a second form of power that came from beyond and inside its edges. Both images of power, as we will discuss, envision ways of interacting across boundaries. Different as the sources of power are in these two conceptions, they are inseparable from each other, with each implying an opening for the other.

The most obvious way to think about space, power, and boundary in late imperial China is through political hierarchy. The boundaries of the administrative system defined one aspect of this. Discrete bureaucratic units began at the level of the county (or sub-county in some cases), and worked their way up a nested hierarchy through prefectures and provinces to the level of the empire. Each level had its own administrative city with its own officials and appropriate rituals. Chinese sometimes referred metaphorically to bringing new lands into the empire, which they often thought of as a process of civilization, as the drawing of administrative boundaries. Classifying space into political order was thus a fundamental property of civilization.

This system in practice was not quite as neat as it sounds, however. First, as G. William Skinner pointed out, economic and social ties in many cases cross-cut political boundaries.[8] The resulting hierarchies often did not nest neatly, because unlike the administrative system, people could visit markets at more than one center. Second, the hierarchy grew fuzzier at the edges instead of coming to a clean break. Throughout much of the southwest, for example, the Chinese state appointed local chieftains to govern, without creating the normal administrative hierarchy. This is consistent with the image of China as an empire where civilization emanated from the center and receded toward the edges. It differs to an extent from the bureaucratic image of officials in a nested hierarchy, but is consistent with the idea of an emperor as the charismatic Son of Heaven.

While the emperor headed the entire bureaucratic structure of officials, he also stood outside it in some ways. Unlike all the officials below
him, his power did not extend from office, but directly from the Mandate
of Heaven. In this, the emperor resembled the Balinese kings that Clifford
Geertz described. Geertz wrote about an image of the "exemplary center"
where power declined out from its central source in many different aspects
of social life.[9] The ruler was like a source of illumination for all around
him, but with an efficacy that declined gradually to the utter darkness that
surrounded his light. Chinese writers sometimes described this as a series
of declining tribute zones with ever weaker ties to the center.[10]

In China, power could be approached but never reached—a receding
center as well as an exemplary one. This appeared, for instance, in the
architecture of the Forbidden City. Rather than filling space with an enormous building, like many European palaces, a visitor who passed through
the Tian'an Gate into the Forbidden City saw a vast expanse of space (now
mostly empty but then normally filled with soldiers and buzzing bureaucrats), apparently focused on the seat of power in a small building far
ahead. On reaching the building, however, it was typical to find that the
emperor was not there. High-ranking visitors might proceed through the
building, only to be faced again with a vast space and another building far
ahead. The same vista might be repeated again on passing through the
second building. The ultimate power always receded into the distance. A
similar trope reappears in other contexts, as in the stories of the truly great
martial arts masters hidden deep in the mountains or of Daoist immortals
similarly always just out of reach.

Many of the same images of central power appear again, refracted
through the lens of local religion. Like officials, most gods rule a territory,
typically defined through periodic temple rituals where parading deities
mark the boundaries of their realms. Most of the time, however, their
power emanates from central points marked by their temples, and from
the wooden images installed there. While visitors can see the god's image
sitting on its altar (unlike the emperor on his throne, for most people), the
altar itself can usually not be approached directly. A bit like the Forbidden
City, larger temples may also be arranged so that visitors have to pass
through at least one building, with its own altar, in order to approach the
main altar in a "rear palace" (*houdian*). Particularly ornate temples
reinforce the receding center again through their ornament, which can
fractally diminish into ever finer and more remote carvings as one looks
into far recesses and distant ceilings.

This kind of power, which radiated down from a receding center, was commonplace. Big landlords and wealthy elites occupied a similar position to gods or the emperor, in their smaller ways. Much about local experience meshed with the idea of separate units under the control of a higher authority: branches of a lineage, tenants of a landlord, levels of a marketing system, or territories of neighborhood or village earth gods within the broader territory of a more important deity. We see it even in the cultural value granted to the foods most closely associated with this form of power—the products of the great rice paddies of the south or the wheat fields of the north. Southerners often claim that they can never get full without some rice at a meal; people in the northwest may say the same thing about steamed wheat bread (*mantou*). These products of lineage and land, handed down from ancestors (the kinship parallel to gods, political officials, or local landlords in this image), and of local systems of economic control formed the central core of any meal, to be surrounded by tasty but ultimately optional side dishes, like decorations around a sturdy building.[11] Note that in this Chinese construction of categories, the definition of the center is more crucial than specifying precisely the placement of the boundary. Civilization in much imperial Chinese thought consisted of centers that faded toward margins. The largest center was China itself (the "central country") with a fading to barbarity beyond the extent of its power. This repeated at ever smaller scales and in regimes well beyond politics. It was reproduced as valleys rose into less governed mountains, as the god's control over his or her territory faded or was challenged by demonic forces, and even as rice was surrounded by side dishes.

Taiwanese funerals make symbolic use of rice in ways that are completely consistent with this. According to Stuart Thompson's analysis, grains of rice represent the continuity of the patrilineage, the prototypical unit of the officially sanctioned image of space and power.[12] The key symbolic contrast at funerals is with pork, which represents the impermanence of ties through women and other aspects of the person that the funeral strips away in favor of the purity of the lineage. The geomancer at the site of the new grave will reinforce the imagery by scattering raw rice and other grains mixed with nails and coins—all objects of hard permanence, and all symbolizing the wealth and eternity desired for the lineage.[13] Like the bones of the body, which will be preserved long after the flesh is gone, the rice is meant to last forever, both as symbolic object and as material resource for future generations.

This was in a sense the goal of this entire structure of notation. The exemplary center, with its ability to create benefits by exerting its power, was far more than just an ideology of imperial rule. It was an entire cosmology. Nevertheless, notation is never complete. The Chinese hierarchy of centers never had a monopoly on power, or even on the imagination of power, and we turn now to its limits.

States have a hard time climbing hills, as James Scott pointed out.[14] He meant that the processes of census and surveillance, which are critical to the maintenance of state power, become increasingly more difficult as the terrain becomes harsher and the costs of control begin to outweigh the benefits. In a place like China, this meant that the power of the center reached its limits at both the external and internal borders of the empire—in the hills of internal Hunan or Fujian as much as at the political edges. These borders typically differed significantly from the rich valleys that defined the prototypical center. They were often ethnically diverse, with a strong presence of non-Han groups. Economically, they did not grow the classic staples of rice or wheat, but instead produced locally consumed staples, like corn or potatoes after the introduction of New World crops, or specialized commercial hill crops like indigo dye, Chinese medicines, charcoal, or opium.

From the point of view of the receding center, such areas indicated a descent into barbarity. They were often not literate in Chinese and were not always within the political jurisdiction of counties and prefectures. Many had a gender division of labor and status that center-based elites found improper, and some lacked patrilineages, another basic marker of civilization.[15] From within the image of the empowered center, such places appeared to lapse into savagery and insignificance. In practice, however, they had a power of their own. Nomadic groups to the north of China constantly harassed across the Great Wall (except, of course, when they constituted a conquering dynasty), and southern mountain dwellers were a menace to travelers. The weak state control over both external and internal borderlands made them into breeding grounds for bandits and rebels, from the Taiping Heavenly Kingdom to the Communists in modern times.

Even more than the threat of violence, however, such regions also provided a power of the imaginary. Images of southern minorities, for example, granted them a wide range of powers that had nothing to do with the possibility of violence in an area of weak central control. Their women were often seen as sexually alluring and powerful. Currently popular forms of tourism based on visits to experience the staged lives of minorities are inseparable from sex, either directly as prostitution or indirectly through song and drinking shows that are mainstays for tour groups. Seen from the Confucian center, this was just a further indication of improper gender roles, but it was the very people of the grain-growing central valleys who found this power irresistible.

We can see this again in a kind of magical power ascribed to these minorities. To some extent, this may have been part of an association between "savage" groups and the powerful mountain landscapes in which they lived. So-called "Miao Albums" (which depicted all kinds of southern minorities, not just the modern Miao) often showed the men almost as forest creatures—hair cropped short (unlike Confucian men but like animals), almost naked on top and wearing a sort of animal-skin skirt. In the mountains of Guangxi in the middle of the nineteenth century, for example, locals of all ethnicities often turned to Yao religious specialists and worshipped at temples with Yao origins.[16] In Taiwan, Gary Seaman shows how local Han in the Puli region would turn to minority specialists when they needed powerful black magic performed for them. Indeed, the "raw" groups of Taiwan's mountains were seen as holding all these kinds of power: they could perform sorcery, their women still constitute a disproportionate percentage of Taiwan's prostitutes, and they were feared for their prowess in taking heads until the Japanese pacification.

Note that this power from beyond the boundary exists in the center every bit as much as at the edges. The Qing dynasty travel literature that described exotic savages was consumed primarily in the center, of course.[17] Modern ethnic tourism also caters primarily to people from the wealthy cities of the east coast. We also see the power of the boundaries directly in the central cities, with phenomena like the "floating" population of migrants who come, often illegally, to take advantage of the booming economy. Blamed for nearly every sort of social ill, these migrants share in the imagined power of the boundary, even though they often stem from poor areas of the plains and live in the core cities. The combined power and threat of beggars was another indicator of the boundary as it intruded directly into the center.

The empowered boundary is just as much cognitive as it is geographical. In the spiritual realm, for example, we find great power associated with liminal categories (as in so much of the world). The unincorporated dead loom particularly large in China. These are the nameless ghosts whom no one worships as either ancestor or god. Unless propitiated at annual rites or in roadside shrines, ghosts have the potential to wreak havoc with our lives, causing sickness and death. We also have semi-natural spirits like fox fairies, whose crimes range from mischief to murder. Iconographically, ghosts often take two quite different forms. First, like fox fairies, they can be beautiful creatures with deadly powers to seduce. The other important image is of the miserable creature of the underworld. Each of these images posits powerful beings at the border between nature and (Confucian) culture.

We can see the imagined power of the cognitive edge in food as well. Rice or wheat may have symbolized the satiating power of the center, but all of the most extraordinary foods came from the margins. Nearly every highly valued food came from either the cognitive or the geographical periphery, and many came from both. Rare dishes for banquets and medically efficacious foods nearly always drew their power from the boundary. Standard banquet foods like bird's nests, shark's fins, or bear's paws came from distant and exotic places, as did important medicines like deer antlers or rhinoceros horn.

Perhaps the most famous recently has been *yartsa*, the Tibetan caterpillar-fungus. In Chinese it is called "winter insect summer grass" (*dongchong xiacao*), and people usually describe it as a caterpillar in winter and a sprout of grass in summer. In fact, it is a larva that has been parasitized by a fungus, which devours the insect while it hibernates underground over the winter, and sends up a fungal sprout in the spring. Dead and alive, animal and vegetable, the yartsa is a classic liminal object, filled with the power of the cognitive and physical edge.

These power-foods are just the extreme case of the standard distinction in Chinese food between the main dish, the rice or grain that forms the heart of the meal, and side dishes, the meat and vegetables that add taste and interest. Most side dishes in practice, of course, came from the same fertile valleys that produced the wheat and rice. The really empowering foods (in both prestige and medical efficacy), however, came from the margins. This contrast recurred in the funeral symbolism that we have already mentioned, where rice represented the continuity of the lineage and pork—a luxurious but not particularly exotic side dish in a peasant economy—represented transient ties traced through women. As Thompson writes, "While rice is 'substance shared' by members of a family, pork is very much 'substance given,' for it is prototypically the foodstuff for exchange and reciprocity between families—it is the primary banquet food."[18]

In fact, this argument could extend even to cover the power of women themselves. As in many patrilineal societies, China tended to offer two quite different images of women, who were both threats to lineage solidarity and necessary to lineage reproduction. The first, consistent with the view from the Confucian center, subordinated women completely to the lineage (first to her father, then to her husband, and then to her son, in the common formulation) and valued them as nurturing mothers to the patriline. The second, reflecting the power of the edge, saw women instead as a threat to lineage independence because they brought in ties to outsiders and because their sexuality threatened to undermine the system. Thus in the Chinese spirit world we get both virginal nurturers like Guanyin or Mazu and sexual killers like fox fairies.

In this sense, the ambiguities and threats from the boundary existed everywhere, not just at the geographical margin. By the same token, the idea of the center could be just as crucial, even for those in the mountains. Both images of power are pieces of the Han imaginary, rather than something that necessarily represented the actual situation of people in specific places. Both forms of power were around all the time, in gender relations, funeral symbolism, beggars on the street, and even at the dinner table. The self both defines and threatens the other, just as the other defines and threatens the self. That is, the idea of a power of the center already implies the power of what lies beyond; the apparent clarity of simple political boundaries hides a far more complex understanding of the ambiguities that lie between self and other. The notational system based on a centralized hierarchy created its own form of counter-power, making room for the acceptance of a wide set of ambiguities.

Conclusion

In both of our examples, we can see the beyond that lies at the root of all ambiguity. This is the beyond that cannot be ordered or contained, cannot be framed or bounded. In *The Bacchae* we see it in the forces around Dionysus, and in the book of Job in the problem of theodicy. For the Israelites it was in death itself, the situation that is beyond any categorization such as "pure" and "impure." In China it is found in the empowered margins that cannot (and need not) be brought into the center. No abstract system of order which posits impermeable boundaries between its entities can account for it. The edges of the beyond can, however, be précised and crossed in the practices of ritual and the negotiations of practice across many different civilizations—as we have seen in Jewish rituals of purification and Chinese conceptions of power. The fractal nature of boundaries appears in any repetitive system like ritual prayer, or like ornament in music or in architecture, which—in their very repetition— recognize the insufficiency and inadequacy of their own orders. Such an understanding of boundaries points to the myriad ways that multiplicity itself (including pluralism) rests on ambiguity.

Systems that make claims to transcendent meaning and cosmic order, as both the Jewish and Chinese examples did in their very different ways, also show an openness and a certain cognitive lability and reflexivity. In the Chinese case, the power of the margins constantly inflicted and inflected the imperially sanctioned power exercised through nested and clearly demarcated hierarchy. This was not just the problem that real power waned at the edges of the empire, because the margins were as much cognitive as geographical, and thus internal to the thinking of people across the empire. There was no escape from the thing beyond the edge. In the Jewish case, too, we find that the very price of theodicy is that true knowledge belongs to God alone, and so we are left at some level with perpetual uncertainty. Human reason is but a poor tool, a fragile reed that cannot in the end know the ways of God or even, as we shall see, the true meaning of our own religious acts. Both cases remind us that unknow-ability and uncontrollability lie at the very heart of the project of knowing and controlling through the production of categories and the construction of boundaries.

3

Ritual and the Rhythms of Ambiguity

WE UNDERSTAND "RITUAL" as a series of formal, iterated acts or performances that are, in Roy Rappaport's terms, "not entirely encoded by the performer."[1] That is, they are imbued by meanings and shaped by conventions external to the performer. We consider such ritual acts crucial to the existence of the relational self, that is to say, of a self who can accommodate ambiguity. This is the result, we will argue, of ritual's ability to both recognize and cross boundaries, and of its rhythmic relationship to time.

Rituals create a subjunctive space, a shared "could be" that constructs individuals in relation to others. This is as true of religious ritual as it is of the rules of civility and etiquette. Ritual, in its formal, iterated, and enacted moments, presents a unique human resource for dealing with ambiguity and the multivocal nature of all relationships—with beings human and divine. Ritual defines and binds entities, times, and spaces. By creating such borders, it also links entities, times, and spaces to what lies beyond their immediate field. As we will argue in this chapter, it presents a coherent and embracing way to live in a plural and hence also deeply ambiguous universe, one where order can never really be known, but still must be acted upon.

When we say that people share a symbol system, or a set of values, or a common idea of the sacred, we in essence assert that they share the potential space of what "could be," a subjunctive world.[2] Much ritual action provides this shared sense of empathy—sometimes even in terms of a shared "what if." When Jews congregate around the Passover Seder table and are enjoined to fulfill the commandment to feel "as if you yourselves have been liberated from Egypt," they create that shared space where the communality of the "could be" becomes the basis of the ongoing collective experience. The Shi'ite enactment of the defeat of Imam Hussein at

Karbala and the Catholic participation in the Eucharist all have similar import.[3] Confucius, famously uninterested in the world of spirits, still insisted that when "he offered sacrifice to his ancestors he felt *as if* his ancestral spirits were actually present. When he offered sacrifice to other spiritual beings, he felt *as if* they were actually present."[4] Maimonides enjoins us to attend to our prayers "as if" we are standing before the Creator of the universe.[5] The moral community that Émile Durkheim outlined in *The Elementary Forms of Religious Life* exists precisely because it shares the potential space of culture created through ritual.[6] That shared moral community is never the entirety of social experience in its full complexity of misunderstandings, conflicts of interest, and incompatibilities. It is instead a subjunctive construct, a shared acquiescence to convention.

In ritual, we subject ourselves to externally given categories of order, whose source can be anything from a transcendent deity (as in Judaism) to the natural ordering of the physical and social world (as in Confucianism). Ritual concentrates on the performative nature of the act, rather than on its denotative meaning. In its purely formal aspect, ritual puts questions of belief or truth aside in favor of the shared world that its action creates and requires. The external, performative aspects of ritual—especially its repetition and recollection of places and times not given to purely rational or instrumental computation—give its potential interpretations a unique lability. Thus ritual encompasses the ambiguity of life in a unique manner. It allows one to "play" with such ambiguity without undue concern with the authenticity of one's actions and beliefs. Ritual unshackles the mind from a need to *believe* in a dogma of our choosing, as long as we act within its conventions.

Ritual allows us to live with ambiguity and the lack of full understanding. In slightly different terms, it allows us to live with the other, with what we do not fully know or understand—as indeed, we can never fully know or understand any other. The presentation of ritual's "as if" universe, the subjunctive, requires neither a prior act of understanding nor a clearing away of conceptual ambiguity. Performance simply and elegantly sidetracks the problem of shared meaning by allowing participants to express acceptance of an order without requiring a full understanding of it. In this way, it resembles all manner of decisions that we must make to take any concrete action, when we accept that we have as much understanding as we are likely to get and that action must be taken even though our knowledge is incomplete (as it always must be). This is true for a medical intervention, a financial investment, a marriage commitment, a declaration of war, or the planning of a highway—for virtually all forms of human endeavor. Through its emphasis on action, on the performative and its creation of a subjunctive universe, ritual creates a world—temporary, fragile to be sure, but not false—a world where differences can be accommodated, tolerance enacted (if not fully understood) and openness to the other maintained.

While ritual activity carries its own form of intentionality, it is important to note that ritual is not necessarily concerned with what we often call "sincerity." In any ritual, as with saying "please" and "thank you," performing the act marks acceptance of the convention. It does not matter how you may feel about the convention, if you identify with it or not. In doing a ritual, the whole issue of our internal states is often irrelevant. What you *are* is what you *are in the doing*, which is of course an external act. This differs significantly from modernist concerns with sincerity and authenticity. Getting it *right* is not, as in the latter cases, a matter of making outer acts conform to inner beliefs. Getting it right is doing it again and again and again—it is an act of world construction. As an ideal type, the self *who does ritual* is very different from the self *who is sincere.*

Unlike ritual, the sincere—to which we wish to juxtapose it—involves a search for motives and for purity of motives. Sincerity privileges intent over action. This concern with intent has become the touchstone of much of our moral reasoning, for instance in Immanuel Kant's writings on the workings of the "good will."[7] As Kant stresses: "The good will is not good because of what it effects or accomplishes or because of its adequacy to achieve some proposed end; it is good only because of its willing, i.e., because it is good of itself." Thomas Nagel and Bernard Williams cogently delineated the limits of this view in clarifying that: "However jewel-like the good will may be in its own right there is a morally significant difference between rescuing someone from a burning building and dropping him from a twelfth story window while trying to rescue him."[8] Nonetheless, from the Puritans of the seventeenth century to the talk shows of the twenty-first, a concern with the inner wellsprings of action and sincerity has become almost an icon of modernist culture. This concern, we would argue, is very much at home in the world of notation outlined above. The search for the singular and unalloyed definition, feeling, impulse, or intent lies at the core of both the search for sincerity and for the pure or impermeable boundary line that defines notation as one mode of parsing ambiguity.

In contrast to this, the realization that our boundaries are only artifice and that the world is fundamentally ambiguous—which we can find in a ritual approach—allows us to accept and even play with that ambiguity. Sincerity seems by its very definition to exclude ambiguity. Recall that its dictionary meanings include "being without admixture," "free," "pure," "whole," and "complete."[9] Samuel Johnson lists among its cognates "unhurt," "uninjured," "pure," "unmingled," and "uncorrupt." Sincerity, carried to its extreme, is the search for wholeness, for overcoming boundaries and positing a unitary, undifferentiated, uncorrupted reality. It is a utopian impulse.

Ritual differs fundamentally, because many of its forms incorporate a degree of ambiguity within its very practice. In moving between differentiation and unity, ritual recognizes the ambiguous nature of reality and registers it, rather than denying it. In some senses, ritual searches for a wholeness like that of sincerity, but it does so by recognizing difference and ambiguity, rather than by denying them. Ritual does more than posit a reality. Rather, its pattern is often the classic dialectic of positing a reality, negating it, and ending up with a "truer" reality.[10] Ritual's opening to subjunctive worlds allows this play with different versions of reality, unlike the singular approach of sincerity. It allows us to recognize the ambiguous nature of empirical reality in a way that the sincere mode would find threatening and overwhelming.

Anti-ritualist attitudes deny the value to this subjunctive of play, convention, and illusion. They seek to root interaction in some attestation to the sincerity or truth-value of all categories or interlocutors. Yet, as we noted in chapter 2, "the map is not the territory." If, for example, our love for each other registers only through our words ("I love you"), then we are caught in the perennial chasm between the words (of love) and the love itself. Words are only signifiers, arbitrary and by necessity at one remove from the event they signify. Hence the attempt to express love (or any other truth-value) in words is endless, as it can never finally prove its own sincerity or truth—its "unalloyed" nature. Ritual, by contrast, is repeated and unchanging. It avoids the problems of notation and sincerity because its visible performance itself constitutes an acceptance of its conventions. Unobservable inner states are irrelevant.

The drive for oneness, for notational wholeness whether expressed in the wish to be at one with oneself and with the world, or for eternal and unchanging truths, will always come into conflict with the reality of existence. A measure of hypocrisy complements any notion of a true self—or any other claim to absolute truths—because we can never fully express an inner being. Worse still, that inner being itself is never unambiguous.

Any attempt to express a pure self is compromised because language and other conventions mediate all social interactions. Shakespeare apparently shared some of this assessment, as we can see from the character of Polonius, in whose mouth Shakespeare puts those lines about "to thine own self be true." He is, after all, a meddlesome buffoon, not above lying and spying on his betters, full of bombast, self-importance, and deceit: a model hypocrite, for his great capacity for self-deception. Single-minded adherence to the "sincere" model of existence in the world does not allow for a somber and realistic vision of just how complicated, contradictory, and ambiguous the sources of action, feeling, claims-making, and intent really are. Rather, it results in the continual production of a hypocritical consciousness that holds up as a model what is essentially a deeply compromised, narcissistic, and unrealizable ideal. It adheres to a vision of wholeness that is not of this world, and attempts to implement it within the world have led to some of the greatest collective tragedies of past centuries. The impulses toward sincerity and notation are similar: both attempt the impossible task of removing ambiguity by clarifying categories and refining intentions.

Such attitudes reject the fundamental messiness of the world in a search for wholeness and totality. And while ritual may teach us to accept and even to play with the inherent ambiguity of the world, the very absoluteness of the notational stance attempts to exclude ambiguity, as we discussed in the previous chapters. The notational and the ritual, we are claiming, are two possible responses to the ambiguity of the world and hence to what is unknown, beyond the self. The differences between them have significant implications for the organization of the social world.

What we usually call the "modern" period, with its emphasis on the notational impulse and its strong "flight from ambiguity," fostered a rare institutional and cultural emphasis on sincerity claims. As a consequence, people now often see ritual from the perspective of sincerity claims, and relegate it to a supposedly "traditional" order that the modern period has heroically superseded. Indeed, these claims have become so pervasive that even "fundamentalist" revolts against this so-called "modern" era occur in the name of finding an even more ultimate authenticity that, at the end of the day, is impossible.

We will argue here, however, that ritual can instead help teach us the tremendous dangers of trying to build a totally coherent world of notation— of authentic, individual truth-claims. It encourages us to recognize the fragmented and discontinuous nature of the world, the endless work

entailed in building and refining our multiple and often conflicting relationships within that world, and the ultimate impossibility of resolving its
ambiguities. And it helps teach us the powers of ethical action based upon
such a vision. Accepting the world's discontinuities and ambiguities
means that the work of building and refining relationships will never end.
Ritual, at least in its relationship to the rest of experience, is never totally
coherent and never complete. Yet doing the work of ritual is one of the
most important ways in which we live in such an inherently plural world.

To no small extent, this work revolves around boundaries and the ritual
propensity not only to construct boundaries—an anthropological "truism"
made famous by Erving Goffman and Mary Douglas, among others—but
also to cross the very boundaries that it constructs. The gavel that calls the
court to order, the *temenos* (that sacred space surrounding a Greek temple),
the opening at Wimbledon, and so on—are all examples of such ritual
framing of spaces, events, and interactions.

Fewer scholars, however, have remarked upon the ways that ritual also
contributes to the crossing of boundaries. Rituals do indeed construct the
spaces of the sacred, but they also require us to enter and exit those spaces.
Boundaries both separate and unite, differentiate and establish contiguity,
as anyone who has ever shared an apartment wall or property line with
neighbors can attest. Ritual, by constructing our categories and their
boundaries, also establishes their modes of interpenetration. Ritual does
this in a second way as well. By creating subjunctive worlds, it reminds us
that otherness is possible, that the world as it appears is not the only possible world.

Repetition is critical to the ways that ritual crosses boundaries. Through
repetition, ritual establishes a formal context above and beyond any particular content or "meaning" of the event, gesture, or locution. We may draw
an analogy here to ornament (dentils below a roofline, patterns on a picture frame, palmettes along a lintel, etc.), which, like ritual, is a formal
repetition of a largely content-free design that exists on and also forms the
boundary of the object it frames.

The key here is the formal quality of both ritual and ornament, as
expressed in Henri Focillon's dictum that "form signifies only itself."[11]
While ornament tends toward pure form, ritual too maintains a strong
formal element in its patterned repetition (though to be sure, not totally
divested from all meanings). This "contentless" form, divested from subject matter or meanings, is the crux of the dual role of ritual in both creating and crossing over boundaries.

Pure content or meaning does not, in itself, allow much leeway for change and the development of the new (except through reinterpretation, the positing of additional meanings). Creeds—the Nicean Creed, the Islamic Shahadah, Maimonides' Thirteen Principles of Faith—do not in themselves allow us to cross boundaries. Quite the opposite, they rather tend toward binary oppositions and reified identities. One assents or demurs. The formalism of ritual, however, to the extent that it is devoid of content (and thus is never complete), allows room for alternative significations. "Empty ritual" may well be a modernist execration, but we are claiming that this seemingly "empty" (but really formal) aspect of ritual acts is precisely what allows us to move from one world of significance and meaning to another. Rather than vilifying "emptiness," we should see the formal qualities of ritual as generating a potential space within which otherness can be introduced and experienced. This is true for the frame around a picture, for the crossing of oneself before receiving communion, as well as for the rituals of courtship as a prelude to love. All enable new experience through the construction of boundaries whose very creation allows us to bridge them. Frame and bridge are one in the formalism of these acts and artifacts.

Some years ago, the psychoanalyst Thomas Ogden analyzed and developed D. W. Winnicott's concept of potential space as that space which exists when an individual can successfully differentiate the three primary aspects of experience: the symbol (or thought), the symbolized (or that which is thought about) and the interpreting subject (the self). For Ogden, "potential space ceases to exist as any two of these three elements become dedifferentiated: the thinker and the symbol, the symbol and the symbolized, or the thinker and the object of thought (the symbolized)."[12] Potential space (what Winnicott also referred to as "transitional space") is a formal arena devoid of its own content or meaning, in which new meanings and content can come to be. It exists only through the differentiation of the symbol, the symbolized, and the interpreting subject. Potential space, in Rosemary Dinnage's terms, allows for the "spanning of the self/other boundary line . . . that permits objective and personal truth to interact."[13] This space is thus critical to the development of all forms of creativity. For Winnicott, it is the necessary condition for all forms of culture and so, we would stress, for the development of empathy as well. A shared culture requires at least some degree of empathy, whether understood as trust, solidarity, or what Durkheim called a "moral community."[14]

Ogden defines empathy as:

a psychological process . . . that occurs within the context of a dialectic of being and not-being the other. Within this context (Winnicott would say "within potential space"), one plays with the idea of being the other while knowing that one is not. It is possible to try on for size one identification and then another (i.e., to play with the feeling of being the other in different ways), because the opposite pole of the dialectic diminishes the danger of being trapped in the other and ultimately of losing oneself in the other.[15]

This trying the other "on for size," being and not-being the self and other at the same time, Ogden argues, is the core of our projective identification with the other and the origins of empathy. Through such fellow-feeling, it is the source of world creation as well. As Gilbert Rose declared: "Both growth and creative imagination are seen as resulting from and facilitating the ebb and flow of losing and refinding oneself personally and endlessly in space-time."[16]

Human creation takes place in the spaces between. Only here lie the possibilities for the emergence of the new or other. The formal or abstract character of ritual creates that space (in constant mediation with the more meaning-embedded aspects of the ritual act) by positing subjunctive worlds that open up a potential space. Such a space opens up the possibility for something new to come to be, something that was not previously represented, symbolized, or imbued with meanings—something that was not previously notated.

The role of percussion—in music as well as in many ritual transitions—recalls how the formal qualities of all frames delineate the boundaries of an entity even as they link it to the world beyond. Rodney Needham pointed out that percussive noise typically marks moments of ritual transition in many places around the world.[17] While he never fully explained this, we see pure noise as an ideal marker of the moment of crossing the boundary between one subjunctive world and another because it has no content. Content is impossible between worlds, and "pure" noise allows us to move from one state to another. Thus, while the myriad meanings of existing rituals keep them firmly rooted in a world already notated, their formal aspects keep them open to what is not yet signified, to what is beyond. Even those already notated and meaning-filled worlds of ritual referents are framed through their very enactment. The iterated performative aspect of ritual, its rhythm, means that it constantly comes in and out of existence. Worlds of meaning and context repeatedly shift as sacred turns into profane into sacred into profane and so on in infinite oscillation. Even the performatives of civility constantly bring into focus alternative realities and continual possibilities of other ways of being.

Ritual and the Boundaries of Time

Ritual's oscillation over the boundaries between subjunctive worlds is often rhythmic and not just repetitive. Rhythm is *predictable* repetition, as in dance music where we know when the next beat of the drum will occur, rather then waiting for the next randomly repeated thump. In this sense, rites of passage like initiations or funerals may not be rhythmic because their timing can be unpredictable, although even that more random flow can be made more rhythmic by initiating groups of people in an annual ritual, for instance. Most other ritual, however, is already rhythmic by design, as with daily prayers, weekly meetings of a congregation, and all calendrical ritual. Most ritual is also rhythmic in a second sense as well: its internal acts have an inherent and predictable flow. That is, the timing of the sequence of acts in a given ritual is similar from one performance to the next. At rural Taiwanese funerals, for example, participants already know how the flow will carry them from wailing grief at the coffin's side, over a trip to the burial ground, through a meal and an afternoon of priestly chanting, to an evening's entertaining performance of the soul's travels through the underworld, and finally to a quiet gathering around a fire of paper spirit money burned for the newly incorporated ancestor. Rhythm characterizes the timing of the flow of individual rituals like this Taiwanese funeral, as well as between one ritual and another.

Rhythm does not simply depend on our sense of time. It may be more plausible to argue just the reverse—that predictable repetitions are what construct our sense of time. Many of our units of time come directly from the rhythms of nature, including the year, the seasons, the lunar month, and the day. Based in cycles beyond human control, we nevertheless mark them with our rituals, like celebrations for the New Year or spring festivals (Passover, Easter, Maypole dances, and the rest). Much of the rest of our sense of time comes from the rhythms constructed out of shared social conventions—rituals. The most obvious example is the modern week, whose global reach began centuries ago with the worship periods of globalizing Jews, Christians, and Muslims. The ritual structure can be secular as well, like the traditional Chinese ten-day week, based on state laws requiring officials to rest every tenth day.

The Jewish intellectual Rabbi Abraham Heschel pointed out that nearly all of the Jewish holidays were tied to natural rhythms, especially the rising and setting of the sun for daily rituals and the waxing and waning of the moon within the cycle of the entire year for the many holidays keyed to the lunar calendar. Only the Sabbath stands as an exception to this pattern, and for Heschel that made the Sabbath in many ways the most important of all. A week of seven days does not represent any natural cycle. Instead, Jews honor the Sabbath because the Creator declared the seventh day to be for rest. It alone is a matter of pure and arbitrary convention—for Heschel, of the direct will of God rather than any pattern of nature.[18]

The rhythms that create time are almost entirely shared, although the group involved may vary enormously in size—the family for a wedding anniversary, the nation for an independence day holiday, and probably all humanity for the days of the year. The result is a shared sense of time at each level. This is not just a convention that lets us use clocks and calendars. It gives us as well a sense of our community (or our various communities) as the people who share the flow of time with us. We are bound not by the present alone, but through our sense of a shared past and a potentially shared future. Each time we mark (and at the same time create) those forms of time, we accept our membership in that community. In other contexts, of course, we can also reject the same communities— the office worker may curse his job and he may cheat on his wife, but he still accepts both the conventions of the economy and of marriage at that moment when he shows up for work at 9:00 each morning and when he buys his wife anniversary presents.

We can carry this a bit further by following the musicologist David Epstein's distinction between two forms of rhythm: meter and pulse.[19] Epstein defines meter as something absolute and universal, independent from anything in the music itself. An example might be a metronome ticking at 64 beats per minute. Pulse, on the other hand, is the unique rhythm generated within each piece. It generally fluctuates around a meter (though not in all music), but may slow down or speed up for dramatic effect, or strike a note slightly early or late to create tension, and so on. When the doctor measures our heart rate at 72 beats per minute, she is talking about a meter. We are never absolutely steady around that meter, though. What our bodies actually have is a pulse, not a meter.

As a musicologist, Epstein of course finds pulse far more interesting than meter. The variable beating of a heart can entrance us in a way that an even tick 72 times a minute never will. Who wants to listen to a metronome tick for 45 minutes? Or even to listen to a Beethoven symphony played like absolute clockwork? Nevertheless, without meter, music would be impossible. This is true first because any kind of musical coordination—dance, duet, or symphony—would be impossible without some sense of shared and absolute time. Meter is purely conventional; it cannot come directly from the heart, like pulse. As we have been arguing, however, shared conventions (of which rituals form a critical subset) allow community to exist, and predictably repeated conventions allow it to exist in time.[20] The second reason that meter is crucial is that pulse only makes sense in relation to it. When we say metaphorically that our heart stopped or our blood raced, we imply a meter—a standard heart rate against which the speeding and slowing makes sense. The same metrical base is required to make sense of musical slowing and speeding, notes held too long or too short, attacks begun ahead of or behind expectations.

Rituals based on natural cycles like the lunar month rely on what Epstein calls pulse, while purely conventional rituals like the Sabbath or the Chinese 10-day week follow the arbitrary (or God-given) conventions of meter. Metronomes may be boring, but the conventions they represent are as crucial to society as to music.

All repetition pushes toward pure form. Metronome ticks are obviously nothing but form, but it is just as true of words repeated exactly over and over. As Maurice Bloch pointed out, even apparently denotative statements convey no actual content if they are pure repetition.[21] Thus a standard American exchange of courtesies—"How are you?" "I'm fine"—appears to ask for and convey new information about someone's health. In fact, however, the answers are almost purely conventional, repeated the same way under all conditions. When someone tells us they are "fine," we thus know nothing about their actual health. We know only their willingness to accept the conventions of that particular courtesy and its implication of friendly social relations. Such heavily ritualized action is thus a very poor tool for making political decisions or scientific discoveries, although it may provide helpful frames for those things. A ritual or a courtesy, repeated over and over, begins to approach the pure form of music, even if it offers symbols and statements subject to extensive interpretation outside the ritual itself. That is, taking part in a ritual means accepting its conventions, just as playing in an ensemble means accepting the meter. Pure repetition offers no new information at all, except that the people involved accept the convention. Here, again, we can see how the rhythms of architectural ornament, ritual, and music converge toward the same thing—an acceptance of something beyond the individual heart, which creates the possibility for a sense of community with a shared sense of time.

The Flows and Absences of Ritual Rhythm

Four thousand years ago, the legendary sage/king Yu the Great discovered a turtle with strange markings on its shell (see figure 3.1). Appearing in myth as a culture hero who learned to control the waters by preventing floods and creating irrigation, Yu realized that the pattern on the turtle's back showed a key structure of the universe: the dots in each of the nine segments of the turtle's shell form a magic square with each row, column, and diagonal adding up to 15.

FIGURE 3.1 Luo Shu

Yiben Qian, *Xiangchao, juan 1*, p. 5. We are grateful to the Harvard-Yenching Library for help in finding this image.

4 9 2
3 5 7
8 1 6

The odd numbers in the central cross are *yang* and the even numbers at the corners are *yin*, showing the balance and flow around which the universe is constructed. Only someone as wise in the ways of the anthropo-cosmic world as Yu could have understood the turtle's significance as a key to the universe as geometer. The pattern has been significant, especially to Chinese literati, through all the millennia that followed. Its nine squares recall the "well-field" system, said to have characterized early agriculture with a division of fields into nine equal units, of which the central one was farmed for communal benefit. Some temples were constructed on a similar pattern, and Daoist priests today still step through the pattern in a ritual dance. Some Chinese thinkers saw it as the basis for the organization of music, architecture, and even the structuring of meals.[22]

This is but one example of a broad cross-cultural tendency to pattern the architecture of creation by imposing something like meter on the pulse of the world. Further examples can be found in the Roman *lustrum* of five years, the 52-year cycle of the Mexican peoples, or the 60-year cycle of China. The cycles vary from a heartbeat to the Indian *yuga* of 1,080,000 years, but repetition is always central to the patterning.[23]

Not surprisingly, repetition finds a central place in the creation stories of the Western world as well, or at least in the second creation, the one that actually endured, following the flood. At the end of the eighth chapter of Genesis, God promises never again "to destroy every living thing, as I have done" (Gen. 8:21) and goes on to commit:

So long as earth endures,
Seedtime and harvest,
Cold and heat,
Summer and winter,
Day and night
Shall not cease.[24]

The new, post-deluvian order was characterized as well by the imposition of moral rules in the form of the Noachite commandments and the reordering of society in line with an explicitly ethical vision (prohibitions on murder, incest, partaking of a limb—or blood—of a living being, establishment of courts of law, etc.). While these later developments (of Genesis 9) are notational, the closing of Genesis 8 is interestingly different. Here God frames the very continuity of the world as repeating patterns: seedtime and harvest, cold and heat, summer and winter, and so on. The promise of mere continuity in Genesis 8:21 does not seem to suffice. Instead, the divine promise also explicitly announces a pattern and a rhythm.

For the Chinese, too, rhythms define the world. Yin and yang are not static principles but alternating cosmic rhythms; the interlocked paisleys of the classic yin-yang diagram show just such a rhythmic flow, rather than the statis that might appear from a simpler diagram like a circle divided by a radius. Such flows occur as well in Hesiod and with the Hopi. According to Piaget, we can find the same among children who perceive frequency and rhythm even before they are acculturated to more linear ideas of temporal duration.[25] While linear ideas of time may characterize every culture to some extent, based on the experience of aging, so do rhythmic ones—the pulses and meters of the world around us.

Rhythm and the patterning of time break up the flow of the world—the endless continuum of events, times, and realities. All matter vibrates with rhythmic patterns of energy—the basis of our quartz time pieces or kitchen microwave ovens. This is the patterning that we have termed "pulse"—the fundamental rhythm of things in themselves. Ritual in the form of meter takes this patterning one step further, moving beyond pulse to impose conventional order through a rhythmic repetition. In this sense, Passover and Easter impose the conventionalized meter of religious ritual on the natural pulse of the seasons. In a similar manner, the practice of *pranayama* (breathing technique) in yoga works with the natural rhythms of the body, but also overcomes them, imposing a formal order on the most intimate of bodily functions.

Examples from all major religious traditions can be multiplied, but we wish to focus attention on just some of the characteristics of these patterns. To form a rhythmic pattern, these ritualizing moments must always be only temporary. They emerge and recede, become manifest and withdraw; this is the nature of repetition. To be repeated, an action (or image or sound) must not only come into being, but also withdraw, only to reappear. There is no Sabbath without the workaday, no holy without the profane, no tracery without transepts, as indeed there is also no day without night, summer without winter, beauty without ugliness. Ritualizing moments are always only temporary.

Jewish purification ritual is a case in point, as we have discussed in our previous interlude (and to which we shall return in our next one). Pollution is part of life: coming into contact with polluting agents, be they menstruating women, women following childbirth, creepy-crawly insects, the dead and those in contact with the dead, seminal emissions, and so on. None of this can be totally avoided or overcome in some sort of Hegelian *Aufhebung*. Any life lived in society, with other men and women, with families and neighbors and caring for the old, sick, and dying, means, by definition, coming into contact with impurity. There were, consequently, myriad ritual injunctions during the time of the Temple, sacrifices and laws concerning purity and impurity and how to move from the latter state to the former. But the attainment of such state was always only temporary. It could not be otherwise. No one could avoid impurity while fulfilling the obligations entailed by life (burying the dead, caring for the sick, propagating the species, etc.). Ritual purification is thus like brushing teeth. It does not solve the problem of filth; it just lets us keeping living in an inherently polluting world as long as we keep up the repetition.

All human societies may have witnessed sectarian movements and groups that attempted to break out of this rhythmic, ritual mode. The Essenes in the Judean desert, in the time of Jesus, are perhaps the most well-known example. Even the Christian idea of a single baptism instead of repeated ritual baths is an attempt to break out of the cycle. Indeed, we see all world-rejecting groups and movements as similar attempts to break free of this endless cycle of corruption and purity, multiplicity and unity, fragility and wholeness that life in the world implies (this is precisely why Max Weber termed them "world-rejecting").[26] The cost of such attempts, of course, is leaving the world and its institutional orders behind. One can reject that world, like the Catholic monastics that Weber described, but then one has also revoked all claims to change it. One can cleave to the oneness of the monotheistic God, but then one leaves the world of men and women and society, and of family and children and parents and the multiple responsibilities (and pleasures) that are our lot. In so doing, one also gives up the natural connection between rhythmic ritual and boundary-crossing. There are no boundaries to cross when all is united in a crystalline One, and ritual's ability to deal with boundaries and their ambiguities is thus lost.

The point of this discussion, however, is not to enter into the theology of a sanctified life, or even (following Troeltsch) a sociology of sect and church, but simply to recognize two important points: (1) life in the world involves an endless oscillation and patterning, a rhythm of times and events, a constant flow and movement in our lives that nevertheless ties to some formal orders; and (2) there have always been attempts to break this movement, to overcome the ritual mediation or parsing of time in an attempt to realize the one, the total, the singular, and the True.[27] This impulse is part of utopian and (in Western traditions) millennial orientations and, to some extent, of such modern political movements as fascism and communism. Eric Voegelin termed these movements modern gnosticism—gnostic in their conceit of arriving at the true knowledge of history's telos.[28]

The rest of us are caught in states of being that are always temporary. The best we can hope for is some patterned predictability that allows order and formal structure. This lasts only until they unravel, only to appear again, through the patterned repetition of whatever ritual frames we use to impose form on the chaos of our lives. Ritual's rhythms can, of course, be more sparse or more crowded together. Daily prayer is different from weekly prayer, as the order of the five required daily prayers in Islam differs from simply going to mosque on Friday to participate in *Juma* prayers, or celebrating the Eid each year. The more dense the ritual patterning, the more intricate the rhythm becomes, as the tensions between states of presence and absence, order and ambiguity, meaning and loss become heightened. There is an aesthetic to this intricacy, but also an ethic that we maintain only by keeping both poles in sight.

Today's increasingly interconnected world forces us to think harder and harder about empathy, because it constantly thrusts difference (and hence the unknown and ambiguous other) upon us. The potential space for the creation of empathy ties directly to this movement between, to the necessarily temporary existence of rituals and so to their inherent recognition (often only implicit) of alternative worlds and systems of meaning that such oscillation entails. The shorter the "wavelengths" of this oscillation, the more we may appreciate just how tied order is to ambiguity, form to mass, the known to the unknown, and ourselves to the other.

Each moment of ordering—daily prayer, purification rite, birthday party—stops the continuum of daily experience, if only for a moment. It reveals and creates a new subjunctive world, even though we know we will leave that world again as soon as we end our prayers, reenter the world of inevitable pollution, or get up on the morning after a birthday. In music, sound orders time. It is abstracted as the beat, an instantaneous stoppage, a geometrical point in time instead of space. Ritual is far more complex than this (as is much actual musical rhythm), but it also fixes the world for a moment and then allows the flow to resume. By being predictable, rhythm defines time itself—it gives sense to the gaps between the claps. We tend to think of rituals just as a series of events or of rhythm as a simple set of repeated claps or the ticking of a clock:

O O O . . .

It might be better, however, to emphasize as strongly the bits between the claps:

—O—O—O—. . . .

That is, the ritualized, ordering moments are not the only things that matter. They are just one of at least two subjunctive worlds that we always cross between. Rhythm is not just tick, tick, tick, but rather tick-tock, tick-tock, tick-tock. Between the beats lies the continuum of life, the potential chaos, the uninterpretable silence.

We can understand any repetition as rhythm only when we can see the broader pattern. That is, we cannot feel rhythm only within the moment of the "tick" or of the "tock." The acceptance of multiple subjunctive worlds and the necessity of moving between them encourage us to take a standpoint outside and above those worlds, to see the entire pattern as it repeats. The philosopher Gilles Deleuze draws on Hume and Bergson to make the similar point that repetition changes nothing at all in the object that is repeated. What changes with repetition is instead something in our minds, the development of a new mental stance that lets us see the pattern from above.[29]

This was Freud's fundamental insight in his classic story of the little boy tossing a toy far away to shouts of "fort" (gone) and getting it back with a happy "da" (there). Freud recognized that this game of repeated disappearance and return allowed the child to conceptualize and thus accommodate himself to his mother's departures and returns. As Freud put it, "Her departure had to be enacted as a necessary preliminary to her joyful return."[30] The absence was as necessary as the presence. The child's repetitive play allowed him the ability to view the whole pattern from above, to realize that the absence would lead to the presence. Repetition provides the armature upon which both tick and tock, absence and presence, can be re-presented. Repetition always creates difference, both ticks and tocks, and requires us to accept that difference.

More than just difference—rhythmic repetition sets up a yearning for the tick after every tock. Comedians, for whom timing is said to be everything, know this when they pause for just a fraction of a moment before delivering a punch line. That extra wait, stretching out the tock while we wait for the tick, helps creates the tension that leads to laughter. Musicians know this just as well, as they constantly play off variations in the pulse of their performance against the rule of the underlying meter. Classical musicians slow down and speed up, delay entrances, hold notes too long, and otherwise manipulate pulse to create tension and excitement. Jazz musicians do this too, as in the slightly late sound that Billie Holiday perfected, or the rhythmic tension between bass and drums that Charles Keil wrote about.[31]

Ritual is no different. The observant Catholic who cannot attend Mass feels the absence of the ritual in a discomfort that is almost as physical as that of the observant runner who misses her jog. That yearning to return to the ritual order or to the musical meter keeps the clock ticking (and tocking).

Flowers and Fruit

Without the spaces between, there would be no repetition and so, of course, no rhythm, either. Without the "empty" bits, there could be no re-iteration of significance: whether the significant is a moment in time (musical note), an act (of prayer), an emotion (love or loss) or a physical space (in the image of dentil ornament). It is thus not only that the "tocks" matter just as much as the "ticks," the empty spaces as much as the marked or noted ones: without both, neither could be repeated. If we are discussing the dentils of architectural ornament, we would say that their repetition depends on the empty spaces; if musical notes, we would say that their repetition relies on the silences between. In each case, however, we recognize the crucial role of difference to the act of repetition.

The complexities of rhythm go beyond such difference, however, because the flux of time and experience makes each tick and tock differ from the last one. The Danish philosopher Søren Kierkegaard argued that these non-repeatable moments lie at the core of repetition when he claimed that: "The only repetition [is] the impossibility of repetition."[32]

Kierkegaard wrote a short book on repetition in which he describes the narrator's failed attempt to repeat a previous trip to Berlin. The quote above comes from his rather tongue-in-cheek description of his return to the Konigstadter Theatre in search of repeating the joyful experience of his previous sojourn, only to discover "that there simply is no repetition," an experience that he "had verified . . . by having it repeated in every possible way."[33] So is there or isn't there repetition? How, we should ask the Dane, could you repeatedly verify the fact that there is no repetition? He provided the answer earlier, where he advised us that "The dialectic of repetition is easy, for that which is repeated has been—otherwise it could not be repeated—but the very fact that it has been makes the repetition into something new."[34] Repetition both is and is not repeated, it both is and is not something new. We can only repeat through change, which does not, for all that, diminish the act of repetition; change is a necessary condition for repetition. Ambiguity is thus built into repetition, both constituting it and challenging it with very single repeated action (or note, or mark of any kind).

Kierkegaard goes on to point out that "If one does not have the category of recollection or of repetition, all life dissolves into an empty, meaningless noise."[35] In our first chapter, we discussed the formation of categories, the division of the world into ordered units. Kierkegaard is reminding us that unless we repeat these categories, they are not categories at all. They are only proper nouns. A world of proper nouns and only proper nouns, a world without general categories, would be no more coherent than one without nouns at all. Notation can only present a coherent universe if it is repeated. If not, Kierkegaard teaches, it is but noise. Repetition is necessary to knowledge and hence to life and yet, for all that, it is essentially impossible. As Heraclitus pointed out so long ago, one cannot set foot in the same river twice.

Just think, though—in the spirit of Kierkegaard—how often we repeat that impossible act. It repeats every time we fall in love, every time we pray, with every promise we make and tear we shed. It is impossible, yet its existence constitutes all the worlds we inhabit. The "tock" or distaff side of all notations, the empty space between the dentils, the stretches of polluting life between purification rituals: these are all but the spatial, temporal, or sometimes aural representation of that impossibility.

The problem of love was in fact the second arrow in Kierkegaard's bow—the first being the trip to Berlin. His short study of repetition describes a young man's retreat from marriage in fear that each day of married life will simply remind him of its distance from his perfect memories of past happiness. Better, he believes, to live in love's recollection—repeating what never really was, rather than face a present continuum that

can never "repeat" the past's perfection. Here perhaps is the real significance of the epigram on the book's frontispiece: "On wild trees the flowers
are fragrant, on cultivated trees, the fruits." Cultivation, hence civilization,
society, life with other men and women, in the world as it is, relies on
repetition. Plowing and seeding, weeding and harvesting are not one-time
activities, but must be repeated each and every year in season—as we saw
in the quote from the book of Genesis above. Grapevines must be pruned
every year. Indeed, the original meaning of the Greek word *hubris* is "un-
pruned" or "uncultivated." To maintain a world and to bring forth its fruit,
we must cultivate: repeat. So, too, for love.

Any activity that wishes to "bear fruit" thus requires repetition, including always the absence that is built into its very sinews. Repetition's
inexorably interwoven character of presence and absence, sign and emptiness, notation and negation constitutes its particular contribution to
framing ambiguity. Ritual is one of the three ways of parsing the ambiguity we have been discussing as inherent to our knowledge and our existence. Its mode of knowledge and of life allows a perpetual crossing of
boundaries (as opposed to the impermeable boundaries posited by notation's mark) through the imposition of its meters on the world. Ritual's
mode of knowing makes no claim to arrive at an essence or constitutive
truth, but rather continually reenacts the known as itself a mode of knowledge. It is Aristotelian *phronesis*, an enacted and embodied knowledge
that, despite its absences, continually repeats itself in the world. Its rhythm
is its logos.

We have already referred to Roy Rappaport's famous definition of ritual
as "the performance of more or less invariant sequences of formal acts
and utterances not entirely encoded by the performers."[36] In this definition we can find both aspects of ritual that we have been discussing—the
repeated and the non-repeatable, the formal bits that are reenacted (and if
anything is to be reenacted, it must have a formal character), as well as
those absences that allow the very act of repetition. These absences are
what Rappaport terms elsewhere the "self-referential" bits of the ritual.[37]
They are self-referential in that they do not signify any formal canon, but
are instead purely personal, individual, and contingent (and hence, analytically at least, not repeatable) meanings, actions, affects, or events. As
Kierkegaard taught us, there is no pure repetition. Everything we recognize as repeated is a construction that counts some parts as if they were
unchanged (Rappaport's "canon") and downplays the differences ("self-
reference"). Both modes are inherent to all ritual.

There is an order to daily prayer. The observant Muslim prays *Fajr* from dawn to sunrise, *Dhuhr* just after true noon, and *Asr* in the afternoon; *Maghrib* is recited from sunset until dusk and *Isha'a* after dark. The Catholic hours, too, have their appointed times: *Matins* (generally sometime during the night), *Lauds* (at Dawn), *Prime* (6:00 A.M.), *Terce* (9:00 A.M.), *Sext* (Noon), *None* (3 P.M.), *Vespers* (at the lighting of the lamps), and *Compline* (before bed). The same is true with the course of all orders of formal prayer. The appointed time frames each prayer, and the prayer is encoded by powers outside the performers. That is precisely what makes them formal, ritualized, and open to being understood as repeated and rhythmic. These are their "notated" moments. But we must not forget that the prayers are recited at these moments and not at others. One cannot pray *Fajr* in the evening, or *Compline* on getting up in the morning. The spirit may "bloweth where it listeth," but at least in these highly ritualized settings, prayer—proper prayer—must be recited at its proper time. This means that there must also be equally structured "empty," prayer-less moments. The rhythmic requirements of ritual may appear constricting and limiting to some, but they also guarantee (perhaps counterintuitively) that there are other times devoid of prayer, empty of presence, when one is not standing in prayer before God. Note how this differs from the highly individualized spirit of some forms of Protestant religiosity that see prayer as coming down to one as the spirit moves. Freed from the discipline of rhythm, they cannot perform the same role in securing the duality of prayer and non-prayer, of tick and tock, of presence and absence.

More individualized and enthusiastic forms of Jewish religiosity, such as Hasidut, are, for example, also famous for praying *Shacharit* (morning prayer) at all times of day (and sometimes night). One can walk into some Hasidic synagogues and view morning and afternoon prayers being recited simultaneously by different groups. In such examples, the personal, idiosyncratic, and non-repeated acts relativize the formal, notated, and ritualized ones. Consequently, prayer may be more "meaningful"—that is, the meanings are more fully self-referential—but this threatens the duality, the very crossing of boundaries that more formalized ritual guarantees.

The duality of ritual is critical to its nature—the enactment of both presence and absence, of *fort* and *da*, tick and tock, formal and self-referential. Both Sigmund Freud and Søren Kierkegaard recognized this in their different ways. Jacques Lacan developed the idea further in his lecture on Kierkegaard and his concept of *glissement* or slipping away—the inevitably non-repeatable aspect of every ritual performance.[38] For Lacan—as for Kierkegaard—the non-repeatable, the "radical diversity constituted by repetition in itself" is its very secret.[39] For him, moreover, it constitutes the essence of the ludic. As we have argued elsewhere, the ludic and the ritual have much in common.[40] Both play with notation, both use it and subvert it at the same time. Both are characterized by repetition, by a strong use of indexicality, both create subjunctive, "as if" universes, both continually cross boundaries—indeed, both frame their boundaries more as "cell walls" than "brick walls."[41] Both subvert notation as well as play with it, although they do so in very different ways. Ritual subverts through the act of repetition itself, while at least one form of the ludic, that of humor, subverts notation through what Umberto Eco termed its "metasemiotic" character.[42] Taking us out and across boundaries (before returning us to them), it gives us a more encompassing perspective than we could ever have if we simply remained within our original boundaries.

Lear's fool knows what the crowned king has forgotten, that knowledge can only be communicated ambiguously. So, too, for trickster myths from cultures far and wide (Loki for the Norse, Coyote in western North America, Anansi in parts of Africa and the Caribbean, and many more around the world). Like the ludic, the equivocal words of the fool or trickster allow a perspective from above. Indeed, according to the great medieval Jewish philosopher Maimonides, even the transmission of the knowledge of God's worship (i.e., rituals) was through the "gracious ruse" of God.[43] Formal, notational instruction in the true practice of worship was not possible, according to Maimonides, among a people seeped in slavery; they could learn only through God's "ruse." There is, it would seem, a strong component of many traditions that claims there is no way to knowledge but through the thickets of the ambiguous—whether in play or in ritual or myriad other forms of absenting presence.

Rhythm, Broken Rhythm, and No Rhythm

Let us conclude with three simple examples: one of an ongoing ritual, the second of broken ritual rhythms, and the third of a repetition that died. Each story presents a different facet of the ways in which ritual parses ambiguity, each giving us a different idea of what is gained, risked, and lost through this process. The Chinese festivities at the lunar New Year are a good example of how the ritualized rhythms of presence and absence create a subjunctive, temporary world, though many other examples would also work. The most important events of the celebrations are purely family rituals, especially on the eve and the first day of the New Year. No priests or religious specialists of any kind need be involved, and there are no sacred texts. Distant relatives return home for the events, and this is the busiest travel time of the year, as almost all work shuts down and people head for home.

Much that goes on in this ritual is purely within the realm of family custom, although those customs tend to be very widely shared, at least in broad outline. We will mention only one key event—burning incense in front of the ancestral altar. While not everyone has an ancestral altar any more, especially in urban mainland China, this rite was crucially important. The act itself was extremely simple, with the male(s) of the oldest generation first offering incense in honor of the ancestors, followed by the women of that generation, then the males of the next generation, and so on through the youngest generation of girls.

This little ritual creates a simple subjunctive world, an idealized Confucian portrait of the family. This family is autonomous and independent. Quite unlike most other ritual occasions throughout the year, reciprocal visiting and feasting is not important on this day. Internally, the family appears as a neatly stacked hierarchy, with the living recognizing their debts to the dead, with each generation respecting the one before it, and with women subservient to men of their own generation. Such a family is in fact created by the very acts and orders of worship, but only for those few minutes of the ritual. It performs and thus creates the way that fathers and sons or husbands and wives should be; it creates the ancestors themselves. Once it ends, however, this imagined hierarchical community may be just one of several different ideal images of family structure, competing, for example, with ideals of gender equality or the benefits of nuclear families. And all of these ideals also contrast with the realities of families as people live in them from day to day— with the absences of members scattered across the world, sulking teenagers who play too many computer games, spouses who drink or gamble too much, or elderly parents who can no longer command the authority that the ritual grants them. The ritual really does shape the family into a particular form, but like all rituals, its performed world soon comes to an end.

This end, however, is not complete. Ticks have their tocks, and the period of absence, of waiting for the next year to turn, is also a kind of yearning for that moment when an ideal family can again be performed.

The rhythm here is crucial, because it lets us know with certainty that the occasion will come again when we can perform that family again, erasing the fights and infidelities, overcoming even the losses and deaths for an image of the family that is forever. Repetition may be an illusion that we continually renew, but it is an illusion that gives us a sense of a shared past and future—and thus of a community.

Our second case comes from rural Taiwanese funerals. The day of the burial in rural Taiwan is both highly ritualized and emotionally choreographed. Daoist or Buddhist clergy read texts for the salvation of the soul all day. At proper moments, descendants offer incense to the deceased, in a way closely reminiscent of the New Year rite. Elegies are read or chanted, and at the right moments the women let their grief out through loud wails at the coffin. The burial follows, and then a muted feast for the participants, followed by more priestly ritual. This includes some public spectacle, concluding in the evening with the priests guiding the soul through the underworld by acting out the trip and its dangers. This involves a whole set of carnivalesque performances— fire-eating, tumbling, and general chasing around—that pull in a wide audience and typically distract even the most distraught mourners. The night ends very late with a large bonfire of burning "spirit money," with the mourners gathered silently in a circle around the flames as they watch the fire go slowly down. From loud grieving to humor to the quiet moment at the end, the ritual takes mourners and neighbors through emotional drama intended, like funerals almost anywhere, to incorporate the dead person in a new status and to reintegrate the living around the hole that death has created. At an ideal death of an aged person with many descendants, they burn red candles—the color of good luck and happiness.

Not all deaths are proper, though. Of the many funerals that one of us saw in Taiwan, the only ritual faltering took place in one where a man in his early twenties had been killed in a mining accident. Because the young man had not yet established a strong social or kinship network of his own, very few people were present. His young, pregnant wife could not bear the conventions of the ritual, and in particular rejected the emotional choreography toward acceptance that the whole ritual entailed. Instead of wailing at the proper times and places, her grief poured out from her, all the time, piercing and inconsolable. The rhythm of the ritual was destroyed, and it accomplished little in creating the subjunctive worlds that can help us heal at such times.

Such ritual failures are, of course, not limited to the world of China. One of us witnessed a similar example in the United States at the funeral of a young man, who had been about to enter a long-sought career and was to be married in the spring. The funeral was packed to overflowing with many friends and family members, horrified at the untimely death. The deceased man's fiancée spoke in front of the crowd as a widow without a wedding gown and at one point even cursed the Creator, and this in front of an audience that included many learned scholars. Here, too, for a moment the ritual's rhythms broke down, but for the assembled company, the structure of meaning held.

In both cases, the individual ritual faltered, but the broader rhythms of funerals did not. Other funerals followed, again offering a performance of family reintegration and fulfillment, creating their subjunctive world even as everyone knew that some tragedies, in coal mines and in so many other ways, would sooner or later occur again. Even these broken funerals could later be constructed as repetitions. Rituals, like hearts, sometimes skip a beat, but the point of rhythm is that we can trust them to work again the next time.

Our final example is personal, and on the far smaller scale of a private ritual between father and son. When one of us was young—perhaps 11 years old or so—his father used to wake him each morning for school with a gentle push on the boy's nose. The boy's eyes would open, he would say "Beep!" and both father and son would smile. We have written elsewhere about how such privately shared childhood rituals can create a safe space to explore images of self and role for which the growing child (and the parent, too) may have little other opportunity.[44] Even this brief and very simple ritual, with its precise daily rhythm, allowed the man and boy to create a little world where they knew they shared a unique connection. The boy's automated "beep," though not really rationalized or explained for either father or son, signified for both the ease and comfort of the transaction, like a machine responding easily to a human touch.

Like many such childhood rituals, the origins of this one are irretrievably lost. The end, however, is very clearly recalled. One day, the father touched the boy's nose and the boy would not, could not bring himself to respond. Somehow all the rest of life—the petty squabbles, the anger at sharing and not sharing an identity with the father, the resentment of the power of fathers over sons, even in waking them up in the morning— outweighed the momentary pleasure of that daily ritual. There was no premeditation at all, just a sudden refusal to play. The two never exchanged a word about this, but the son caught a look in his father's eye, or maybe it was the other way around, and the ritual was never attempted again.

Sometimes, rituals fail to create a subjunctive world, and sometimes they end altogether. In this case, we can see the death of the ritual as part of the maturation of the child. Entering his teens, the boy was eager to abandon the "as if" worlds of childhood. All rituals change, as all societies do, but the loss of this particular ritual signals a different kind of crisis. With the natural rejection of the rituals of childhood, do we have something to put in their place? Relations between fathers and sons (and, of course, mothers, daughters, siblings, spouses, and all the rest) are as ambiguous and troubled as relations between neighbors or strangers. We often lack the rituals that might replace the ones that we outgrow, and thus may struggle to find ways to cross the boundaries and bridge the ambiguities between self and other. This is one of the great crises for American families, especially as scattered meals, divergent social worlds, and the isolations of new media threaten many of our family rituals and rhythms. The Chinese New Year rites, and even their funerals, remind us that ritual solutions to that problem still remain open to us.

Ritual's rhythms, the construction of a predictable repetition, create a vital sense of shared and social time. Agreeing that we repeat means agreeing that we share a past, and knowing when to expect the next ritual "beat" means that we also share some sense of our future together. This sense of time shapes us into a community of the imagination. Its pulse of absence and presence is one way of living with difference while accepting the ambiguities that it entails.

Our third interlude deals directly with this sense of what can and cannot be shared. We will begin by continuing our study of the rite of the Red Heifer (or at least of later day rabbinic interpretations and exegesis), which shows how ritual can move across boundaries and thus foster a profound sense of empathy. Ritual purity, we find—at least in the rabbinic reading and at least in matters of ultimate concern (death)—encompasses an arena of affect, moral action, and shared concerns that brings Jews and Gentiles into a shared semantic field, even if that would seem almost unimaginable for many today. After that, we will return to Chinese cases, again to show how boundary crossing is crucial to the very rituals that create those boundaries.

Our fields are so accustomed to think of ritual in terms of separation and in-group solidarity that we felt it salubrious to bring examples to the contrary. In both Jewish and Chinese cases, we are certainly not discussing anything like an unbounded, totally open ritual, in which all are invited to partake and join. Yet the very structuring of the rite (or sometimes the text) allows for the crossing of boundaries, for the move from center to periphery, from the edge to the core, Gentile to Jew, barbarians to Han Chinese. All of this occurs in a traverse of ambiguous fields where order meets that which can never be ordered.

Interlude: Crossing the Boundary of Empathy

AS OUR PRIOR chapter noted, generations of anthropological and social scientific thought have taught us to view ritual as boundary construction and so as crucial to the establishment of group identities and solidarities. This is often the more commonsense view of ritual as well. When offered from a secular perspective, this popular view understands almost all ritual as religious and disdains it. When religious, such views tend to feel comfortable within their own ritual boundaries but tend to look at the rituals of others with a much more jaundiced eye. One would only need to recall Slobodan Milosivec's exhumation and pilgrimage around southern Serbia of King Lazar's remains as prelude to the wars of 1992–1995 to substantiate such a view.[1] The outpouring of anti-Semitic sentiment in medieval Europe around the time of Christian Easter or the use of Purim (Jewish carnival) by right-wing Israeli settlers in the West Bank to perpetrate anti-Palestinian outrages shows just how widespread such orientations are across religious civilizations. They thus seem to justify these negative attitudes toward ritual.[2]

If ritual were no more than boundary construction, however, empathy could function only among non-ritualized peoples and civilizations, and we would be forced to understand empathy and fellow-feeling as only possible outside a ritual order. By this logic, the modern era, with its strong devaluation of ritual, should be the most comfortable with empathy. Yet such a position is clearly absurd. The antiquity of the concept of empathy across many civilizations, the empirical evidence for its presence across cultures and times, not to mention the horrific and tragic failures of empathy in the modern world, make clear the foolishness of such an understanding of ritual as somehow essentially antithetical to empathy.

We have attempted to argue the opposite, that ritual orientations present a unique resource for the development of empathy and an openness to the other, to what is ambiguous and not known. Our argument revolved around the claim that since the formalized repetitive acts of ritual create the boundaries of an entity (or category) they also delineate what is not of that category: defining the tick, they bring the tock into focus as well. Rituals also continually oscillate between both, not just defining boundaries but crossing them.

Empathy, we have been claiming, resides in this oscillation between self and other, known and unknown, the notated and the ambiguous. Below we discuss two cases of such movement. In the first, we return to the theme of the Red Heifer, broached in the second interlude, and explore the prominent role played by Gentiles in four Aggadic (i.e., non-legalistic, more philosophical Rabbinic writings) stories devoted to the Red Heifer, the Parah Adumah. We then turn again to the Chinese case and explore the ways in which the powers of center and periphery, which we also discussed in the previous interlude, intertwine with each other by allowing people to cross back and forth over the boundaries between them. Some of this crossing is physical, as in pilgrimage, but much involves the experience of such things as eating a meal or getting married. We end this case with a brief discussion of Chinese alternatives, mostly from the twentieth century, that instead universalize categories. They thus make boundary-crossing irrelevant and, we argue, empathy more difficult.

Gentiles and the Red Heifer

The first story that we present is from Tractate Kiddushin of the Babylonian Talmud:

> When R. Ulla was asked, "How far should honoring one's father and mother extend?" he replied, "Go and see what a certain heathen named Dama ben Netinah did for his father in Ashkelon. Once, the sages sought some merchandise from him involving a profit to him of sixty myriads [of gold dinars]. But the key to where the merchandise was kept was under his [sleeping] father's pillow, and he would not disturb him."
>
> [In the style of many of these tractates, the story then begins again:] R. Judah said in the name of Samuel: When R. Eliezer was asked, "How far should honoring one's father and mother extend?" he replied, "Go and see what a certain heathen named Dama ben Netinah did for his father in Ashkelon. Once the sages sought some

precious stones from him for the *ephod* at a profit to him of sixty myriads [of gold dinars]. But the key to where the stones were kept was under his [sleeping] father's pillow, and he would not disturb him."

The following year, however, the Holy One gave him his reward. A red heifer was born to him in his herd. When the sages of Israel visited him [intending to buy it], he said to them, "I know about you. Even if I were to ask all the money in the world, you would pay me. But all I ask of you is the amount I lost because I honored my father."

R. Hanina said: "If one who is not commanded [to honor his parents] and nevertheless does is rewarded thus, how much more by far one who is commanded and does so?"[3]

The second story is from the Sifre Zuta, a commentary on the book of *Numbers*:

The elders of Jerusalem were informed of a gentile who had a red heifer and they went to him. He requested one thousand gold [coins]. He said [to himself] tomorrow the Jews will say, a heifer that has never seen a yoke. He then put a yoke on her. The Jews paid the price and requested to see the heifer. He took the heifer out and showed it to them whereupon they said to him, "She is useless to us [as she had been yoked]; return to us our money." Because they took from him his money, he went to the top of the roof, fell and died.[4]

The third story is from the Pisikta d'Rav Kahana:

It happened that Israel had need of a Red Heifer and could not find one; at long last they found one at a heathen's. They went to him and said, "Sell us the heifer you have." He replied, "Give me my price for her and take her." "And what is your price for her?" "Four gold coins at the most." They replied; "We shall pay it." While they went to fetch the money, the heathen guessed for what purpose they needed the heifer. And so when they came back and brought the money, he said to them, "I will not sell her to you." They asked. "Perhaps you wish to increase the price? If so, we will pay you all you require."

When the scoundrel realized that they were pressing for the heifer he kept raising the price. Whey they said, "Take five gold coins," he did not want to. "Take ten, take twenty, take thirty, fifty, a hundred," he still refused to sell, until they reached a thousand. He consented to sell them the heifer for a thousand gold coins. Having finally come to an agreement, they once again went to fetch the gold coins for him.

What did the wicked man do then? He said to another heathen, a boon companion of his, "come and see how I fool these Jews. The only reason they are trying to get the heifer from me and are willing to pay me all that money is because a yoke has never been put on her neck, I will take the yoke, put it on her neck, and have some fun at their expense, and get their money just the same." Here is what he did: he took the yoke and put it on the heifer for the entire night. Now, this is the sign that shows that a heifer has never borne a yoke: on her neck, in the place where the yoke is set, are two particular hairs which stand upright as long as she had never borne a yoke. But as soon as a yoke is set upon her neck, the two hairs are at once bent down. And there is still another sign of her never having borne a yoke. As long as no yoke has been on her, both eyes look straight ahead. After a yoke has been upon her, her eyes have an anxious look as she turns her head and rolls her eyes, straining to see the yoke.

When they came back with all the gold in their hands, to take the heifer from the heathen, he went in and, first removing the yoke from the heifer, led her out to them. As soon as he led her out, they proceeded to examine her and saw that the two particular hairs that should have been straight were bent down and that her eyes were rolling back because the yoke has been on her.

They said to him. "Take your heifer. We cannot use her now. We will not accept her even if you give her to us for nothing."

When the wicked man saw that they were returning his heifer to him and that he had come out with hands empty of all those gold coins, the very mouth that had said, "I will have my fun at their expense," proceeded to say, "Blessed be He who has chosen this nation." Then he went into his house, strung up a rope and hanged himself.[5]

The fourth story is as follows:

A heathen said to Rabban Yohanan ben Zakaai: "The things you Jews do appear to be a kind of sorcery. A heifer is brought, is burned up and is pounded [into ashes] and its ashes are gathered up. Then, when one of you gets defiled by contact with a corpse, two or three drops of water mixed with these ashes are sprinkled upon him, and he is told, 'You are now cleansed!'"

Rabban Yohanan asked the heathen, "Has the spirit of madness ever possessed you?" He replied, "No." "Have you ever seen anyone possessed by the spirit of madness?" The heathen replied, "Yes." "And have you seen what you people do to the man?" "Roots are brought, they are made to smoke under him, and water is splashed on him, until the spirit flees."

Rabban Yohanan then said, "Do not your ears hear what your mouth is saying? A man defiled is like a man possessed by a spirit. This spirit is a spirit of uncleanness. When water of lustration is splashed on it, it flees."

After the heathen left, Rabban Yohanan's disciples said, "Our master, you thrust off the heathen with a mere reed of an answer, but what reply will you give us?"

Rabban Yohanan answered, "As you live, the corpse does not defile, nor does the [mixture of ashes and] water cleanse. The truth is that the rite of the Red Heifer is a decree of the King who is King of kings. The Holy One said: I have set down a statute, I have issued a decree. You are not permitted to transgress my decree. 'This is a statute of the Torah.'" (Num. 19:2).[6]

Whatever else, these four stories certainly seem to mirror the structural ambivalences of the Red Heifer sacrifice analyzed in our prior interlude (generating both purity and impurity, sacrificial in nature but not within the Temple precincts, etc.). Certain texts register this ambivalence even more explicitly.[7] In a debate between R. Eliezer ben Yaakov and R. Meir over the inclusion of Gentiles as beneficiaries of the rite of the Red Heifer, R. Meir advocated their inclusion in the community of people to be purified by the ashes of the Red Heifer. On the other hand, R. Eliezer ben Yaakov argued that their inclusion could occur only after they had converted to Judaism to become part of the covenanted peoples. R. Meir's view preserves one meaning of the Biblical text (Numbers 19:10) which says: "And the one who gathers the ashes of the cow shall rinse his garments and shall remain unclean until the evening. And this shall be—for the sons of Yisrael and for the stranger who has entered their midst—as an everlasting statute." While R. Meir's view is not the legally accepted one, the debate itself points us to the core issues that structure the rite of the Red Heifer in general, and the place of the Gentiles in the above stories in particular. The issue pivots on whether Gentiles are within or outside the primary system of social ordering. R. Meir clearly includes them: they live among the Israelites, even if they are not "of" them, and are thus to be included in this rite of purification. His argument understands them as enough part of the community—even as they maintain their status as strangers—to benefit from this rite that purifies from death. Death, after all, is the fate of all human beings, not solely of the covenanted community. Death is the negation of social order, not solely Israelite order. It is the challenge of meaninglessness posited against all systems of human ordering, not solely that revealed to Moses on Horeb.

R. Meir's position, while maintaining the distinctions between Israelite and stranger, nevertheless includes the stranger's humanity in that ritual whose goal is to reassert the human/divine nexus in face of the abyss that death opens up. For him, in other words, the ritual creates the grounds for empathy. Not so for R. Eliezer ben Yaakov. His boundaries are much clearer and hermetically closed—no common humanity in the face of death, no recognition of the need to purify the stranger from contact with that which eviscerates all meaning. Only when the stranger has converted, only when the stranger has become one with the covenanted community does he become eligible for the ritual of purification. The stranger, regardless of the fact that he is living among the Israelites, remains totally outside and beyond the system of shared meanings that define community. Beyond the system and its limits, there is no need to include him in its rites of purification. Other is other, beyond is beyond, outside is outside. System limits are clear, not fuzzy, and not given to ambivalent categories (a stranger who remains a stranger yet benefits from rites of purification). Order is to be maintained by keeping the boundaries clear and rigid. The rite of the Red Heifer is ultimately all about keeping order in the face of that event which is the most threatening of all—death.

The different Rabbinic positions thus contrast significantly in their understanding of the nature of the system of meanings and of its boundaries. The disagreement reflects very different attitudes toward the stranger as either included within these meanings or excluded. The precise meaning of ger ("stranger") is not stable within the Rabbinic tradition. R. Meir's position (that the stranger is a resident alien) is one meaning; the other, less empathetic, is that the ger is a convert to Judaism (and hence, of course, no longer a stranger at all).

In different ways, the Aggadic stories quoted above are ambivalent about this issue of the boundaries of the system of meanings, and of who resides on these boundaries. Note that in these stories a Gentile, a heathen, supplies the Israelites with the Red Heifer. The common theme in the first three stories is the role of the Gentiles as suppliers of the Red Heifer to the Israelite community. Now while this may represent nothing more than supply and demand curves in the bovine market of late antiquity, it seems more likely that something more significant is afoot. After all it is quite some time since we have taken the Aggadic literature in the Talmud to have unqualified ethnographic value.[8] By representing the Gentiles as suppliers of the Red Heifer, these stories incorporate the Gentiles to some extent within the Israelite system of meanings and of ordering. Even if the Gentiles do not profit from the purificatory aspects of the ritual, they have a critical role in making it possible in the first place. One can certainly argue that by not being eligible to partake in the ritual, they are excluded. But there are different forms of exclusion, and it is clear that they are not excluded as irrelevant, as beyond all borders, as totally Other. Rather, their very narrative inclusion—and recall, all Rabbinic narrative was composed after the destruction of the Temple, when the ritual was no longer practiced—as the suppliers of the Red Heifer places them somewhere on the boundaries of the collective experience. They may not be properly included (as with R. Meir), but they are not wholly excluded either. By acting as suppliers of the Red Heifer, they clearly play a role on the boundaries, neither fully included nor fully excluded. In fact, the stories recognize Gentiles as necessary for the existence of community. In some sense, this state mirrors the deep structural ambivalence that characterizes the rite as a whole.

This should not be surprising. Mediating between life and death, and so between order and chaos, between meaning and its failure, the ritual itself is not open to human understanding, as Rabban Yohanan reminded us in the story above. Recall from our earlier interlude that the Red Heifer does not easily adhere to any of the other ritual categories (it both is and is not a sacrifice, it is not in the Temple but does refer to it, it both purifies and generates impurity, it does not invoke intentional action as most sacrifices do, etc.). This more general structural ambivalence is consistent with the role of the ritual—mediating between order and nothingness, it necessarily partakes of both. Still, the attributes of nothingness that adhere to it must somehow be well circumscribed and guarded against. That is why, we suggest, those who prepare the ashes generate impurity. On the level of cosmic or ontological reality, the many legal (Halachic) formulations that preserved the purity of the Red Heifer also help emphasize order over the abyss: never yoked, never subjected to any human action (even so much as resting one's arm on her shoulder), prepared by those never in contact with the dead (such as children raised in special enclaves), totally red with no white hairs, and so on, and so on.

While the Halacha struggles with the structural ambivalences of the Red Heifer in terms of cosmic ordering and its limits (in death), the four Aggadic stories quoted above struggle with a parallel ambivalence related to the social system and its limits. This ambivalence no longer resides in what is beyond all meaning, but in what is beyond the social or communal system, whether Gentile, heathen, or stranger.

We begin with the clear implication of the first three stories, that the Jewish ritual obligations cannot be fulfilled without Gentiles. However outside the Gentile may be, he is thus fully implicated in both the material life (markets and exchange) of the Jew, and in his spiritual or religious life as well. While an insular orthodoxy today may reject such a proposition, the textual material itself points to a much greater ease of intercommunal contact, living on the boundaries of one another's community rather than totally separate and apart. After all, the first three stories (and clearly stories 2 and 3 are versions of the same, though with small differences) only achieve their rhetorical impact by describing the Gentile as a provider of ritual necessities. Gentiles provide that supremely important component of the most critical of all rituals of purification, one that is so unique as to be beyond cognition, beyond all understanding and notation. In this sense, these Aggadic stories represent life itself— we cannot exist without the other. We need the one who is not us, who exists on our boundary, neither us nor totally other, and nonetheless fully implicated in our material and social existence. Of course, if we fully admitted the other into our own system of meanings and ordering (as in R. Eliezer's position), then he or she would be admitted as well into our system of social justice, equity, and rules for the sharing of resources, distribution of goods, and so on. Our own codes of notation would fully encompass them. They would no longer be totally other. Yet, in these stories, the totally other is also fully notated—as an other, that is, as one outside our system of meanings and notations. The status and understanding of the "stranger within our gates" advocated by R. Meir thus speaks significantly to an expansive understanding of precisely that boundary between us and them.

The presence of Gentiles in the stories of the Red Heifer is more than simply a Rabbinic trope. Rather, they represent a structurally necessary component of the whole development of the Red Heifer theology—of maintaining order in a world of fuzzy boundaries (between meaning and nothingness, life and death, between the community of the covenanted and the stranger). The Rabbinical dispute over the definition of "red" as realist (no white hairs at all) or as nominal (where a certain number of white hairs could actually be plucked out, as advocated by R. Akiva) addresses this issue. R. Akiva's position recognizes that the nature of our categories must be congruent with the nature of the world. This is a world that includes Gentiles as purveyors of the Red Heifer (and by implication other needs as well). It is not a realist utopia of a world with all truly Red Heifers without a single white hair, and all Jews without a single Gentile.

In the first three stories, the Gentile figures step outside the system of expected action and transcend the expected categories of order. In the first story, the Gentile's act is positive and virtuous, doing more than is expected of him, not only the first time (in not waking his father), but the second time as well (in not requesting an exorbitant price for the Red Heifer, which was his reward). In the second and third stories, the Gentile's act is evil, unnecessary and for no expected reward (he had already agreed on a price with the potential Jewish buyers). In these stories, the Gentile's actions transcend the categories of rational, market-oriented action (which would, presumably, not threaten expected profit through an act of egregious maliciousness). The Gentiles in these stories are either supererogatory when virtuous (which the Jewish tradition calls *l'fnim mishurat hadin*, literally, "beyond the letter of the law"), or simply motivated by evil intention (*l'hachis*) when negative. In all cases, they act beyond the given constraints of the social system—that is, the system of our notational categories—and so illustrate and define what exists at its borders (both the good and the evil). Not insignificantly and in line with what we have presented above, the acts of Gentiles illustrate these boundaries, precisely through their existence on the boundaries of the covenanted community.

In the first story, the Gentile's actions point beyond the boundary, defined through positive virtues. His virtue is so great that he does not even benefit fully from his reward (in the price he could have asked for the Red Heifer). It can be said that he accepts the universality of our interconnected worldly existence. He would be a model member of the Noachite community of peoples (who share normative principles of something akin to natural law). He shares in the same problem of death (that problem of

theodicy for all believers in a transcendent law) and of the meaninglessness that death creates. Standing in the same existential position as the
Israelite, his actions point to the way of righteousness and to the overcoming of the absurdity of death in the fulfillment of moral dictates that
transcend the law.

The second and third stories present a very different scenario. Here,
too, the boundary figures, the Gentiles, point beyond the law through their
actions—even the relatively simple law of honest market exchanges and
rational, interest-based calculations. They point, however, to vice rather
than virtue, to evil and to the workings of the evil inclination. On the
boundaries of the system, the Gentile does not move to include himself
within it (as did the first). Rather, he quite purposefully excludes himself
through his spiteful actions, oriented to no rational result but only to evil
for evil's sake. The Gentile in these stories places himself firmly outside
the moral and legal systems. He cannot play the role of the Gentile posited
by R. Meir. He no longer is on the boundaries of the community, and his
individual actions did not bring him closer to a shared system of orderings, meanings, and visions of justice. Rather, they take him further away,
beyond all possibility of inclusion—certainly beyond the realm of life-
affirming purification that is the very purpose of the ritual. It is significant
in these stories that death appears (in marked contrast to the sleep of the
first story). In both stories, death is perhaps the only possible result of
such evil actions—reaffirming theodicy, but in very different terms. Only
death can meet these Gentiles' attempts to destroy that purity which itself
negates the annihilation of death.

In these stories, the use of the Gentile allows the Rabbinic tradition to
explore what the system of ritual rules, regulations and notations cannot
fully express. Supererogation means, after all, going beyond the necessary
categories of order. As such, it poses serious difficulties for a rule-ordered
moral or ethical system such as Judaism.[9] In the two stories of evildoers, the
desire to make a homiletic point may have necessitated the use of the Gentile for something that would have been too painful to express if the character had been an Israelite. Rhetorically killing off an Israelite in the two
stories that ended with the death of the evildoer may have been simply
too harsh. Had it been presented as the act of a Jew, both the punishment
(of death) and the very act of separation (in the protagonist's desire to scorn
the potential purchasers of the Red Heifer, to humiliate them without
their knowing) would have been too threatening to the categories of order
and identity. The Rabbinic tradition shows a marked trend to mitigate the

presentation of sinful acts on the part of Jews, to present them as acts of unpremeditated lust (*mumar l'teavon*) rather than reasoned and carefully thought out acts of religious non-compliance (*mezid*). The use of the Gentile thus allowed the redactor of the stories to make the necessary theological point without portraying Jews in too unfavorable a light. Here, too, the argument loops back to the necessity to live and interact with others, with those beyond one's own boundaries—sometimes in order to express the very essence of what the boundaries themselves define.

The final story is much more complicated and deals with much more difficult and complex issues, but it has a similar dynamic. The ambivalences and tensions here point to the core of our understanding of religious praxis. It presents two views. The first compares Jewish purification to the Roman's magic, as efficacious action geared to the material (or natural) world. Religious action appears here as a tool, an implement, in this case one made to serve medicinal needs (madness): Prozac for the ancient soul. The story, needless to say, rejects and makes light of it as something that one told Gentiles (who presumably could not appreciate the subtleties of the Rabbinic mind), but with no real commitment to its veracity.

The second reason that Rabbi Yohanan gives to his students touches the very essence of a traditional Jewish religious life. It affirms the transcendent authority of the Almighty, whose ways cannot be known to mankind, and whose decrees must nevertheless be abided by. There is no play of reason, no possibility to ascertain a rationale for the commandments. The commandment resists the give and take of the world and its myriad modes of exchange, understanding, negotiation, or even its conception of necessity. The commandment *is*, just as God *is*. Just as significantly, R. Yohanan argues that whatever you may have imagined as the natural etiology of impurity and purity is pretty much nonsense. Corpses do not defile, nor does the Red Heifer grant purity. Here the text moves a significant step beyond a simple reaffirmation of the sovereignty of God. Rather, it posits the realm of religious action and meanings in general as beyond rational order, not given in any sense by the demands of the empirical world. Magic in this sense is rational. It may be mistaken in its premises, its assumptions, and its implementation. Its efficacy may be open to doubt, but it assumes a reasoned set of interventions in the world. Transcendent religion, we are told here, is utterly different.

Corpses do not defile! This is perhaps the most significant statement in the whole narrative. After all, in the world of Rabbinic Judaism of the period, nothing else approached the degree of impurity caused by contact with the dead. Death is a perennial threat to all aspects of humanly con-structed order; it negates human existence itself. Yet, corpses do not defile! There is nothing inherent in the corpse, perhaps even in death itself, which defiles. We are not—we are told—dealing with natural phenomena, with things as they are, with the world as it presents itself to our senses and intelligence. We are, rather, dealing with the nominal world as consti-tuted by the Almighty, a world whose conventions do not grow out of ma-terial experience.

This aspect of impurity as a godly act opens a whole additional layer of meanings. In Judaism, things, objects in themselves, do not transfer im-purity. (Recall that even the dead themselves are not impure, though people who come in contact with them are.) Objects can only transfer im-purity after they have been fashioned by human hands, will, intention, and labor, after the material has actually become implicated in the human world. Of course, there are myriad debates in the Talmud over defining the moment in the construction of an artifact that impurity begins to adhere to it. This is true of clay utensils, wrought iron, already harvested crops (as opposed to those still in the ground), and so on. Impurity is thus dual: it is an aspect of an object (as, at some point, things do transfer im-purity) and also a relationship, a status. These two aspects of impurity, moreover, stand in constant tension.

This realization allows us to consider the answer to the Roman in a more subtle light than our first reading. As is often the case, it is signifi-cant that the Rabbinic text still preserves and presents the answer to the Gentile. R. Yohanan's assertion that corpses do not defile and the Red Heifer does not purify would not have its tremendous force without its contrast to the commonly accepted view that corpses do in fact defile and the Red Heifer does indeed render pure. (After all, to this day, Jewish people wash their hands upon leaving a cemetery.) R. Yohanan implicitly argued that less-than-critical Jewish ritual practice is thus not that far from Roman magic.

In this story, too, the Gentile plays a critical role, here embodying one pole of the Rabbinic tension between realist and transcendent understandings of religious action. The Gentile understands religious ac-tion uncritically (as the Roman understands his magic) in terms of an empirical efficacy (natural or supernatural). This common understanding then allows the leap to the much more radical transcendence of R. Yohanan, which subsumes such understanding in the principle of a transcendent a priori.

Monotheistic religion has left its most significant mark through this position of radical transcendence, relativizing and trivializing the words, orders, and notations of the world in light of something beyond all human ordering. This position was reiterated close to a millennium later, in another work that also rests on the interaction between Jews and Gentiles— R. Jehuda Halevi's *al-Khazari*—which argued that: "the approach to God is only possible through the medium of God's command, and there is no road to knowledge of the commands of God except by way of prophesy, but not by means of speculation and reasoning."[10] Radical transcendence, beyond reason and reasoning becomes accessible only through the "opening" of prophesy.

With this fourth story, the structural ambivalences of the theodic vision, the problems of supererogation and of evil intent that we dealt with in the first stories begin to pale in significance. Before, we analyzed the role of the Gentile in Aggadic stories that sought to express what could not be totally expressed within a system of order, but here we find ourselves in a much more difficult position. In essence, R. Yohanan declares that the very system of religious meanings cannot express itself in its own terms. Or perhaps, phrased differently, nothing that can be expressed is fully true. The terms of truth lie forever beyond us. The system's terms (here of religious ritual— corpses defile, a Red Heifer purifies) are only human, and thus incomplete, fragile, limited. The Rabbinic system privileges such terms. Rabbis may have the last word, but they do not have the only word. Even more importantly in its very incomplete, fragile, and limited nature, the Rabbinic system recalls the Roman's own understanding. The Roman's conception of the cure for madness still captures a truth of our shared, embodied humanity—and so also of both the necessity and limits of notation.

In a subtle twist, the Gentile can stand in for the human position *tout court*. He is the negation of the Israelite, but he is just as human as the Israelite. His humanity shows in his acts of goodness and in his acts of evil intent. He is human in his inherently limited understanding of what we do when we "do" religion. The voice of the other is nothing in these stories but the unexpressed, repressed voice of the self. When poised over the abyss, the other reminds us of our deepest truths and innermost selves.

The worlds of the original biblical text and those of the post-Temple Rabbinic exegesis come together in concern over the shared human condition. We have pointed in our previous interlude to the importance of *hazayah*—"sprinkling" as a dedicatory act—in anticipation of Death's threat to the order that humans impose on the world. In an analogous manner, the later Rabbinic focus on the role of Gentiles with respect to the Red Heifer may be understood as a kind of dedicatory sprinkling that co-opts and tames the threat of its own day—the destructive power of Roman armies—and domesticates them into the system. Rabbinic culture of this period shifted its weapons—from spears to words. Rabbinic sacred space is textual, not geographic. To create *their* version of the ashes of the Red Heifer, they must go "outside the camp"—into the world of Gentiles, offering their words as a dedicatory act. They celebrate a common humanity, the sanctity of embodiment, of filial love and respect. By giving honor and offering the dedicatory words offered, the rabbis tamed chaos and brought it back into the Rabbinic geography—the textual sacred space of Rabbinic meaning.[11]

All this takes place in the subjunctive *as if* space provided by both ritual and the ritualized exegesis of God's word.[12] These stories and their Rabbinic interpretations provide one kind of grounding for empathy, for an ability to deal with others with mutual respect while not denying that they are fundamentally different. We turn now back to several cases from China, which also show how both ritual and daily life require rhythmic crossing between known and unknown, center and margin, self and other. This view, like the Rabbinic commentaries on the Red Heifer, contrasts with alternatives that make boundary crossing—and thus empathy—irrelevant or impossible.

Crossing Chinese Boundaries

Human history so far has granted us no guarantees of living in harmony, either with those like us or with the stranger perennially living inside our gates. Nevertheless, we are suggesting that ritual may have an important role in allowing us to live with difference without denying it. The Jewish, Confucian, and other ritual-oriented traditions recognize real boundaries, real differences among us, but they also help us learn to cross them. In doing so, they contribute to the public good in a way that is not often recognized.

The early Confucians in particular theorized the core idea that ritual was the key to creating harmony. Ritual allows humanity to cross over its differences—between ethnicities, classes, and even individuals (often through etiquette, which is the interpersonal side of ritual). For Xunzi in particular, *li* (typically translated as "ritual") was the discipline that allowed humans to create a society beyond raw power or self-interest.

Secular or sacred, *li* is what lets us deal with the other. Much later, the neo-Confucians of the Song dynasty encouraged a popularization of *li* by authoring manuals of how to perform ritual properly at home.

According to the *Analects*, Confucius himself argued that "among the functions of *li* the most valuable is that it establishes harmony" (1:12).[13] He clarified a bit later when he said that the "superior man harmonizes without being the same, the inferior man is the same without harmonizing" (13:23). This is often taken to mean the obvious fact that an advisor who agrees all the time is not very useful. At a deeper level, though, the idea gets at a core role of ritual—not to reduce people to identical units, but to allow them to live together with genuine difference. The commentaries of the *Zuozhuan* expound at greater length on this, using the metaphors of food and music, both of which require the careful combination of difference to please us, and both of which collapse into banality without it.

This early emphasis on ritual explains why the Board of *Li*, one of the main national ministries in later dynasties, was responsible for a set of practices that seem unrelated to modern eyes. These included overseeing obvious rituals, like the annual cycle of ceremonies, led by the emperor, at altars around every administrative city. Yet they also included responsibility for the reception of tribute from foreign lands, because this, too, was a way of dealing with difference. They supervised the civil service examinations as well, because these determined candidates' understanding of *li* as the human relationships that negotiate across our internal social differences of parents and children, rulers and subjects, or friends. Ritual, in this view, allows us to live together, even in an imperfect world riven through with significant differences of identity and interest.

Here we want to return to a few specific examples of how this worked in practice in Chinese societies, all based around the differences between center and periphery, between self and other, which we outlined in the previous interlude. There we discussed two Chinese images of power that coexisted, one descending from a center like the emperor and spatially idealized in the lineage land of fertile valleys, and one coming from beyond the margins of those valleys, imagined in mountain peaks and "uncivilized" peoples. Together these forms of power represented a fundamental imaginary of difference in China, often discussed in Confucian terms as "civilization" and "barbarism." In both these forms, however, the boundaries are open to play and manipulation, rather than annotating a clear and precise line like a political boundary or a defensive moat. People in

China regularly crossed the gap between center and periphery in both physical and mental space.

We will begin with pilgrimage, which was an obvious way to cross between the different powers of edge and center, at least temporarily. Late imperial China, like modern China, allowed for a great deal of religious mobility. Supporters of a local temple might visit a mother temple elsewhere or an allied temple in another town. People would make longer journeys to visit temples with a particular reputation for efficacy. While important temples that attracted pilgrims existed in a wide variety of geographies, from distant peripheries to major cities, the most famous and important pilgrimages were to the temples of China's "sacred mountains." Almost all of these sites were in areas that were difficult to reach: China's internal borderlands that fell between the major political and economic units. Even for those mountains that were not so far off, climbing up the mountain itself offered a taste of the physical hardship and geographic/ecological change that characterized the more distant pilgrimages.

Part of the appeal was the altered environment—the palpable experience of difference—which elite pilgrims tended to comment on as much as they did the temples themselves.[14] They admired the rugged peaks and wondered at the strange lights and fogs that illuminated the sky. Their descriptions help us remember that the empowered edge was a general experience of otherness, not strictly a religious one. The temples were important, but so was the companionship of friends in a strange place, the alien aura of an unfamiliar physical and social environment, and the idea of retracing the steps and experiences of important people who had already visited and written about these places. Seen in this light, religious pilgrims are not really very different from more modern boundary-crossings toward the empowered edge, like nature or ethnic tourism. In all cases, the experience reminded people that differences were real and that, at least temporarily, they could be bridged. And that realization, we are arguing, lies at the heart of a capacity for empathy.

While trips on such extended pilgrimages were rare for most people, they still had a clear rhythm of seasonality, where one could watch the neighbors going or watch strangers passing through each year. One could even argue that worshipping at a purely local temple was much the same kind of rhythmic crossing between kinds of power, even with no significant physical movement. This is because gods usually combined both sorts of power. They showed the power of the imperial center because of their titles (often bestowed by the worldly emperor), because their images and temples shared a great deal of iconographic significance with magistrates and their official compounds, and because people quite often made the direct comparison of gods to bureaucrats.[15] Yet most gods also included an unruly aspect, some form of power from well beyond imperial and bureaucratic proprieties. They included drunken and lascivious monks, children, fierce warriors, suicides, murderers, and a great many women.[16]

Thus, while no one uses the word "pilgrimage" to discuss it, a trip to the neighborhood temple brought people to the borders and ambiguities between both forms of power in a way not so very different from a long pilgrimage to a sacred mountain. One could even argue that just lighting a stick of incense for gods on a home altar did the same thing. Here the rhythms of boundary crossing are even clearer, occurring each day at home for some people, or on the first and fifteenth days of every lunar month. The orderly progression of ritual tick and tock ordered time just as powerfully as the agricultural cycle. These rhythms help to ritualize the process of crossing boundaries (between human world and spirit world, between valley agriculture and mountain wildness), creating a shared time that eases the crossing.

People also flowed from physical periphery to core, of course, more for economic and political reasons than for spiritual ones. Typical examples include beggars, sojourners, and the people who make up the current "floating" populations. While such people hope to capitalize on the economic power of the center, they also bring to the center a bit of the power of the edge, adding a hint of fear to the loathing that local people often feel toward them. All of this movement—from center to edge and from edge to center—is usually intended to be temporary. That is, it does nothing to negate the differences between the two forms of spatialized power, but simply allows people to intertwine the boundaries for a while, playing with the edge but not dissolving it.

In a very different way, a late imperial Chinese garden also accomplished a kind of pilgrimage in reverse, bringing the empowered edge to the center. Many gardens featured miniatures of the exotic landscapes of the periphery. Twisty paths might mimic in miniature trails through rugged rocky landscapes, allowing a garden stroll to conjure up thoughts of Daoist immortals wandering hidden paths in sacred mountains. Unusual objects that clearly showed the wild flow of hidden energies (*qi*) in unusual stones (*qishi*) or twisted trees helped reproduce the feelings of being at the edge of the world. It was not even necessary to leave the house to get a taste of the empowered edge through miniatures of such objects placed on a desk or shelf. One could thus stay home and still experience both sides of this fundamental difference between center and edge.[17] Empathy may not be directly involved here, since gardens are not humans, but the conclusion that the world is fundamentally plural, and that very great differences can have a place even within each of us, is an important step toward dealing with other people in an empathetic way.

The boundary between center and edge in China is not an absolute line, but it is absolutely necessary to both ways of imagining power. It is always there, yet it can also always be crossed. In a sense, the two kinds of power offered multiple identities, so that people could associate themselves with the power of the center (worshipping their ancestors, perhaps) and then with the edge (going off to enjoy their garden). This is parallel to the work of ritual. Ritual, at a minimum, draws a boundary between the world that ritual itself creates through its performative actions and the world outside the ritual context. At the same time, it allows us to cross back and forth over that boundary.[18] Most crucially, the inherent ability to cross boundaries without dissolving them forms part of the ability to empathize, to imagine oneself as if one were the other, while still recognizing the fundamental differences. In that sense, it may be vital for all human society.

Chinese authorities sometimes tried to cut off this possibility, at least in the immediate physical sense of trying to make it impossible to travel or trade between center and edge, between civilization and barbarism. The Great Wall was such an attempt, as were the many ditches that were constructed in late imperial times to try to cut off all connections between Han and indigenous groups.[19] The idea was to prevent the Han from taking economic advantage of the indigenous people, and to prevent indigenous violence against the Han. None of these barriers worked very well, however, at restricting either trade or violence. In the end, Chinese most of the time accepted the powers of both center and edge, with the boundaries between them, and with the dangers and opportunities of crossing back and forth.

We can see one example in the public processions and festivals that villages and neighborhoods across China have long organized. Neighboring communities often had tense relations with each other, where disputes over land, irrigation water, livestock damage, marriage disputes, and all the other tensions of daily existence could easily blow up into violence. Within a village, mechanisms through lineages or temples could often help resolve such disputes, but these possibilities weakened quickly outside the local community.

Processions of local gods often cross community lines, and thus have close ties to intercommunity relations. These traditions of processions continue or have been revived across many parts of China, Taiwan, and Hong Kong. Processions and other major temple rituals often require complex coordination and may attract tens or sometimes hundreds of thousands of worshippers. They are a strong indication of local society's capacity to organize itself without the direct involvement of the state.

Much of this religious mobilization of local social capital fits a standard Durkheimian view of ritual as a way of marking boundaries and increasing solidarity within the group. This is particularly clear when gods leave their temples in processions to tour their territories, carefully marking the edges of their turf. These events recall, and to some extent mimic, late imperial magistrates touring the extent of the areas they controlled. Just as a touring magistrate would bring an escort of civilian aides and military guards, gods bring their own retinues of heralds, secondary gods, and spirit soldiers. While the god is typically embodied in a wooden statue and carried in a sedan chair, the retinue consists of local young men (and occasionally women) dressed in appropriate costume and makeup. Infused with the power of the god, some performers may bloody themselves with ritual weapons (especially in Taiwan and the far south of China) and others perform intricate martial routines, complete with spears, swords, and shields.[20]

Boundary creation is clear here, yet processions and festivals also bring us directly to the boundary-crossing work of ritual. Visits between temples provide one way in which this occurs. Among the most elaborate of these are visits back to a temple of origin. This has been increasingly important in Taiwan as the possibility of a deity's return to a mother temple on the mainland has opened up. The small Taiwanese town of Lukang is home to an important temple, the Tianhou Gong, which is one of the oldest in honor of Mazu, the predominant goddess on the island. When one of us was doing research there in 2006, the goddess was just returning from a visit to the mother temple in Meizhou, Fujian. As part of the welcome, the temple organized a massive procession that included dozens of young men blowing long trumpets, 108 women dressed as the Buddhist arhats, countless people dressed as Qing dynasty yamen runners, and many other performers of all kinds. It was easy to see the enormous reserves of social capital that this temple could mobilize. Leading the procession were performing groups from other temples, along with their own gods in sedan chairs. That is, gods were greeting each other across temple boundaries, rather than Mazu simply reiterating her own boundaries. We should also recall that the visit to the mainland itself was a crucial boundary crossing, an unrecognized but vital part of how the tense relations between China and Taiwan are actually being negotiated on the ground.

On a smaller scale, something similar happened in front of the Lukang temple almost every day during the research, as gods from all over Taiwan would come to visit. The details varied widely from one group to the next, but the basic structure of the ritual was always the same. The visiting deity, sitting in his sedan chair, would stop before the entrance to the temple while his retinue exorcised the temple plaza and showed its respect (and the visiting deity's power). They accomplished this through the performance of traditional martial displays like a dragon dance or the popular form in Taiwan called the Eight Infernal Generals. Possessed mediums would also perform until their blood flowed. Finally, the visiting god would approach the temple in three rapid thrusts and retreats before finally entering, the equivalent of a kowtow. The visiting god's followers were close behind, and they would burn incense to honor the host goddess. Community boundaries are certainly marked here, but in a way that allows them to be crossed through godly versions of human etiquette.

There was, of course, always the danger that these forms of spiritual etiquette could break down—just like secular etiquette. Gods, like humans, can snub each other by refusing to visit each other or to act respectfully. Martial performance groups from different villages usually dealt with each other with ritual care if they happened to meet during their processions, but could occasionally come to blows. Ritual is no guarantee of peace or even of empathy, but it does at least offer a stage on which empathy between different or even opposed groups can occur.

We can see this in another form in the display of armed chickens in figure 3.2. The chickens march in a military formation called a *Songjiang Zhen*. Groups of male performers, marching along with gods, often reenact this same formation. In this case, the chickens are offerings laid out for the major summer ritual held to pacify the hungry ghosts, who have been temporarily released from the underworld. That is, rather than patrolling the borders of a god's territory like the humans, they both mark and cross the boundaries between the living and the dead. Their rhythmic array, marked by the pulse of each chicken repeating the next one without ever being identical, recalls the rhythms of the ritual itself.

FIGURE 3.2 Chicken Formation
Photograph by Robert P. Weller.

Conclusion

There were other ways of imagining power in China beyond the duality of central and peripheral power and the ritual crossings between them. Perhaps there are many additional ways of thinking about power, but let us add just one here: a de-spatialized and universal conception in which distinctions of center and edge are no longer relevant, and there are no significant boundaries: the world is homogeneous. For imperial China, this occurred especially in some Buddhist conceptions of the universe. While secular differences in political and economic power certainly existed in a Buddhist understanding of the world, all those distinctions were really just illusory. At a more fundamental level, the Buddha-nature existed in exactly the same way in all of us, locking us into the suffering of reincarnations but also offering each of us the possibility of an escape into nirvana. The Buddha's own wanderings, reiterated later by monks who wandered from one temple to another, fit with this view where specific spaces were relatively unimportant.

By the twentieth century, however, other universalisms began to outweigh Buddhism. These were the tropes of a globalizing modernity. Its
images had roots in the European Enlightenment, and had spread rapidly
from the nineteenth century as a set of claims about universal civilization
based on the notions of individual autonomy, equality, and rationality. All
of these values, as loudly proclaimed in pivotal documents like the American Declaration of Independence of 1776 or the French Declaration of the
Rights of Man and of the Citizen of 1789, saw people as essentially the
same over space and time.

There were still boundaries in this conception of the world, of course.
This period had, for example, brought a hardening of political boundaries
as the concept of a nation-state replaced earlier notions of the polity, including the Chinese one. The ideology of the nation-state provides a good
example of how universalism and boundary creation could go together. In
great contrast to the idea of an empire, every person within the boundaries
of the nation-state was fundamentally the same as all the others, with the
same rights. This peaked with the "one race, one language, one culture"
conception of the nation-state that became so important in the late nineteenth century, and whose consequences still echo in ethnic cleansings
around the world. Taken to this extreme, we see a universalism applied
only within the boundaries of the ethno-political unit; others are not fully
human, or at least not citizens, and so do not have the same rights. At the
same time, the boundaries become tighter, less permeable, more like
brick walls. Empathy beyond the border is lost, along with the rhythms of
boundary crossing.

The alternative—seen in Marx's vision of Communism, for instance—
was no boundaries at all. The entire globe became a single nation-state.
Modern money, in a sense, accomplishes the same thing. It recognizes no
boundaries and makes no discriminations. Rock-hard boundaries or no
boundaries (that is, boundaries drawn around the world as a whole) are
not really so different, however. Both deny any fundamental differences
among people of one's own group, and absolutize differences beyond
them (either over the border or between humans and other creatures). In
either case, the openness to boundary-crossing of a space-based conception of power like China's was lost.

To some extent, as many studies have documented, the unbounded
globalization of the last century has had a certain effect of flattening the
world and making all spaces the same.[21] Even something as apparently
trivial as the rise of the hamburger is only the surface evidence of a much

deeper change. A meal at McDonald's does not just substitute meat patties and French fries for rice and bamboo shoots; it changes the structure of the meal itself, where the contrast between the staple starch and side dishes—between center and periphery—is lost in favor of the fast-food version of the standard American meat and potatoes. More than this, the rise of the hamburger points to the new kinds of time discipline that change eating habits, to the rise of a youth and child culture that demands new kinds of public spaces, and even to imported notions of health and hygiene. In practice, however, these globalized and universal ideas have not utterly replaced what came before them in much of the world. Certainly they have not done so in Chinese societies, where most meals still center on a staple, and where consumption of powerful foods from the edge is probably higher than ever. This new conception of the world, however, challenges earlier notions of space and power by making all spaces appear alike.

We can see this just as clearly in the world of religion, where the twentieth century brought increased popularity for a wide range of universalizing religious ideologies, all very different from the strongly place-based nature of China's local temple religion. Christianity, especially Protestantism, is the most obvious example of a set of ideas meant to be equally true for all times, places, and peoples. While never as successful in China as in some other parts of the world, it has had a significant impact both through direct conversions (perhaps currently accounting for 5 percent of the population) and by leading other groups to emulate some of its techniques.

It is not merely coincidence that the Protestant movement, especially at its origins, also ushered in a powerful anti-ritualist sentiment, seen most clearly in the radical cleansing of Europe's churches that wiped out thousands of images of saints, reduced art and music to the service of pedagogy, and destroyed the altars themselves in favor of unadorned spaces. The resulting emphasis on purity and sincerity of notated belief rather than on ritual action had an enormous influence around the world. It shows up in China most clearly in the early twentieth century, when the Nationalist government adopted a Protestant-inspired definition of religion based on belief that includes neither local temple worship nor Confucianism itself. The Communists accepted much the same framework, and both regimes repressed expressions of local ritualism.

The importance of universal ideologies, and perhaps the indirect impact of Christianity, also helps to explain the extraordinary popularity of new forms of Buddhism, especially those growing out of late twentieth-century

Taiwan. Buddhism remade itself from an escape from the secular world to allow personal cultivation, and from a provider of ritual services to the people, into a powerful and successful way for people to live in a booming market economy. Many of the redemptive sects—syncretic groups with strong Buddhist connections—that have thrived especially since the early twentieth century also transcend all the earlier understandings of space based on center and edge. Both the Buddhists and the sectarian groups have pre-modern origins, of course, but their great success over the past century certainly relates to the new conceptions and realities of market and politics that were coming in from overseas.

All of these universalisms, in China and beyond, in spite of their differences from each other, treat boundaries quite unlike the powers of center and edge. They leave very little room for substantive differences among people. In the public sphere, at least, all citizens are identical, and any differences (from religious loyalty to sexual preference) are purely private matters. The problem in practice is that those differences have in reality often turned out to be both public and intractable, as we can see in the violence of parts of the Middle East, the Balkans, and Africa, but also more mildly in conflicts over gay Episcopalian bishops or head scarves for Muslim students in France.

The universalism that has globalized since the late nineteenth century is in some ways less constrained than the ones that preceded it in China, like Buddhism or the sectarian religious traditions. Backed up by the global economy and widely shared political understandings (like the nation-state as the basic unit of international organization), current universalisms have more power than anything comparable in late imperial China. Nevertheless, they have never fully succeeded, and people on the ground have met them with combinations of acceptance, resistance, replacement, reinvention of tradition, and creative bricolage. Whether we examine food, religion, or any of the other topics touched on here, the new ideas have added another possibility for people rather than causing the wholesale loss of what came before.

One crucial contrast between these universalizing ideas and a spatially rooted dynamic of center and edge, as we have argued, is in the conception of boundaries and how they can be traversed. Boundaries are inevitable in the center/edge understanding, but can be negotiated across in all the ways that we have discussed. The universal world instead imagines either no boundaries (all the world as Christendom or all as a free trade zone, for instance) or impassable boundaries (all the "world" of the nation-state as Serbs with no room for Croats, for instance).

Empathy requires a double move—a recognition that other people are fundamentally different from "us," but that they also share enough common humanity with us to allow recognition. We saw this in both the ritualization of potentially dangerous intercommunity relations in China through parades of gods, as in the Rabbinical reworking of understandings of the most important purification rites in Judaism. The rhythmic shaping of space and time through ritual is especially clear in the Chinese cases of pilgrimage and procession. For the Red Heifer, the rhythms occur not so much in the ritual itself (which has not actually been performed for millennia, if at all) but in the repetitive descriptions in the texts and in their study.

Mechanisms that allow us to communicate peacefully across boundaries include much that we have discussed here: rituals that cross boundaries between human and spirit, between counterposed communities, between Jews and Gentiles. This ability to live with and across boundaries is crucial for society—it is at the heart of the capacity for genuine pluralism and for human empathy. Modern universalisms have tended to leave the problem of boundaries unsolved, and sometimes even unrecognized, because everyone is seen as an autonomous individual rather than as a member of a community. The continuation and adaptation of older ways of understanding the universe may yet prove important as we still struggle to learn how to live with genuine difference.

4

Shared Experience

THE UNIVERSALIZING DISCOURSES that we brought up at the end of the previous interlude hark back to our earlier discussion of notation. Universals, by definition, abstract away from the particularities of time and place. They set up categories within which all people are the same, but where the boundaries between categories can be quite difficult to cross—the nation-state and its "folk" as opposed to the alien others, or the saved versus the damned. They deal with ambiguities by trying to minimize them. This attitude differs significantly from the ritualizing effort to construct alternate subjunctive worlds, dealing with ambiguity by making it possible to cross between worlds, to accept more than one version of reality.

Ritual, which puts brackets around particular contexts, thus contrasts with universalism, which dissolves the particularity of all contexts. Scholars of language have long made a similar kind of distinction, and following some of their arguments will help us distinguish a third way of dealing with ambiguity that differs from both notation and ritual. We can begin with Basil Bernstein's famous and controversial proposal that we distinguish between two major forms of language use, which he called an elaborated code and a restricted code.

An elaborated code, for Bernstein, is flexible in a way that makes it difficult to predict what syntactic alternatives a speaker will choose; such language is labile and variable. A restricted code, on the other hand, draws from a much narrower range of alternatives, and defines the choices much more rigidly. This is not a matter of having an impoverished vocabulary, but rather of the context determining much of what will be said in a restricted code.[1] For example, Bernstein pointed to the frequent use of words like "this" and "that" in restricted codes—words that cannot be understood apart from the immediate context.

The most controversial element of this proposal was the way in which Bernstein rooted the two forms in very different social matrices. Elaborated codes, he argued, work well in the kind of complex, open, and ever-changing environments and social systems of the modern city. Restricted codes instead tie to clearly demarcated systems of social roles. Bernstein thus saw a kind of *gemeinschaft* and *gesellschaft* of language. While he was careful not to pass a value judgment, his assertion that the British working class is held back in part by socialization into restricted codes has been very controversial, even as it has strongly influenced some educational policy to promote standard varieties of language for all children.

How then should modern, urban people deal with social and personal boundaries? Bernstein implies that they need to rely on linguistic codes that are detached from the immediate context, that deal with individuals rather than social categories, that offer abstracted and universalizing reasoning rather than rules bound by tradition. In answer to the child's demand to know why she has to come to dinner, the user of an elaborated code explains the importance of good nutrition, or cites the various studies that show that family dinners correlate with children who have fewer behavioral problems. The user of a restricted code can just say "Because I'm your mother and I said so." In a way, then, Bernstein's work suggests a social grounding for a language built for notation on the one hand, and a relatively ritualized and repetitive language on the other.

While restricted codes are somewhat ritualized, however, they are not rituals. Compared to a ritual like Jewish morning prayers or Chinese ancestor veneration, that is, they are not rhythmically repetitive, not purely formal, not entirely restricting of the individual's choices, and do not have predictable outcomes. William Labov, a sociolinguist who has been a important critic of Bernstein, argued that the more notational elaborated codes in fact conveyed little more substance than restricted codes, and that in actual use they are as much "turgid, redundant, and empty" as they are flexible and analytical.[2] By the same token, restricted codes in practice express a wide range of meanings and are quite flexible in context.

We do not need to follow through on the details of their argument, nor do we have the expertise. We bring it up, however, because it moves us toward a third way of thinking about how people can live with ambiguity. Sociolinguists like Labov have insisted that the particulars of addresser and addressee, and of setting and event, are crucial to understanding every linguistic statement.[3] While abstract notational codes make any utterance possible in theory, real speech always brackets out many of those possibilities to position communication within a particular context.

It is possible, for example, to learn to tie knots through an abstract language of bights and overhand knots. We can thus describe a bow as tying an overhand knot, followed by forming bights out of the two ends and tying a second overhand knot. In fact, however, nearly no one learns to tie a bow through such a language. Instead, we learn to tie our shoes by watching our parents and imitating their actions. The only knot that most of us learn through language is a bowline, in which we make a rabbit hole and use the end of the rope to have a bunny come out of the hole, run around a tree, and dive back into the hole. A story of rabbits hopping in and out of holes uses a completely different kind of language than that of bights and overhand knots. It is a highly restricted code that does not generalize at all beyond its immediate use. Sailors and other knot-tying virtuosos may require the language of abstraction, but for the needs of most of us, imitation and bunny stories are far more memorable and useful.

This kind of shared experience—of parents showing children how to tie their shoes or to make the bunny go around the tree—forms the main topic of this chapter. Like ritual and unlike notation, shared and contextual experience deals with ambiguity in part by bracketing it temporarily away and allowing the context to define a subjunctive world. Unlike ritual and like notation, however, this kind of interaction is open-ended and goal-oriented. We are not so interested in knots, of course, but in the sorts of interactions in which Muslim and Orthodox Christian Bosnians, or Han and Uyghur Chinese, can put aside their deep differences and painful memories, and instead just find a way to build a hospital or a school to-gether—in short, shared experience.

Context and Flexibility

Experience is always particular. It is rooted in a context, a unique configu-ration of actors, actions, interests, and forces (natural as well as human). The perennial question, however, is how much of that very concrete expe-rience we can abstract to serve as a basis or model for behavior and predic-tion in other experiences. Experience also carries with it its own ambiguities. We can never know the full extent of all of the actors, actions, interests and forces at work in any given situation, as we saw in our earlier discussion of Job. We do the best we can, in the hope that it will be good enough.

Notation and ritual are, as we have seen, two historically significant ways of dealing with the ambiguities of life. Notation, in its most abstract form, attempts to impose a preconceived grid on experience—an interpretive template drawn from some ideal set of all previously similar experiences that will provide an ideal context and interpretive vision for it. This is sometimes enormously helpful. For example, if we can identify the tool in front of us as a screwdriver regardless of its size, color, or the handle's material, then we can also identify the relevant purposes of the tool (tightening screws). In other cases, however, such notation can be tragically fallacious—for instance, if we take the uncivil behavior of our neighbor to be just another example of what we already "know" about all Jews, or Muslims, or Blacks, or whichever group we may have prejudiced feelings toward. The shortcut to knowledge provided by our invocation of predetermined categories (notations) can be, depending on the relevant realm, a great boon or a blinding prejudice.

Notation tends to work better with inanimate objects than with individuals or groups of individuals, invested with "free will." Free will imbues every human situation, encounter, meeting, and dialogue with an ontological openness that no category can ever fully circumscribe—however subtle or sophisticated. Of course, we use notation just as often in our dealings with humans as in our dealings with screwdrivers; it just does not work as well. Notate though we will, we still fall in love, we get into fights, we (hopefully) change our opinions, we learn, we forget. Every day we tickle and get tickled, splash in the mud, break into an imitation of a famous singer or actor, and in short constantly show the impossibility of notation as sole indicator and guide to human behavior and interaction.

Ritual serves as an additional and critical tool that lets us be together despite the openness of all our encounters (and hence the limits of any externally imposed category of interpretation). Ritual's formalism and its repetitions provide a vehicle for human sociability while not denying the ambiguity that is part and parcel of sociability itself. Ritual factors in ambiguity, as we pointed out above, in the example of the tock that is inherent in every tick. If it were truly biologically or neurologically impossible to step outside roles and social expectations, there would be no need for civility, courtesy, or the rules of etiquette. The rules apply precisely because such possibilities are always with us—sometimes threatening, sometimes beckoning, sometimes both at once.

Ritual's rhythms provide predictability and so create an arena where people can interact and share a world. They create what we have termed a "shared subjunctive"—as when entering a theater or concert, or for that matter a tennis court or baseball stadium or court of law. Bracketing out myriad aspects of reality, defining them as extraneous to the actions of ritual, allows us to construct a shared experience, despite the inherent limitations of notation per se and its ultimate insufficiency in providing the basis for world construction.

Like notation, however, ritual too can break down (as discussed in chapter 3). Much of the world is today, for better or worse, much less ritualized than it once was. We have already discussed how notation has increasingly taken the place of ritual as the primary enabler of human interaction in many societies—though we tend to be skeptical as to just how efficient this may in fact be. The inherent limits of notation and the rather de-ritualized nature of much social life today suggest that it may be especially fruitful to return to the particularities of experience and its contexts. Hence we will attempt to sound out shared experience, to take its pulse free of any imposed ritual meter or externally defined criteria of meaning through notation. We hope in this way to show its resources for dealing with the ambiguity that adheres to all experience.

As a beginning, let us return to Basil Bernstein's critical idea of elaborated and restricted codes of speech—as modes of directing behavior, organizing experience, and controlling impulse. He sees them, in brief, as ways of organizing the various forms of ambiguity that accompany experience. Rather than starting from his rooting of the two codes in different social structures, however, we will carry the idea in a different direction. The most famous reworking of Bernstein's categories was Mary Douglas's identification of two dimensions of variation: *grid* (to represent the degree of elaboration of categories, loosely based on Bernstein's elaborated and restricted codes) and *group* (the degree of social pressure toward conformity, revised from Bernstein's variation between positional and personal forms of family control). These two continua led Douglas to an all-encompassing ordering of virtues, sins, ideas of self, and forms of art.[4] We also propose two dimensions of variation. Like Mary Douglas, we move away from Bernstein's reduction of linguistic variation to class-based social structure, but we also vary from her version.

For our purposes, the most revealing difference between elaborated and restricted codes is between content-free and content-rich grids of understanding—between more and less abstract systems of thought and organization. Bureaucratic organizations and the language through which they are explained, enacted, maintained, and sanctioned are examples of the former, while the lived structuring of kinship as it varies across the world shows the latter form (no matter how much anthropologists may analyze kin groups by abstracting from context). The same difference holds with, for example, with the organization of a Starbucks franchise as a case of the former, and a drug deal of the latter.

We find it useful to bisect this continuum with another dimension—not exactly forms of social control (as in Mary Douglas's idea of group), but the attendant value of flexibility and inflexibility. That is, we distinguish whether our systems of ordering, or even the way in which we respond to information, are more flexible, or if they tend to be rigid and imprisoned within preexisting categories. We mean here information of whatever kind—social or natural, formal or informal—anything from a passerby's "Good morning" (or failure to respond to our salutation) to the shifting ground of an earthquake, from a message from City Hall concerning our water meter to a group of people doing the *salat* at the airport.

We can imagine the resulting grid as a matrix on which to map the responses to ambiguity that we have been presenting, as in figure 4.1. Ritual appears in the upper left-hand corner, as a form of highly context-bound and inflexible response. Ritualization involves formalization, and thus has relatively little room for variation within its appropriate context. What we have been calling shared experience is also highly contextualized knowledge (positional, in Bernstein's terms) and thus lies above the horizontal line, like ritual. Yet it is also highly flexible and unlike ritual in that sense. This is a critical distinction, because following Bernstein and Douglas, the default has often been to identify context-specific forms of knowledge with inflexible ones. This, as we argue throughout this chapter, is not necessarily the case. It is possible to develop a highly contextualized mode of response to ambiguity without it being necessarily ritualized or otherwise inflexible.

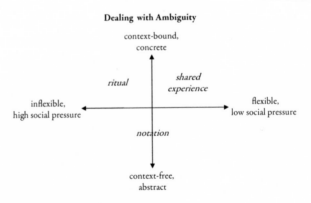

Dealing with Ambiguity

context-bound, concrete

ritual   *shared experience*

inflexible,   flexible,
high social pressure   low social pressure

notation

context-free, abstract

FIGURE 4.1 Dealing with Ambiguity

What of notation? On the one hand, notation finds its place below the horizontal line, as something that is relatively context-free. That is, after all, the point of notation and categorization—the construction of more or less abstract orders that transcend time and place. More abstract knowledge in theory applies in many different situations because it has been freed from specific contexts. This is a vital function, though as the communitarian critique of liberalism has made clear, it comes at a very heavy, perhaps even unsupportable cost, at least in the realm of morality and definitions of the public good.[5]

On the other axis, however, notation can vary greatly. Think of the differences between the common and civil law traditions as occupying different places on this continuum. Even more striking would be juxtaposing the principles of equity to law. Equity, by Aristotle's definition, mediates the more abstract, generalized notational principles of law by more context-specific attention to the particularities of the case at hand. As we shall see a bit later in this chapter, abstract principles—of law, business organization, public policy, religious doctrine, and even craft production—must always be mediated by concrete, contextualized knowledge in order for them to succeed in properly organizing the relevant body of knowledge for the attainment of their purported goals.

Notation can also take an even more flexible form. While few notational systems contain the flexibility referenced in the well-known Sid Harris cartoon (figure 4.2), many forms of notation do carry a relatively high degree of inherent flexibility. Think of how difficult it is to follow a recipe without bringing in a great deal of prior knowledge that is not encoded in any set of rules but just comes from hours of experience in the kitchen. Much the same is true for following a sewing pattern or playing Baroque music. It is the case also with the visual arts that combine sophisticated notational referents with an openness to interpretation and contextualization. Natural science too rests on twin commitments to notation and to the possibility that all categories are open to revision.

At a certain point, however, notation may also become quite inflexible, even ritualized. This ritualized notation can, depending on circumstances, lie at the foundation of a world-historic religion (the repetition of the Islamic *Shahada*, the Jewish *Shema*, or the Nicene Creed), or it can form the core of a particular form of autism or neurotic obsessional behavior. Notation can be fetishized; it can become an idol. Recall the story we recounted in the previous interlude of the Red Heifer and Rabbi Yohanan ben Zakai's statement that "As you live, the corpse does not defile, nor does

"I THINK YOU SHOULD BE
MORE EXPLICIT HERE IN STEP TWO."

FIGURE 4.2 Ambiguity and Notation
Sidney Harris, ScienceCartoonsPlus.com, with permission.

the [mixture of ashes and] water cleanse. The truth is that the rite of the Red Heifer is a decree of the King who is King of kings." R. Yohanan clearly recognizes here the limits on the flexibility of notation within the Jewish tradition. Notational rules, he argues, have only nominal, not ontological reality; his remarkable statement asserts that they are in fact nothing more than a form of ritualized notation. They still must be observed, but one must also understand that observing them does not open the possibility of further creative notation through rational thought.

The very abstract and context-weak nature of notation gives it a unique lability. It can, when backed by the coercive power of the modern state, play a significant role in organizing the frames through which we see and understand reality. This was Jim Scott's point in his influential book, *Seeing like a State.*[6] In fact, the elective affinity of notation and state power goes back to the origins of historical notation, where writing was first introduced in the great agrarian empires as an auxiliary to statecraft and bookkeeping in the great river empires of Mesopotamia.

Brackets

Context—without the addition of extraneous factors like state power or ritual practice or notational elegance—creates its own subjunctive. By abstracting away from specific contexts, notation in its ideal forms moves away from such subjunctive worlds. At an extreme, it approaches the unachievable project of an ideal language of the kind sought by philosophers like Bertrand Russell or the early Ludwig Wittgenstein—a language that would be complete and consistent, with everything subject to proof from basic axioms. Such a language of no doubts and no lies is impossible in daily life; Gödel's incompleteness theorem showed that it is impossible even for mathematics.

The alternative—limiting interaction to a specific context—means accepting restrictions on the ability to generalize. Contextual truths are only partial and temporary, limited to the situation at hand. As we have argued, ritualization involves marking these lines especially clearly by bracketing out the ritual context, often with very clear markers of the boundary. Raising the curtain at the theater, applauding for the conductor, or standing for the entrance of the judge brackets off a particular space, time, and social world, just as much as purifying a sacred space or announcing "Let us pray." As we discussed in chapter 3, every ritualized act involves crossing into a subjunctive world, and crossing out of it again later.

Here we argue that shared experience also brackets out many features that could potentially be relevant to people in other contexts, even if the interaction itself remains unpredictable and not very ritualized. Bracketing allows us to lay aside the full complexity of life. This is what happens when the extended family sits together at Thanksgiving, for instance, as if there were no squabbles, simmering resentments, or active feuds. It happens as well in a classroom, where students and teachers alike put aside other roles they sometimes play, even in relation to each other (as members of the same club, for instance). Actual conversation around the dinner table or in the classroom need not be ritualized at all, of course. It can be quite unpredictable and open. Nevertheless, bracketing out other relationships, emotions, and identities is what allows it to take place.

The work of the International Summer School on Religion and Public Life (ISSRPL) offers an interesting example of such bracketing. For ten years the ISSRPL has been running two-week seminars in difficult and contested cities and countries around the world with highly divergent and diverse groups of scholars, activists, religious leaders, political elites, and teachers. It has met in Croatia, Bosnia, Bulgaria, Indonesia, Turkey, Israel, Cyprus, the United States, and the United Kingdom. A typical year (2010, for example) would bring together fellows from Bosnia, Bulgaria, Congo, Cyprus, Germany, Indonesia, Israel, Kosovo, Morocco, the Palestinian Authority, Sri Lanka, Turkey, Uganda, the United Kingdom, the United States, and Zimbabwe for a fortnight of intense study, site visits, and reflection in small groups around the problem of "living together differently."

One of the primary tools of the group is to circumscribe and bracket out received wisdom and presumed knowledge of the Other. The school attempts to limit knowledge claims to the specific context of interaction. The point is to recognize difference rather than to find commonalities. The hope is to distance fellows from their established "truth-claims" to establish an arena of interaction that can be compared to the "as if" of ritual space, which we discussed earlier. As an arena of shared experience, however, it does not attempt the formalized and repetitive rhythms of ritual. Instead, it is a very clearly bracketed subjunctive arena where interaction grows from the pulse of the context itself. The ISSRPL provides a laboratory for the practical pedagogy of tolerance and living with difference in a global society. It seeks to break down taken-for-granted assumptions about the other and to replace them with a practice informed by the suspension of judgment, tolerance toward that with which we disagree, and a practical, non-ideological set of attitudes based as far as possible on tangible experience rather than prior assumptions about worlds that we do not share.

The major mechanism for this is a form of de-centering of self, in which the self not only sees the other, but sees the other see it, and sees herself or himself see the other. The only real substantive rule of the school is that all participants must act as if they did not believe that their own group had any moral claims based on the "unique" nature of that group's historical suffering. If you think for a moment on how many groups make claims based precisely on this—Jews, Blacks, Palestinians, Muslims, Serbs, gays, women, and so on—you can realize just how daunting the observance of this rule may be. Participants are not asked to give up such a belief in the moral superiority or historically unique suffering of their group, but only to act as if they did not believe that it assured them any unique entitlements, moral or otherwise. The school is devoted to this kind of circumscription of meaning to immediate context.

As one might expect from the reliance on context, concrete cases of decentering and of boundary questioning in the school most often happen accidentally, rather than being thought through in advance. Undoubtedly, bringing together two or three dozen individuals from many different countries, ethnicities, religious traditions, and practices to share an intense two weeks together in a foreign country calls boundaries into question and makes the retreat into established and comfortable presuppositions and ideological frames difficult.

In the 2006 school, the visit to a former Bone Hospital on the outskirts of Stolac in Bosnia/Herzegovina illustrated this vividly. Here Bosnian Croats, self-identifying as Catholics, tortured hundreds of their Muslim fellow citizens and townsfolk. The ISSRPL group included a Catholic from Croatia, now working at a U.S. university—for whom the moment of standing on that ground, which certain of her co-religionists and co-countrymen had turned into a vast torture chamber, was the most difficult of the entire two weeks. No retreat into existing ideological, social, or historical constructions was possible at that moment. The result, in her own words, was a profound de-centering of self.

A similar but less dramatic moment happened in 2005 at the Israeli Defense Force (IDF) cemetery at Kiryat Anavim, where the citizen soldiers of the nascent IDF who fell in the struggle over the Jerusalem corridor in the 1948 war were buried. At that moment (and one cannot extrapolate beyond that moment), the Palestinian Israeli fellows could not, one felt, look at the Jews only as oppressors and conquerors, but also as young, fallen men and boys.

In these and similar cases, the experience did not question a specific, discrete event within the context of the school, but instead undercut the taken-for-granted reality of a more general orientation or disposition toward the other, which the participant had to recalibrate in the wake of the school's experience.

While these are rather dramatic examples of such processes, they happened *in minora* often, and to many participants in different ways. So for example, a Pakistani Muslim woman was surprised when staying with Muslim hosts in Stolac that her hosts were warmer toward and identified more with her Palestinian Christian fellows than with her. The identification as fellow sufferer clearly, in this case, trumped that of fellow Muslim.

In another case, an Israeli orthodox woman who had an eight-hour layover in Budapest on her way back to Israel from Sarajevo told her husband (over the phone) that rather than stay in the airport, she would spend the time in Budapest itself, do some shopping, and so on. When asked who would accompany her (as orthodox Jewish women do not often travel alone in strange cities), she said "Ahmed and Salam" (Palestinian Israeli fellows on the same flight), and her husband was shocked. Reflecting on this, she pointed out how much she herself had changed in the two weeks—for such a reality would have been inconceivable to her beforehand.

A similar dynamic of being forced to reconceptualize the boundaries of oneself, one's other, and one's group would happen again and again: going into the Cambridge mosque and having some members of the group separate to enter prayer, entering Trinity Church in Copley Square to have one group member go up for Communion.

In Adam Seligman's case, it was a moment in 2006, leading prayers in the orthodox Jewish synagogue in Newton. The group of fellows entered about 10 minutes into prayer and suddenly all was silent. The usual murmur that is so comforting and such a pleasing and enveloping aspect of Jewish prayer suddenly ceased. It was clear that in one way or another, one group was distancing itself and marking some mistrust from another group. For Seligman himself, however, both groups were equally "self"— the synagogue (and, by implication, the Jewish people) to which he belonged, and the ISSRPL fellows, for whom he had a great responsibility and strong feelings of loyalty.

Each case profoundly shook the boundaries of inside and outside, us and them, and where the self belongs and to whom. Even if only for a moment, boundaries were in flux, and definitions of group and membership were placed in question. In all cases, the particular contextual and bracketed experience allowed this profound—if temporary—shifting of boundaries and the new consciousness that emerged from it.

This issue of boundaries goes beyond the perception of group membership and the limits of inclusion. The question of the "taken-for-granted" goes to the heart of our shared social life. The summer schools have made painfully clear just how much we do not share, even though we rarely confront that fact. The taken-for-granted is precisely the unexamined. Indeed, it could not bear such scrutiny on a permanent basis, for if examined it would prove to be much too fragile and too confused to support the assumed shared meanings that we impute to it.

A good example of this happened in Mostar in 2006. Mostar is still a tragically divided city, even though the famous bridge that President Tudjman's forces had bombed and destroyed had been rebuilt in 2004. The city center was rebuilt and thriving, though 200 meters away, the city looked like Stalingrad after the siege. On the hill overlooking the "Muslim" side of the city, a huge, immense cross had been constructed. It had not been there before the war and presented itself as a provocation and incitement, hardly in that context a mark of the savior's humility. Walking with one of the fellows, a Catholic priest, Adam Seligman put his hands on the priest's shoulders, pointed out the cross on the hill, and said something like: "That is a bad one, eh, Padre?" At this, the priest, with whom Seligman was and remained very friendly, became visibly upset, crossed himself, and said, "How can a cross be bad?! Say it is poorly placed, say it is here provocative, but a cross cannot be bad." Indeed, for a Catholic priest, a cross cannot be bad. For most observant Jews, the calculation is quite different.

Here is a good example of what we are referring to. We both use the word "cross," we both think we mean the same thing, but in fact we do not. We have just enough shared meaning and shared resonances to allow the minimum necessary to maintain interaction and social communication in most circumstances. But the depth, resonances, symbolism, identities, and affectual relations with the word are totally different.

In most circumstances of daily life, this is irrelevant, for at least two very different reasons. First, even when we have different affectual, symbolic, historical, and meaningful relations to the same word, concept, symbol, or artifice, we can still act "as if" we understand one another. There may be no need to go into the full resonances that the actors have of the word, concept, place, or thing, because nothing makes them think about the differences. Context and experience allow the communication to work effectively, even though each person brackets out or leaves ambiguous much of its significance. This can last, unless we are pushed in some way, breaking apart the taken-for-granted aspect of the context.

The second way of making divergent meanings irrelevant is when we explicitly or implicitly (or usually some combination of both) define the context of our mutual interaction to limit the range of meanings to a tightly circumscribed, shared, and hence mutually relevant field of meanings that allow the interaction. Thus, for example, the person who sells the house where she has lived for 40 years, the house where she raised her children, from which she set out to bury her parents, to divorce her husband, and so on, has a very different attitude toward that collection of brick, stone, wood, and plaster than the contractor who is purchasing it to tear it down and put up a condo. This difference is irrelevant to their interaction, for both agree to limit their meanings to the very thin surface of the commodity form—the price. Again, it is context that defines the needs and limits of meaning.

This contextualization of meanings suggests that we do not so much share meanings as share use of words. As long as we can construct a shared usage for the purpose at hand (buying and selling, proceeding with a history seminar, participating in a Mass, etc.), we can lay aside other connotations and evocations of words. We do not ever have to share meaning "all the way down" so much as we have to agree on a common use of the word. Similarly, lacking a hammer, someone may use a handy rock to knock a nail into the wood of her porch. After she gets tired, you might help by taking the rock up and using it in a similar manner. You need not reject your preexisting definitions of rocks and hammers, but need only agree to work together to solve this problem—getting the nail into the wood with no hammer in sight—by using the rock in this manner. We need to share usage, not necessarily meanings, or at most only partial meanings.

Entering into situations of dialogue, we often feel that we have to arrive at shared or common meanings. Yet this is often illusory, frustrating, ultimately destructive of one set of meanings, resonances, identities, and symbols. It is simply senseless, for instance, to wish a Muslim from Mostar and a Catholic from Mostar to arrive at the same associative meanings on viewing a cross. It is also, at the end of the day, deeply disrespectful of differences. If meanings must be truly shared in their entirety, then all parties must hold them in common. Difference is lost—in meanings, symbols, resonances and so on. Shared usage, however, does not compromise the different meanings.

There are purely technical tasks in which this whole problem does not much arise. When we discuss lawn mower parts or staplers with a retailer, for instance, the overlap of meaning may approach 100 percent. Usage and meaning coincide, and there is little potential for misunderstanding. This is not, however, a beneficial state for anything that is beyond the realm of spark plugs or staples. It is certainly not something to strive for when discussing those matters that we each most intimately identify with—what for each of us represents the core of truth, belonging, and meaning in life. To do so destroys the personal and group meanings that one seeks to preserve, through which one's own selfhood and being in the world are made manifest and meaningful.

In one way, the ISSRPL is an attempt to implement a notion of shared usage. It does not foster an illusion of shared meaning, whose very fragility threatens to destroy civil interaction as soon as it is put to the test. Nor does it attempt to dissolve real difference by insisting that meanings be entirely shared. It instantiates instead a practice of shared usage, painfully reconstructed concept by concept, place by place, artifice by artifice—rethinking everything from scratch and recognizing the boundaries between what can be shared (usage) and what need not (meanings). In short, it offers experience as a shared subjunctive, bracketing out difference while leaving it intact.

Shared usage minimizes the need to insist on shared meanings. It allows us to admit that much is not shared—that differences matter. The conscious goal of the school is to set out a circumscribed and deeply contextual understanding of what is shared. This is quite different from what typically happens in our churches, synagogues, mosques, and schools. Those contexts instead assume that we share meanings—hence the acrimonious debates over evolution in American school curricula, divisive arguments over gay priests in the Anglican communion, and the assumption—probably false, and certainly not verifiable—that the person sitting next to me in the pew is experiencing the same meanings of the prayer that I am, as we recite or chant the same liturgy.

The experience of the ISSRPL suggests that it is possible to live together without such shared meaning, as long as we agree to shared usages, which are always highly contextual. Bracketing out—even temporarily—the need for shared meaning could perhaps allow us to begin a process of questioning, playing, reframing, and reshaping boundaries that might allow us truly to live together without being identical, to make our life with other people less filled with friction, feelings of betrayal, and mistrust. Such bracketing enhances the possibility of creating shared experience out of common context.

Ritual and Shared Experience

Shared experience enables us to work across boundaries by bracketing out irreconcilable differences, as the summer schools do by taking claims for a monopoly on suffering off the table. This process can even extend to the point of not attempting to come up with shared meanings, as long as we share enough sense of shared process and shared goals to work together. In many ways, this resembles the techniques of ritual that we discussed earlier. Both shared experience and ritual bracket out a subjunctive space in which we set aside many of the differences and concerns of life in other contexts. Both can even sidestep the problem of shared meaning because, for both shared experience and ritual, the actions themselves put participants on the public record as accepting the particular context as defined. This remains true, even if they share very little in their interpretations of the meanings of their actions. It is even true if they take part hypocritically, as long as their actions fit the context.

These subjunctive worlds are only temporary: participants will leave ISSRPL and the particularities of its interactions, just as a Muslim will eventually stop facing Mecca and get on with life between prayers. They are able to cross and renegotiate boundaries in part exactly because they are *temporary* in the most literal sense; they exist only as delimited by time. Permanence, in contrast, is beyond time, but thus also beyond real change. Its boundaries are firm, clear, and lasting—the ahistorical boundaries of notation.

Ritual and shared experience do not, however, create exactly the same kinds of time. Ritual, as we discussed earlier, relies on meter. That is, it exists through an externally defined and unchanging repetition. This creates time—a shared sense of past and future—and in that way makes social worlds possible. It does not, however, create history. Ritual's time creates the rhythms of a shared life, but its repetitions offer little flexibility in reacting to the needs of day-to-day life. The very qualities that allow ritual to create a shared sense of time, of past and future, also make it less sensitive to the constant change around us. Rituals claim that today's event is fundamentally the same as yesterday's and tomorrow's.

Shared experience offers a very different relationship to time. Experience has its own rhythms, but they are more the natural and constantly changing rhythms of pulse than the conventional regularities of meter. This is just like a heartbeat that will speed and slow in response to changing contexts, or like waves whose lapping is loosely rhythmic from one to the next, but whose exact timing we cannot predict because it is subject to broad environmental and physical variables of which we sense little. We can often see such things in our own workplaces—not in the conventional meters of 9:00 and 5:00, but in the informal coordination, for instance, of how we might time a trip to the coffee pot to coincide with a friend's schedule. We can see it again in two colleagues who decide to write a book together. Like any discipline, this benefits from a rhythmic repetition that will force progress (or at least a struggle toward progress) to continue by having to meet the next deadline for reading or writing. Yet that rhythm will not be strictly conventional. It will vary from week to week, depending on travel schedules, writing burdens, pleas for mercy, and demands to see progress. Even the work sessions themselves develop an unplanned and loose rhythmic regularity in how much small talk is allowed (or required) before getting to the work, or when the two relax the pace with a joke or an irrelevant observation. At least as the two of us have done it, there is no meter—no agreement that we meet every Monday at 10:00 for two hours, no matter what. There is, however, a pace, a sense that pages should appear at a pleasing rate: every day is too fast, every few months is too slow, but there is a lot of room for flexibility between.

Transitions among Experience, Ritual, and Notation

Shared experience creates history because each reiteration is different. Ritual's metered repetitions instead create time that transcends history. The two senses of time are not always so easy to separate, however, because they interact with each other. One consequence of this interaction is that there is a tendency for experience to become ritualized. The baseball player who wears yesterday's unwashed shirt and hits a home run will wear the dirty shirt again the next day. Instead of trying to coordinate the work rhythms of the morning to run into friends at the coffee point, the worker shows up every day at 10:32 and feels a breach of etiquette if the friend is not there, too. If we keep repeating experience to the point where we expect that the future will always repeat the present, history has been lost to a different sense of time.

The push from experience to ritual, for example, appears in the early expansion of China's Taiping Rebellion, a massive rebellion of the mid-nineteenth century that claimed to be returning China to a primordial Christianity and that eventually resulted in uncounted millions of casualties.[7] During its early years of organization in the rural hinterlands of Guangxi Province, this highly improvisatory religious movement solidified its ritual forms beyond their immediate context, and thus laid the groundwork for a social organization that would support the rebellion.

Their leader was a failed civil service examination candidate named Hong Xiuquan. Hong had picked up a very early missionary tract after one of his trips to Canton to take the exams. Reading it years later, he realized that it explained a dream vision he had experienced while very ill, in which he was taken to heaven, purified by having his internal organs replaced, and led to meet his true family—a bearded father, a mother, and an older brother. The Christian tract offered him the key to the vision's meaning:

the man was God and Hong was thus Jesus's younger brother. The Protestant translation of their concept of God into Shangdi—an ancient Chinese term for a high deity—fostered the idea that Hong's duty was to bring China back to its original monotheistic and Christian understanding.

Hong recruited a tiny number of followers in his home village, whom he baptized as best he knew how. The village elders, however, soon found themselves challenged by Hong's iconoclasm, leading ultimately to his departure for the mountainous and dangerous wilderness to the west. He ended up in northern Guangxi, an ethnically mixed area that at the time harbored very active groups of river pirates and where government control had become very weak.

Here Hong's God Worshipping Society, as they called themselves at the time, had to adjust rapidly to the local context. Among the most significant changes was that some new recruits began to be possessed. They relied primarily on forms of spirit possession with a very long history in the area, but the possessing deities now included innovations like God and Jesus. As a partial result, the group suddenly began to attract massive numbers of followers, soon rising into the thousands.[8]

The limited Taiping documents that we have on these events suggest that the possession episodes were wildly exciting, and could have been one of the most important reasons for the group's success. They were also, however, extremely chaotic, with many deities appearing at once and often pronouncing heavenly truths that conflicted with each other. It is no coincidence that much of this happened while Hong was away for long periods of time. We have neither notation nor much ritual here. Instead, the early Taiping was embedded in the local context, even as the movement was utterly transforming it. Starting with a poorly translated biblical tract and a visionary leader from another place, it had become tied to purely local traditions of spirit possession and to purely local social dynamics between groups that were quite different from many other places in China.

It may be thrilling as one god after another speaks, but it also became confusing as all these possessed statements did not always mesh with each other. Exactly because this was so tied to context, it was impossible to extricate the statements of the deities from the struggles among the spirit mediums for positions of power in what had become a formidably large movement by then. The new local leaders sensed the possibility of a descent into chaos—of nothing but context with no sense of shared past or future through repetition. When Hong finally returned from his travels (surely with some surprise about the changed scale and nature of his movement), the local people asked him to impose some kind of order, to validate their experience. He did this by announcing that one leader was truly possessed by God, and another by Jesus, but that all the rest were demonic and would be punished by death if they ever claimed to speak with the voice of the spirits again. This was an attempt to end the inconsistencies of the mass possessions, to make them predictable and thus repeatable: a move from experience to ritual, from pulse to meter. It is no coincidence that other forms of ritualization emerged at the same time, like creating leadership ranks and titles, along with flags and other symbols of power. The Taiping eventually developed an entire court culture, including a civil service examination system and all the rest that was governed by the Board of Rites in late imperial China. This constituted the transformation into a clear political movement that intended to take power by armed force.

Hans-Georg Gadamer pointed to this pressure toward ritualization when he wrote, "Experience is valid only if it is confirmed; hence its dignity depends on its fundamental repeatability."[9] Experience thus has to be validated by repetition. The Taiping accomplished this through a relative ritualization of spirit possession, which allowed them to create a political community out of the threat of chaos.

The reverse of Gadamer's point about the necessity of repetition for experience, however, is just as important and pervasive. That is, unique and singular experiences constantly invade ritual, pulse threatens to overtake meter. We see not just ritualization out of local context, as in the Taiping, but also contextualization that can ultimately threaten ritual. To some extent, this happens every single time that we repeat a ritual, because no true repetition is really possible. There is always an element of improvisation: a child knocked over a candle, someone released an enormous sneeze during the moment of silence, the Red Heifer had a white hair. The ritual survives anyway by making clear that some crucial bits—the canonical part of the ritual, as Rappaport puts it—count as if they were unchanged.[10] At some rituals in Bangalore, India, for example, the performer does everything possible to be sure of the correct time for the performance and makes the strongest effort to begin at exactly the appointed second.[11] Nevertheless, his first ritual utterance is an apology to the deity for getting the time wrong. This is a recognition that the flow of historical time—pulse—can never match the ideals of ritual's meter, that context will always interfere.

Every ritual tradition has ways of adapting to this problem through methods that allow people to declare that whatever is essential about the ritual has been repeated, and that the many variant details are irrelevant. Sometimes, however, a context changes so very drastically that the ritual itself teeters. One of the most extreme examples of this was Judaism after the destruction of the second Temple. Before that point, the entire tradition had been constructed around sacrifices conducted by hereditary priests and centered in one most sacred space. After the destruction and with no hope of rebuilding, the close tie to a particular but lost place made it impossible to continue performing those rituals and to call them a repetition. The result was a move from sacrifice to text, from priestly intermediation to Rabbinic interpretation, from Jerusalem to the world of the Diaspora. The rabbis who worked for generations to accomplish this managed the extraordinary feat of allowing Jews to maintain a feeling of continuity with the past, a feeling that in some fundamental sense they were still repeating the most important essence of their religion, even though nearly every detail of ritual life had to change.[12]

In China during the eleventh and twelfth centuries C.E., Confucian scholars took on a task that must have seemed almost as daunting, although the cause was less traumatic. Deeply immersed in a ritual and political tradition that was roughly a thousand years old by then, these scholars (who later came to be called neo-Confucians) realized that the gradual pressure of history on ritual over a millennium had caused an enormous amount of change to creep in almost unnoticed. This was not the sudden transformation that Jewish leaders faced after the loss of the Temple, but instead was the result of the endless erosion of centuries, of one petty compromise piled on top of another until they, too, had the feeling that no one was any longer truly repeating. The core of the tradition, they felt, was in danger of dissolving away entirely. The result was a thorough rethinking that involved moving away from the gradual and largely unreflective political and ritual changes that the centuries had brought. They pulled away from the weight of experience and history through both notation (textual reinterpretation of how the original Confucian corpus should be understood) and developing new ritual regimes. In what may seem remarkable to modern eyes, they published both virtuosic textual studies to edify the elite and manuals of household ritual and daily etiquette aimed at guiding the population as a whole. Some of those manuals, especially Zhu Xi's *Family Rituals*, remain in print today and are used exactly as he intended—by ordinary householders.

The reformers did not claim simply to be reproducing the original intent of the founders or restoring the nation to its ritual essence.

Instead, they explicitly recognized that the social and cultural context of life had changed greatly after well over a thousand years. Much as they might have wished for a return to the exact ritual descriptions in ancient texts, they realized that such a thing was completely impossible. Like the Jewish leaders after the demise of the Temple, they were finding ways of justifying claims to continuity by readjusting a ritual tradition to the world of experience. As Zhu Xi put it in the preface to his *Family Rituals*:

> During the three ancient dynasties the classical texts of the ritual were fully adequate. But in the texts that survive today, the regulations . . . are no longer suited to our age. . . . In my ignorance, I . . . took on the task of reviewing the ancient and recent texts [on ritual]. I started by identifying the major structures that cannot be changed and made minor emendations. . . . In writing this book, I presume to follow Confucius's idea of carrying on what came from our predecessors.[13]

Notation and Shared Experience

Context or experience tends to stand in an uneasy relation to notation, just as it does to ritual. At its most abstract extreme, notation obviates all particular contexts and provides only the most general (and generalizable) grids for all experience. In use, however, context almost always mediates notation. Sometimes context can even explode notation. Aspects of this can be found in the insights of Marshall McLuhan on the role of the media in the conveyance of any notational message.[14] Walter Ong proffered a similar insight in his classic book *The Presence of the Word*, where he noted that "sound is more real or existential than other sense objects, despite the fact that it is also more evanescent"[15] (we might even add—recalling the tock/ tick of ritual—precisely because it is more evanescent). The spoken word, after all, exists in real time, thus partaking in time's quiddity. Sound is rooted in the particular moment, in the real apprehension of experience rather than its notation (modern recording devices notwithstanding). In many instances, it not only reflects the context, but is an essential element of any particular and hence evanescent context. At the same time, we modulate sound in the present to produce new realities, whether in street brawls or over romantic dinners—not to mention in more ritual contexts. Words spoken are often inseparable from action: in the Hebrew Bible as well as in aural cultures and the workings of magic and the evil eye. The oral/aural component provides a context to the words that makes them an event.

This is, after all, the meaning of prophecy. The "event" of prophecy is less the message than its articulation, which can, often does, break the bounds of the normatively acceptable. This breaking is itself the meaning. Isaiah, Amos, Jesus—all prophesied in speech, not through written notation. Indeed, in Hebrew, the root *d-b-r* is the source of the word for both speech and event. The spoken word of God created the world, we recall, in the canonical books of our civilization. Similarly, the mystical syllable "om" was the original vibration of the divine at the creation of the world, as described in the Upanishads. While notation is timeless, sound only exists in time, and it is no coincidence that so many traditions link sound so closely to the origins of time.

As Ong reminds us, the spoken word is always context rich (the context of its speakers and listeners), while the written word communicates to those who are not there at all. Oral speech is rich in complexities and the messiness of everyday life, including the fuzziness of our thinking on the spot and in dialogue with others (as anyone knows who has ever attempted to transcribe and publish any taped discussion). All anthropologists writing up their field notes for the day, or even more, rereading them at a later date, no longer in the field, have the awful sense of having lost something critical in the move to notation. Trying to recreate the experience is often like reaching back for a dream upon waking, only to have its wisps trailing through our fingers. This may be the reason that so many cultures that greatly value oral testimony are so suspicious of the written word. Indeed, our very word "testimony" shares a root with testicle (*testis*), which some trace to a Roman tradition of placing one's hand on the genital organs as an act of loyalty and fidelity. The word thus refers to an action in context, rather than to something notated in a text. We find this again in the story of Abraham and Eliezer, when Abraham commanded his servant to find a wife for his son Isaac only from his kindred family and not from the daughters of Canaan. Eliezer swore by placing his hand under Abraham's thigh (Genesis 24:2–3). In a rather pale mirroring of this, we swear on the Bible—the most profound attestation to oral culture and the spoken word that we can muster. In both, the deed and the word are bound together.

Context almost always mediates notation and it can, on occasion, explode notation as occurs in the radical potential of prophecy. Yet there is another side of the story as well, because context is always also moving toward notation. As soon as we wish to remember something, or to teach it, we tend to move toward notation. As soon as we wish to instruct, to share and impart knowledge, we invoke an "ought," whether in cooking or morals, crossing the street, or playing an instrument. We tell the novice how she ought to hold the bow of the cello, to look both ways when crossing the street, to keep the dough under a towel as it is rising, never to steal or lie, and so on. In all these cases we make use of the "ought" form, which is not, in itself, notation. Yet, the use of the "ought"—especially when it is continually repeated—carries a very strong default to move from "ought" to "Ought" and hence from context to notation: from experience to abstraction.

There are, for example, all sorts of things that we do in a particular way simply because it is our habit. This can include how we brush our teeth, play piano, pray to God, plant in the garden, cook dinner, clean the dishes, and get to work. If we do not perform these activities in the manner in which we "ought" to do them, we may feel that something is not quite right with the world. We make no claims to legal, transcendent, metaphysical, or even rational reasons, no claims to universal strictures—it is just the way that we do things, the praxis of everyday life. Many people (including these authors and their spouses) have very particular ways of being in the kitchen, and while no one has the presumption to claim that there are no other ways of handling a complicated dinner, in our kitchens with Rob, or Rahel, or Alice cooking, there is only *one* way to sauté onions, although it may not be the same way for each of those cooks. This is what we mean by "ought" (with a lower-case o). The lower case reminds us that this ought is subjective and contextual. While we would be much aggrieved if the matter at hand was not executed in the manner to which we are accustomed (as people attempting to help in the kitchen will attest), we make no claims to any broader legitimizing framework. As we come to write such things down, however, to notate them, the lower-case o often transforms into an upper-case O" The ought takes on very strong normative connotations and moves from "this is the way I do it" to "this is the way it should be done" or "this is the right way of doing it."

Our sons and daughters following us around in the kitchen, however, learn to cook in a manner very different from gaining the same knowledge from a cookbook. By following us around, they experience the event (sautéing the onions) in context of the whole meal and all the preparations involved, the size of the onions, the quality and quantity of oil used, the heat of the flame, the thickness in which the pieces were cut, and infinite additional details.

In the early 1990s, Haym Soloveitchik wrote a very influential article (reproduced in multiple forms and variations) on precisely this move from what he termed "mimesis" to text in the practice of observant Jews over the twentieth century. He stressed how the loss of a taken-for-granted way of life brought in its wake an outpouring of textual, that is to say, notational injunctions, parsing the details of daily religious observance in absolute terms. Observant Jews bought and read these texts on a mass scale, and they have now reshaped the texture of religious life. His point was very similar to our kitchen analogy above. He described how myriad practices that had no basis in actual, written law, but which were passed down from father to son and mother to daughter, came to be evaluated, legitimized, or delegitimized through a massive legal and notational (and publishing) enterprise that prescribed to the observant Jew every facet of every action in terms of God's law to Moses from Sinai. Soloveitchik argued that Jews in earlier times had simply absorbed much of their way of life, their *halacha* (which is the term for Jewish legal and ritual practice and literally translates as "path" or "way to follow"). Today, instead, they *learn* it.[16] Learning the way of their forefathers, rather than absorbing it, has, according to Soloveitchik, significantly transformed the way in which Jews live a religious life. Notation has made the *halacha* less flexible, less capable of dealing with ambiguity. Notation has replaced experience as the ultimate validator of religious life, he claimed—for both orthodox and ultra-orthodox Jews. To quote Soloveitchik:

> The shift of authority to texts and their enshrinement as the sole source of authenticity ha[s] had far reaching effects. Not only has this shift contributed, as we have seen, to the policy of religious stringency and altered the nature of religious performance, but it has also transformed the character and purpose of religious education, redistributed political power in non-Hasidic circles, and defined anew the scope of the religious in the political arena.[17]

It is not only in the hands of the state that notation is a powerful force for transforming cultures and social practice.

The process remarked on by Soloveitchik in the Jewish community is at work in many parts of the Muslim world as well. For instance, in those areas once under Communist hegemony, like the Caucasus and Central Asia, Islamic practice was often highly mediated, often legally naïve in the ways of Sharia, and generally syncretic. Observant Muslims survived

Communist rule often through clandestine practices, only to find them-selves attacked in the final years of the twentieth century and today by a new breed of textual exegetes—often with only rudimentary knowledge of Arabic and perhaps a very few years training in the Gulf, or by mission-aries from Saudi Arabia or North Africa.[18] These missionaries, home-grown or imported, attack, delegitimize, and often manage to destroy traditional practices in the name of a purer Islam, untainted by the corrup-tion of history—an Islam authenticated solely by its texts. Here, too, the move from practice, context, and experience to notation and elite interpre-tations of texts has led to far-reaching transformations in the texture of religious life—in people's ability to deal with the foreign, ambiguous, and liminal. In all cases, a notational "Ought" replaces the contextual "ought."

Each of these cases, while driven by different forces, seeks to preserve one set of particular practices (sometimes by replacing other contextual-ized practices, as in Central Asian Islam) through notation. Preserving practice in and through time involves writing, freeing the practice from its context in order to preserve it. Doing so also transforms and generally ri-gidifies the practice, leaving it less open to the ambiguities and contradic-tory demands of any present reality.

We can distinguish, however, between notation per se and the pro-cesses of symbolization and abstraction that are inherent to it. Notation carries with it, by necessity, a degree of abstraction, yet one can (albeit with effort) notate in such a way as to include a great degree of context and in so doing minimize the force of abstraction. Notation bears an elective af-finity with abstraction but no absolutely necessary correlation. If and when it is an issue, we can work to minimize the force of this move toward ab-straction—and with it the move from "ought" to "Ought." One important reason to do so is that the more we understand, represent, and teach in terms of "Ought" rather than "ought," the more our categories and defini-tions become separated by rigid boundaries. This was the process that Soloveitchik discussed concerning the changes in the practice of contem-porary Orthodox Jews.

Changing Levels

Another way to get at the tension between notation and context is to explore how social actors actually coordinate their activities. Throughout this book we have argued that boundaries, which are necessary to the very existence of discrete entities, always involve ambiguity. Yet, boundaries also imply difference—whether they are binary, as is often the case when notational forms are introduced to define them; or relational, as we are claiming is the case with ritual; or fractal, as in embodied and contextualized experience. This is what leads to the ambiguities. The boundary of an object is determined by both its center and by what lies outside.[19] Objects are open to what lies beyond their meaning-giving frame. Boundaries retain ambiguity because they are vulnerable to what is different, in addition to being constituted by whatever they enclose.

Difference, however, presents us with a practical challenge. If we have to solve a concrete issue together (where to dig the hole, how to grade the paper, who should do the dishes, how much to spend on the education budget, etc.), difference is an obstacle to action. If we wish to act without coercion, we feel that we have to agree. When we do not agree, we often dig down beneath the concrete issues at hand to find "deeper" or most substantive disagreements on first principles, or values, or broader orientations. In such cases, we reinterpret the concrete in terms of more abstract, notational system of meanings that stand between us and that appear to demand resolution in order to move forward with the concrete problem that we face. Often, then, a concrete disagreement may turn into a full-blown ideological confrontation, making agreement impossible.

Donald Schön spent his career examining just such situations in which professionals must solve problems together with clients and other professionals, with whom they may share few common frames of reference (little shared notation, in our terms). He was a critic of what he saw as a major trend of professionalization over the course of the twentieth century: the idea that technical rationality alone allows us to solve problems. This attitude, which he dubbed "expertise," encouraged professionals to claim knowledge in the face of invariable uncertainty and to expect deference from clients.[20] One could think of the example of some physician-patient or architect-client interactions. This is dangerous, however, because it can easily blind the practitioner to the full set of needs of the client, to the complexities of the actual context, and to the possibility that this iteration may turn out to have been quite different from others in the past. The professions, in our terms, are caught between the need for notation to pull practitioners out of what Schön calls the "swampy lowlands" of muddling through each unique case, and the "high ground" of a technical rationality so narrowly defined as to risk missing all the real complexities of life.[21]

Schön's response is to suggest "reflective practice," a kind of dialectic between what he calls "knowing-in-action" (the kind of knowledge that lets us play the violin or whip egg whites) and conscious reflection about those actions. This involves complicating the notational knowledge of a doctor or urban planner, for instance, with the complexities of the full context. And this is followed by reflecting on the new experience to alter the notational world.[22] Rather than dealing with clients or patients from a set position of claimed knowledge, the practitioner constantly interacts with them to rethink the context as a whole.

This is one of the reasons that we refer to boundaries in this form of shared experience as "fractal." While we do not mean this to be taken too literally, we want to emphasize the infinite complexity and involution of these boundaries, rather than seeing them simply as lines of bifurcation. Benoit Mandelbrot famously argued that the coast of England was infinite because, even though we might approximate it as an oval, the line was actually lengthened by a large number of inlets, lengthened again by mini-inlets within the larger ones, which were in turn lengthened by micro-inlets, and so on forever.[23] Similarly, the boundaries within the shared experience of reflective practice—those between practitioners and clients as well as those between notation and context—are constantly being renegotiated.

In later work (co-authored with Martin Rein), Schön added the possibility that frames of analysis themselves could change in the process of negotiation among multiple parties to a context. He gave the example of the various state agencies, public activists, and potential beneficiaries when Massachusetts tried to create a new policy toward the homeless in the 1980s.[24] This negotiation did not necessarily mean that all participants would come to share the same frames, but rather that negotiation was possible in spite of differing frames. It was enough that in the Massachusetts case "the actors' conflicting frames did not *wholly* color their visions of the policy situation."[25] This left enough room to respond to the situation itself, even though their frames led them to emphasize different facts and cling to different arguments. This is very similar to our argument that we can bracket out many of our intractable differences and disagreements and simply respond to the context at hand.

Schön and Rein warn further that the language of technical rationality can cause serious problems when it tempts us make all of our assumptions explicit in an effort to find complete common ground with our partners:

This language suggests that we must climb *up* the ladder of abstraction in order to reflect *on* the contents of the levels below. But meta-cultural frames are embedded in our habits of thought and action. As we attend to the material at hand, we may succeed in reflecting *through* it to frames that are implicit in our understanding *of* it. Those who are adept at climbing up the ladder of abstraction are not necessarily better equipped to reflect on metacultural frames than those who have acquired a feel for the frames built into concrete materials and practices.[26]

Here they identify one critical mode of dealing with differences by seeking agreement on the level of the notational or the abstract principle. This mode moves "up" from the concrete, gradually invoking more and more abstract, general levels of argumentation until we can find a level upon which we agree: as co-teachers, we might disagree about the grade, but we do agree about the criteria for giving grades, or perhaps one of us is against grades at all, so we have to move up to agreement on the role of the university, or educational institutions, and so on. Note, too, that such argument usually involves not one notational principle but many—thus creating gray areas between overlapping principles. Entering these gray zones creates a place of play and creativity and the ability to move between notational systems and so get beyond any one of them. By invoking many, we problematize any single one as ultimate or absolute (while not rejecting notation out of hand).

Actually solving the concrete problem at hand, however, requires that we must also be able to move "down" the ladder and re-engage with the concrete problem on the basis of the agreement on the notational/abstract level. When we don't have to go "up" too far, this is usually possible. However, when we have to move all the way up the notational ladder, it becomes very difficult to re-engage at the level of the concrete problem in an efficient manner. This is often the problem with so many of the conferences, workshops, and meetings devoted to "inter-religious dialogue." The monotheists can generalize past their differences to agree that all are the "children of Abraham." If Buddhists are added to the mix, everyone is forced even higher up the levels of abstraction, reducing their rich religious traditions to a shared belief that we must do good and behave ethically. All this is fine, except that the problems that led to the meeting are never abstract and theological, but are usually very concrete and practical—relating to a particular bit of real estate in the Middle East, or the veiling of women, or clitoridectomy, and so on. Just concurring that we are all children of God or should do what is good does not help us solve any of these problems.

Moving up levels of abstraction tries to resolve the difference by seeking an agreed-upon a priori. Put another way, we search for the commonality that analytically—or notationally—precedes our differences. Yet this is often a futile exercise, because to achieve commonality and consensus we have to go so far up the notational ladder that we have no way to get back down to the concrete context of the decisions before us as members of the city council, or hospital ethics committee, or town planning commissions.

There is, however, another mode of dealing with the concrete problem we face—improvisation or bricolage within the context of shared experience. This stresses action, the doing within particular contexts and their histories. Here, participants do not seek an a priori, but rather organically begin with difference to produce an evanescent solution to a particular problem (evanescent, because it is always a particular and unique problem). This solution often ends up being temporary, for as soon as we attempt to generalize from any particular solution to other problems we are willy-nilly engaged in the making of a new notational system.

A particularly interesting example of this dynamic can be found in Richard White's description of relations between the French and Algonquian peoples in the Great Lakes region of North America in the late seventeenth century.[27] Both French and Algonquian societies prohibited murder, though both put this prohibition aside in times of war (for the killing of enemies). We can see this shared orientation as somewhere on the "top" of that notational ladder shared by all societies. But here the confluence of orientations ends. The French would release prisoners of war at the end of hostilities. The Algonquians, however, disposed of enemies at all times and in any way possible (unless they were "ritually protected"). When dealing with a murder within society, the French held the individual murderer responsible, to pay with his life for his deed if found guilty. The Algonquians, however, dealt with "death at the hands of allies," the equivalent of a murder within society for the French, by either the offer of slaves or material goods in compensation. The provision of this compensation was, moreover, the responsibility of the whole tribe or clan of the murderer and not of one individual. Failure to make such a provision turned allies into enemies, who could thus be killed with impunity.[28]

Such divergent attitudes—just one or two notches "down" the notational ladder—do not allow shared action or a common practice, no matter how much agreement can be reached on either the evils of killing or its necessity in times of war. Rather than a shared notation, what actually emerged out of this interaction was instead a hybrid or syncretistic set of actions marked more by their underlying ambiguity. French/Algonquin relations gravitated toward improvisation and "indecision," rather than seeking to attain clarity and agreed-upon meaning. As White put it, "neither French nor Algonquian cultural roles fully governed the situation."[29] Summing up one such incident in 1683, White explained that the result was "in the end fully in accordance with neither French nor Indian conceptions of crime and punishment. Instead, it involved considerable improvisation and the creation of a middle ground at a point where the cultures seemed to intersect, so that the expectations of each side could find at least some satisfaction."[30]

While relying on notation to resolve differences locks us into one role, using improvisation plays with the boundaries of role(s) to arrive at a solution, and it thus leaves open the possibility of more complex and creative role-playing. This is especially important at the frontier of different cultural and social orders, but is true for all sorts of other boundaries as well, including those between social actors in the same culture and society. This improvisation can have many aspects. We can, for example, step out of the roles that this concrete situation places us in (let us say, teachers arguing over a grade) to invoke other roles (a friendship long established); we can stay in our roles but negotiate favors given or received; or we can project future contexts of continued interaction and hence the need for cooperation. This is often interpreted as politics or collusion, though anyone who has ever served over time on any number of committees, either in universities or legislatures, knows that much of the world works this way. We can sometimes reframe the context (redefine the whole educational imperative) and thus, in essence, reframe the way in which we approach the problem. Or we may de-cathect from the problem (I don't care that much, you do, let us do it your way). There are nearly infinite ways to work within contexts when freed from the constraints of an a priori notation, because each situation is slightly different. In such contextual improvisation, we are able to solve problem "b" by drawing on lessons of context "a" without using notational systems.

This is really where creativity comes into play. Some people are better at it, some worse, and some contexts more open to it (think of a successful marriage) than others. Merleau-Ponty describes the following fascinating experience of Matisse painting:

A camera once recorded the work of Matisse in slow motion. The impression was prodigious. That same brush which, seen with the naked eye, leaped from one act to another, was seen to mediate on a solemn and expanding time—in the immanence of a world's creation—to try ten possible movements, dance in front of the canvas, brush it lightly several times, and crash down finally like a lightning stroke upon the one line necessary. Matisse, set within a man's time and vision, looked at the still open whole of his work in progress and brought his brush towards the line which called for it in order that the painting might finally be that which it was in the process of becoming. By a simple gesture he resolved the problem which in retrospect seemed to imply an infinite number of data. And yet, Matisse's hand did hesitate. Consequently there was a choice.[31]

Perhaps creativity is all about choosing well, if not necessarily consciously.

The creation of notational systems, however, predisposes us to think about how to use them to solve concrete problems, which may be a huge mistake if overdone. Notational systems increase efficiency by storing knowledge (no longer evanescent) and allowing its transmission over time and space (no longer local). Developing such systems and relying on them, however, also necessarily reframes reality itself, often with unintended consequences. This would be much less the case if we relied on the improvisational mode of dealing with problems. Yet, relying just on this approach condemns our solutions to the ephemeral and is, consequently, much too time consuming and labor intensive for the liking of most.

At some point, however, the context inevitably makes itself felt. This happens, for example, when we begin to move "down" to context from within the notational mode after our move "up" the notational system. When we move back "downward" after the move up (which, as stated, usually involves invoking more than one notational system), we often contextualize the case before us to such an extent as to make the problem facing us idiosyncratic and hence, in essence, outside notational systems. This is the significance of the example we gave of French/Algonquian relations. Tellingly, this move downward often occurs in the context of those most primary of all human experiences: sex and violence. Such "bracketing out" of notation allows improvisation to play a role, even if it is not admitted as such. Most solutions to concrete problems probably involve something like this process.

In the real world, we never actually solve any problem by relying on notation alone. However, we do almost always invoke notation when we need to legitimize action, or present it to others, or explain it. In this sense, authority rests on notation—whether it is the authority of the state, of science, or of any formal body of knowledge. Yoga may well be practice par excellence, but the different schools offer certification with hours studied and curriculum accomplished, signed by individuals whose names carry weight within their community of practitioners, and so on. As soon as practice and improvisation move beyond performance, some notation and authority are called into play.

Redrawing Boundaries

A grid of action and context, made up of infinite boundaries of possibility can, by its very complexity, temporarily question the very idea of boundaries, which are there and not there at the same time. The pervasiveness and quiddity of boundaries-in-context can make them almost irrelevant in any practical sense (like water for the fish). Like ornament, which in its repetition marks presence and absence at the same time, they too are present (to consciousness) and obscured at the very same time. The normative challenge is to find a way of legitimizing these infinite possibilities and the messiness and muddles that go with them, without turning them into abstract and absolute rules. We could say that the key would be to note them without Notating them.

Such an attempt to reconceptualize boundaries would be crucial, for example, in the case of national and other forms of collective identity. As long as people have lived in communities (that is, from time out of mind) there have been boundaries between these communities. The nature of these boundaries—their relative flexibility, porousness, the extent to which people could exist on those boundaries, and so on—has not, however, been a historical constant. Daniel Boyarin in his important study of *Boundarylines* analyzes the slow and highly negotiated process through which Christianity and Judaism split off into separate civilizational endeavors.[32] The worlds of Al Andalus, of Ottoman Salonike or Edirne, are well-known examples of communities living side by side, not without friction and sometimes with violence, but also with boundaries that were wider, more flexible, and often more porous than those of the high modern nineteenth- and early twentieth-century nation-state. The practice, common through-out many Mediterranean and North African communities, of sharing saint's tombs—between Jews and Muslims (in North Africa and Ottoman Palestine) and between Orthodox Greeks and Muslims (in Crete before World War I) is a fine illustration of such fuzzy boundaries. Even in the early 1950s, as Iraqi Jews made their way to Israel following their expulsion/flight from Iraq, a contingent was caught for close to a year in Irbid in northern Jordan (just south of the Golan Heights). They spent the year praying in the local mosque—despite the 1948 War, the Nakba, and the continuing hostilities between Israel and its Arab neighbors.[33] Such fuzziness and sharing across communal boundaries became impossible with the crystallization of identities in national and statist terms—a process that, while it began with the Peace of Westphalia, became paramount in post-Napoleonic Western Europe. It spread to Central Europe in the mid-century "Springtime of the People" (1848), to the Balkans with the first and second Balkan Wars in the early twentieth century, and to the Middle East with Zionism and the anti-colonial struggles after the end of World War I.

Nationalism and the nation-state redraw boundaries and reconstitute collectivities through a high degree of abstraction and notational interventions: maps, passports, treaties, stamps, bureaucracies, flags, and all the rest. The Peace of Westphalia ended many decades of horrific warfare across intractable religious boundaries, and in the process began to turn a Christian Europe into one of independent national communities. Over time, these new nation-states grew bureaucratized and heavily notated; as their communal identities became ever more highly abstracted and symbolized, they unleashed a murderous force of their own, as the entire history of the twentieth century shows, right up to the horrific wars that accompanied the breakup of Yugoslavia in the 1990s. In such a world, context and experience can be crucial as people attempt to mitigate the dangers of abstraction, even as their own elucidation and development lead invariably along the very same road.

We have seen throughout this chapter that the three modes of dealing with boundaries and ambiguity that we have identified—notation, ritual, and shared experience—are no more than ideal types. Looking at shared experience has shown how much pressure there always is, in both notation and ritual, to adjust to particular contexts. At the same time, contextual behaviors can only be regularized into long-term social resources through ritualization or notation. The interactions among all three are continuous.

Even so, shared experience brings its own characteristic ways of dealing with ambiguity. Reminiscent of ritual, it brackets out many of the boundaries that might otherwise be intractable, and that cause problems for notational modes. Unlike ritual, though, it opens up a nearly infinite tessellation of possible new boundaries, which we can argue over, negotiate, and set into continuous new patterns. In the process it also opens up its own mode of living in time, different from the timeless truths of much notation and from the metered repetitions of ritual. Its rhythms are instead more like the pulse or ocean waves, or the way that two people walking together may gradually begin to match their steps. The rhythm is there: never repeated in exactly the same way twice, always open to the historically unique (hills to climb, rocks to avoid), but also allowing us to bring the wisdom of our previous steps into the path that remains ahead of us.

Our final interlude addresses the tensions of experience and notation. More specifically, our examples, again taken from Jewish and Chinese cultural contexts, illustrate how the thick particularities of life always mediate, often rather severely, the abstract categories of our notational systems. It is not that practice explodes codes or categories, but that it continually mediates them. Codification, notation, and the creation of conceptual distinctions are but one end of a dynamic characterized by the continual abrogation of these distinctions and the creation of new ones or new ways of understanding existing ones. In China we see how the acts of governance tie closely to a recognition of the highly mediated nature of its own legal categories and the endless process of messy negotiation that the workings of context and experience impose. In Judaism we see law almost self-consciously reflecting on itself—aware of the ambiguous nature of the experience that it attempts to order and so mitigating its purported absoluteness in the midst of its very pronouncements.

Interlude: Experience and Multiplicity

THE ARGUMENT FROM context and experience is, not surprisingly, at least as old as Aristotle. In Book V of his *Nicomachean Ethics*, he compares the principles of equity (meaning contextual judgment, as opposed to following a universal rule) to a certain builder's rule used on the island of Lesbos, which—being made of lead—"was not fixed, but adapts itself to the shape of the stone."[1] The rigidities of universal laws and principles could only go so far in providing justice and needed to be adapted to particular circumstances, like the leaden builder's rule on Lesbos. In fact, Book VI of the *Nicomachean Ethics* is devoted to Aristotle's understanding of *phronesis*, which provides a unique type of knowledge, distinct from both theoretical knowledge (*episteme*) and technological, productive know-how (*techne*). A difficult term to understand and translate, often rendered as "prudence," *phronesis* is closer to the prudence-brought-on-by-experience-of-the-particular. It bears a strong family resemblance to the argument that we are making here for contextual knowledge.

Theoretical knowledge was, for Aristotle, something very close to our idea of notation; it was "ideal, a-temporal and necessary"—like the principles of geometry, for example.[2] To these he contrasts practical knowledge, that is, knowledge that is "concrete, temporal and presumptive." Theoretical reason begins with universal premises and works down to particulars, while practical reasoning begins with concrete problems, avoids formal deductions, and seeks reasonable correspondences between the problem at hand and similar, past circumstances as guides to action. In Aristotle's own words:

> It is apparent that prudence is not scientific knowledge, for . . . it concerns the last thing [i.e., the particular], since this is what is achievable in action. Hence it is opposite to understanding. For

understanding is about the [first] terms, [those] that have no account of them, but prudence is about the last thing, the object of
perception, not of scientific knowledge.[3]

Scientific knowledge, that is, theory, is for Aristotle totally abstract and
general with no worldly relevance, while prudence (*phronesis*) is eminently
practical and action-oriented.

He divides practical knowledge into two kinds: together with *phronesis*,
Aristotle counted *techne* as a form of practical knowledge. Technical knowledge is the ability to synthesize former experience into workable precepts
to produce good effects. Technical knowledge is productive, tied to the act
of making (*poiesis*) rather than to action per se (*praxis*), which is in the
realm of *phronesis*. An excellent technician is one who can instantiate general rules (of carpentry, say) in different circumstances. The expert technician can construct general rules from past experience and bring them to
bear on new ones—in the manner of any accomplished craftsman. *Phronesis*, however, takes us some ways beyond this form of knowledge. This is
because *phronesis* grows out of and reflects back on experience without
solidifying it into general laws. It is, to quote Joseph Dunne, "a perfected
form of experience in that it is the virtue which makes the experience of
some people not just the accumulated systematization of their past actions and impressions but a dynamic orientation to bring this systematization into play and allow it to be tested by present circumstances, to draw
from it what is relevant and to see where it does not fit—in the former case
consolidating it and in the latter extending or modifying it."[4] Phronesis is
less a set of general rules and more an orientation toward action and so
toward new forms of particular experiences.

Code and Commentary

This orientation toward the particular, which defines the action-oriented
forms of knowledge, lies at the heart of our argument on experience. As opposed to the linguistic analysis of Basil Bernstein, who saw the context-bound
as inherently limited and limiting, we are claiming that the context-bound
may also provide an experiential richness that constitutes not only its own
form of knowledge, but following Aristotle, its own virtue as well.[5] Ambiguity here is neither denied as in notation, nor "précised" as in ritual, but is
rather continually negotiated in the endless profusion of new experiences, a
mosaic of boundaries, rather than their binary or relativized representation.[6]

To play this role, however, experience must be rich and deep. Aristotle himself says that young men cannot be wise in *phronesis*, for they have not been around long enough to accumulate the necessary amount of experience.[7] Context requires time, and time becomes experience through narrative. It is thus not surprising that for Robert Cover narrative played a constitutive role in informing (and sometimes, in pluralistic societies, challenging) the most normative and notated orders of society, that is, their legal systems. Cover's seminal essay on "Nomos and Narrative" showed us how legal orders exist within much more extensive temporal and narrative frameworks of communal meaning and belonging that make up an embracing *nomos* of which law is but one element. These narratives, he taught, locate and contextualize the law and give it meaning. In his words: "For every constitution there is an epic, for each Decalogue a scripture."[8] And it is these narratives, he argues, that make the law "not merely a system of rules to be observed, but a world in which we live."[9] Narratives, no less than law codes, he shows, establish "lexicons of normative action" and paradigms for behavior.[10]

After developing this argument, Cover goes on to show that the existence of very different interpretive communities within a single *corpus juris* can lead to continual contestations and widely divergent understandings of what had been assumed to be a shared *nomos*. Divergent narrative traditions—that is to say, the divergent experiences and contexts (of the Amish, or the Church of Latter Day Saints, for example) lead to very different understandings of the normative or legal order. Without shared experience, the *nomos* is but a system of rules and not a world.

Cover argues that the move from rules (norm) to *nomos* must involve context and experience. Sharing *nomos* must involve shared experience, and so a shared narrative as well. That is why his descriptions of such a shared narrative draw richly on religious groups (both historical and contemporary) and their narratives of the *longue durée*. As he points out:

The divinely ordered normative corpus, common ritual, and strong interpersonal obligations that together form the basis of such a paideic legal order may indeed be potent. They combine to create precepts and principles enough to fill our lives, as well as to fit those precepts into the common narratives locating the social group in relation to the cosmos, to its neighbors, to the natural world. The precepts, then, not only are there—they are also infused with the full range of connotation that only an integrated set of narratives can provide.[11]

The ritual component is important in binding norms to *nomos*, obligations of "ought" to those of "Ought," and so in the creation of the shared subjunctive that stands at the foundation of so much of our sociability. Shared ritual binds disparate elements by mediating the tension between them. In the broadest of terms, there is always a tension between the terms of a legal order—of abstract justice—and the demands of community and shared narrative. This is not simply the tension between justice and equity that Aristotle discussed, but is closer to that between truth and trust. All legal systems serve both masters—or perhaps mediate between them. There is, as all would agree, a demand for truth, and an understanding that justice requires ascertaining the "facts" of the case at hand. Together with the demand for truth, there may, however, also be a complementary demand to maintain the bonds of solidarity and community within society—trust. This need to maintain community does not always square with a straightforward demand for truth, especially when understood in the most abstract and general terms.

Jewish law, for example, clearly recognizes that justice, without the quality of what we are calling "trust," is a dangerous entity; it splits mountains and can destroy human well-being. Justice must be mediated with peace—a mediation that is achieved through compromise, which is always the preferred mode of resolution of differences, rather than any appeal to "pure" justice. Peace in this context means social peace—the maintenance of the bonds of mutual well-being and solidarity that make human society possible.[12] Justice—abstract, cold, avenging justice—is a quality of God and thus not always advisable for mere mortals to dabble in. The more commonplace distinction between justice and mercy is roughly a subset of that between truth and trust. It is one form among many through which the contradictions and tensions between truth and trust work themselves out.

A second mediation—one within the textual corpus itself—mirrors the continual mediation of abstract justice by the needs of empathy and community. This is the mediation of what may be called "code" by "commentary"—not too distant from Cover's ideas of *nomos* and narrative. Within the Jewish legal corpus, this has been developing for close to two millennia, from the very origins of legal codification in the Mishnah. Given a continual push toward notation and codification, there has been, over the centuries, an equally strong counter-push toward commentary, toward greater and greater contextualization of the code, and its mediation by the citation of alternative rulings, divergent explanations, minority decisions, and an expansive amplification of possibilities beyond those codified. In the telling words of Isadore Twersky:

> Attempts to compress the Halachah by formal codification alternate with counter-attempts to preserve the fullness and richness of both the method and substance of the Halachah by engaging in interpretation, analogy, logical inference, and only then formulating the resultant normative conclusion. Any student who follows the course of rabbinic literature from Geonic works of the eighth century through the Mishneh Torah and Turim and on down to the Shulkan 'Aruk cannot ignore this see-saw tendency. The tension is ever present and usually catalytic. No sooner is the need for codification met than a wave of non-codificatory work rises. A code could provide guidance and certitude for a while but not finality. . . . A code, even in the eyes of its admirers, required vigilant explanation and judicious application.[13]

While codes, such as that of Maimonides, sought to eliminate divergent rulings and interpretations, commentary thrived on the never-ending addition of context, detail, and the plethora of conflicting explanations and interpretations. Maimonides sought in his code to abstract purely formulated behavioral norms from the Talmud. This attempt, however, downplayed the problem that these can become a shared world only by being embedded in their contexts. Maimonides sought to excise precisely those more contextual parts of the Talmud from the curricula of study.[14] In just the same way, the utility of major codes such as Joseph Karo's *Shulkan 'Aruk*, which to this day remains normative, did not prevent them from being questioned and seen by many as giving too short a shrift to the often "incommunicable values and aspirations of religious experience and spiritual existence."[15] What made this debate possible and prevented it from ultimately leading to the growth of communal schism—to what is termed "two toroth" (literally, "two laws")? We suggest that as radically divergent as were the understandings of the role of a code in the practice of Judaism, the practice of ritual and its shared experience united all parties to the dispute. This itself mediates the purely abstract nature of any code, as we saw in the article by Haym Soloveitchik as quoted in chapter 4. True, the debate over Maimonides's *Mishneh Torah* was especially virulent and was part of a much broader debate over the role of philosophy that pitted various Jewish communities in southern France, Spain, and Ashkenaz against one another.[16] But such tensions both predated the Maimonidean controversy and outlived it. They are an integral part of that particularly Jewish communal narrative within which the *nomos* is grounded. The thick bonds of shared ritual are themselves an interpretation and contextualization of code, even as the continuing and collective study of commentary provides both armature and ornament for both.

The myriad ways that context and experience mediate notation reach well beyond the dynamics internal to any one tradition. The experience of shared context—of living side by side, sharing neighborhoods, business deals, and public spaces—has historically imposed its own logic of mediation. The needs of the hour have, again and again, greatly circumscribed the course of strict notation, as have the contexts of lives shared across different notational systems.

Jewish legal texts dealing with the legitimacy and illegitimacy of Gentile courts (*arka'ot shel goyim*) offer a potentially rich arena for viewing this dynamic. While Jewish law, from the Amoraic period onward, has included the dictum of *dina d'malkhuta dina* (the law of the state is the law), the understanding, circumscription, interpretation, and enactment of this legal principle has varied in different periods.[17] Generations of legal theorists from the seventh century until today have debated how, for example, to accept its implications in principle without losing the specificity of the Jewish legal system. Does the law pertain only to matters between the king and his subjects (and not, for example, in matters of torts or family law)? Is it restricted to matters of taxation, punishment, or eminent domain?

Further complications arise in matters of contracts. Contracts drawn up in Gentile courts are valid in Jewish law, with the exception of divorce decrees and the manumission of slaves. Yet the scope of these exceptions and their meaning has been understood very differently at different times and in different places of the Jewish diaspora. Jewish legal decisors continually debated and contested all these matters and more from early medieval into modern times. The generally accepted view—as evinced clearly in the legal codes of Moses Maimonides (*Mishneh Torah*), Jacob b. Asher (*Ba'al HaTurim*), Joseph Karo (*Shulkan 'Aruk*), and others— makes clear that recourse to Gentile courts is prohibited in the strictest of fashions. Yet a closer reading of texts and commentaries mediates this harsh view. The very different sets of extenuating circumstances, exceptions to the rule, and principled recognition of non-Jewish courts add a complexity to the binary view that has dominated much of medieval and modern understandings.

For example, in matters of damages, recourse to a Gentile court is, in the general run of things, strictly forbidden. Such recourse is likened to a revolt against and desecration of the Law of Moses. Yet, despite this rhetoric, the prohibition appears to rest more on an incongruity of procedure between Gentile and Jewish courts than—as is so often assumed—a categorical condemnation of Gentile judicial systems. This is because in Jewish courts two witnesses are needed to effect the transfer of property from defendant to claimant, while in Gentile courts one witness is sufficient. In those situations where Jewish law admits the evidence of one witness only (as in the case of a witness for the defense), a Jew is permitted to give testimony in a Gentile court because in such a case the requirements of Jewish law are satisfied.[18] Here then we can see the interesting possibilities of how different legal systems may accommodate one another when forced to by the context of their shared experiential world.

In a similar manner, a close and comparative reading of rulings about contracts that specify their possible adjudication by Gentile courts raises very probing questions as to how the Halachic system viewed the system of Gentile courts and their potential role in disputes between Jews. These rulings reject such adjudications, but in subtly different ways, and with different emphases. Somewhat surprisingly, at certain points and among certain decisors, there seems to be a willingness to adopt (or accede to) discrete non-Jewish practices, such as the swearing in of witnesses, which was a Christian practice that certain Jewish communities, perhaps out of ignorance, accepted as the law. In such circumstances, these decisors argued, Jewish courts could admit these practices.[19]

All such features of the law, as well as the exceptions to the blanket prohibition on Gentile courts (the most important being the permission to go to Gentile courts when dealing with a man of known violent inclinations) lead us to believe that we are looking at a number of critical mechanisms of accommodation and even (partial) legitimation of at least certain aspects of a foreign notational system. Such alien notations can thus become useful and possibly transferable to other legal systems at other times. While much further study is necessary to support this claim, it is clear from study of *responsa* literature, Rabbinic court records, and communal legislation (*takkanot ha-kahal*) that at least by the late eighteenth century, and in a departure from the late medieval period, the relationship of Rabbinic courts and Gentile ones tended to be cooperative.

For example, recent research by Jay Berkovitz has illustrated this adaptive capacity of Jewish culture, through his investigation of the relationship of the Metz Rabbinic court to the French judiciary in the latter part of the eighteenth century. Containing nearly 1,200 cases, the Rabbinic court register brims with details of commercial transactions, family law, and modes of jurisprudence.[20] The authority to adjudicate civil cases was very salient in Jewish communal life prior to the nineteenth century. The main focus of his study is the procedural cooperation between Jewish and general courts and the precise strategies for navigating between the competing jurisdictions of the two systems. In Metz, the Jews encountered the challenges of legal pluralism on a daily basis, and they met these challenges by adapting to the prevailing system of law. Their efforts were predicated on the idea of legal centralism, that is, the theory that foreign systems must subordinate themselves to state law. Prior to the Revolution, and with the encouragement of the state, law functioned as a homogenizing force. The result was a powerful impulse to coordinate with the French legal system, and although there are no signs of either coercive pressure or capitulation, this was felt keenly in every area involving monetary exchange and contractual interaction. The integration of Jews into a unified legal system was not synonymous with civil-political equality, nor did it confer freedom from prejudice. However, as Berkovitz has shown, the realm of law offered Jews a framework from which emerged rules of engagement between the Jewish minority and the surrounding society and culture.

Thin Disguises and Local Governance

Context-driven adjustments between two or more quite different notational systems illustrate how dialogue between notational code and contextual commentary has allowed people to live together in spite of their different traditions. In addition, however, very different forms of contextual ambiguity may be at work, even within a society organized around a single regulatory code. China's history has many cases in which the state insists on a unity of rules and a single narrative. Nevertheless, local officials and residents find ways around them, as long as people disguise their activities enough to give local officials the ability to say that the laws are being implemented, and as long as local officials are willing to rule with "one eye open and one eye closed," as the common Chinese metaphor puts it. That is, the notational rule is clear and accepted by all, but like the "leaden rule" that Aristotle described, bends greatly to fit the shape of particular contexts.

There is an old adage in China: "hanging up a sheep's head but selling dog meat" (*gua yangtou mai gourou*). It speaks to more than just false advertising, where a butcher announces that he is selling mutton, but instead has only dog meat, which is much cheaper and less prestigious. The customers know perfectly well that they are buying dog, so in a sense there is nothing "false" about the advertising. Instead, they want to buy their cheap, low-prestige meat in a way that allows them to save face. Butcher and customers alike can claim the benefits of acting as if they were buying and selling mutton, even though everyone knows it is something else altogether.

Something similar characterizes many aspects of governance in China today (and in Taiwan, especially before its democratization after 1987). We will discuss religious examples in particular, although it is also true in other realms. For roughly a century, under both Communist and Nationalist rule (and even under Japanese colonial rule from 1895 to 1945 in Taiwan), China's legal system has guaranteed nominal freedom of religion, but with severe restrictions in practice. First, under European legal influence, religions were defined along roughly Protestant lines, as voluntarily joined systems of belief with sacred texts and trained clergy. Confucianism was ruled out, as was most of the local-level worship in small temples and on home altars. The remaining religions were to be organized on roughly corporatist lines, each with a centralized administration closely tied to state supervision. That list in China today includes only five legal religions: Buddhism, Daoism, Islam, Protestantism, and Catholicism. All temples, mosques, and churches must register through the appropriate national association. This notational system of regulation makes it extremely difficult to practice local popular religion, which was regularly condemned as "feudal superstition" until recently. Probably several hundred million people nevertheless take part in such activities at least a few times in the course of a year. It has also caused great difficulty for tens of millions of Catholics and Protestants who reject state control over their churches and ordinations.

The result in many cases has been a kind of governance by turning a blind eye, a mutually agreed-upon hypocrisy in which people hang up a sheep's head of respectability for the state to see, but everyone knows that the meat is actually dog. One rather early but well-documented example stems back to the first decades of the Japanese occupation of Taiwan (1895–1945). Chinese almost everywhere hold a major ritual in the seventh lunar month—the Universal Salvation (Pudu)—to feed the hungry ghosts who are released from the underworld at that time. During the late nine-teenth century, Taiwanese (like some other Chinese on the mainland) in-cluded something called "robbing the lonely ghosts" in which unattached young men would compete to retrieve flags and offerings placed at the top of very tall bamboo poles. As a contemporary missionary observer described it:

> A very unspiritual mob—thousands and thousands of hungry beg-gars, tramps, blacklegs, desperadoes of all sorts, from the country towns, the city slums, or venturing under cover of night from their hiding-places among the hills—surged and swelled in every part of the open space. . . . Screaming, cursing, howling, like demons of the pit, they all joined in the onset. . . . It was a very bedlam, and the wildness of the scene was enhanced by the irregular explosion of firecrackers and the death-groan of someone worsted in the fray.[21]

The Japanese rulers were not fond of this sort of chaos, and made this particular custom (but not the Universal Salvation as a whole) illegal. In at least one township, villagers told local officials that they would comply. Not only that, as loyal subjects of the Japanese emperor, on the day of the ritual they would substitute an athletic competition as part of the new Japanese emphasis on physical education. The particular competition they held set teams of young men against each other to climb tall bamboo poles and retrieve flags and other offerings at the top.[22] In other words, they kept doing exactly what they had done before, but called it something else. Was the government fooled by this? Almost surely not, because the govern-ment offices in this town are just a few minutes walk from the temple plaza where the ritual took place, and many of its employees, even under colonialism, were local people.

Such techniques of diplomatic hypocrisy—I will pretend this is an ath-letic competition if you will pretend to believe me—occur over and over again. Something almost identical happened after the Nationalists retook Taiwan in 1945, and campaigned against the superstition and waste of popular religion, just as the Japanese had. In this case, they tried to dis-courage people from offering whole pigs as sacrifices on the birthdays of their most important deities. In one town, the custom was for people to try to raise the fattest pigs possible, and the most enormous ten—pigs so big they could not stand up or even roll over—had the right to be displayed in front of the temple. As the government campaign began, the response in this town was again to announce acquiescence and this time to substitute an agricultural competition. The ten fattest pigs—now claimed to represent the farmers with the most advanced agricultural practices rather than the most pious believers—were honored in front of the temple. Once again, the local people did not actually fool anyone, but just offered up this very thin disguise in exchange for local officials turning a blind eye.[23]

In 2007, when one of us was interviewing people elsewhere in Taiwan, one township official said that they had a full list of all local temples, along with information about founding dates, major deities, and so on. When asked if they would share a copy, the various officials in the room looked at each other rather sheepishly and finally said "no." Many of the temples, they explained, had never registered with the government, even though registration was legally required. As officials, if they knew about all those temples, they would have to enforce the law. Sharing the results of their research, they felt, counted as admitting that they "knew." Both eyes would have been open, and the status quo of ruling by turning a blind eye would have been broken.[24]

Mainland China today does this so systematically that it makes sense to think of it as a mode of governance. Perhaps the most obvious example in the religious realm is the Christian "house church" movement. House churches refer broadly to those congregations, both Protestant and Catholic, that have refused the authority of the state-approved corporatist structures for their religions. As unregistered religious groups, they exist outside the law and could in principle be repressed at any time. Nevertheless, these are the religious groups that have grown most rapidly in China, especially the Protestants. They now outnumber members of official churches by very roughly three or four to one, accounting for tens of millions of people. They were severely repressed during the Cultural Revolution, but the last 30 years of reform have seen a general trend for the local government to look the other way. As a result, there is no longer anything underground about these groups—many have built large churches in major cities, clearly marked with a cross, and attracting hundreds of worshippers each week.

We see something very similar in local temple religion, which is equally outside the law. One Hong Kong–based spirit medium, for instance, raises money to build new temples in the mainland. When she comes for their opening ceremonies, she coordinates with local officials, who are then able to make sure that they are away on business during the ritual.[25] There are also several documented cases in which local people in China have raised money for temple reconstruction by telling officials that they are building a museum of local culture, and telling local residents that they are building a temple.[26] In one such case, a sign at one side of the entrance proclaims "Museum of Dragon Culture" and one on the other side says "Temple to the Dragon King." As in the Taiwanese cases, there is no possibility that local officials were actually misled by techniques like not registering a church while meeting in a large building with a big cross on it, or burning incense and praying in a "museum."

This kind of thing can occur at the national level as well. For example, in 2009 one of us asked a monk who was involved in one of the most important Buddhist charitable foundations in China—the Ren'ai Foundation—how they had registered, given that religions were not supposed to carry out non-religious activities like charity. He explained that they simply had not registered as Buddhists, but instead asked some lay followers to register the group with the Civil Affairs Bureau as an ordinary non-governmental organization (NGO). When they go to give aid, as after the devastating Sichuan earthquake in 2008, they do not use Buddhist symbols on their banners and other information, but he said that they make sure to have clergy there so that people make the association. Their web site makes no effort at all to hide the Buddhist connection. In fact, many thousands of NGOs in China (both religious and not) have registrations that are not strictly legal. Some register as for-profit businesses, because it is so much easier. Some register with an inappropriate organization. Others do not register at all.

For NGOs, just as for the temples and churches, officials are calculating that they have something to gain by feigning blindness toward these developments. In particular, they realize that such groups offer many important services (old age care, as just one example), can provide independent sources of information to the government (like environmental monitoring), and have close ties to local social structures (especially true for local temples).

If these compromises are so useful for both state and society, why not simply change the laws and regulations? Some of the reasons are unique to China's history and current politics. Without democracy, there are only very limited forms of feedback through which popular pressure might lead to changes in the law. In these particular cases, where relatively non-confrontational means have been found in order to live with the situation, there is little pressure at all. In addition, a freeing up of the registration procedure for religions or NGOs may imply more room for an independent civil society than China is currently willing to risk.

Other reasons that people choose to live with hypocrisy, however, are much more widely shared with other places. One need only think of prostitution in most Western countries. The practice is illegal in the great majority of them, but is tolerated in some forms in all of them. The reason is that the law is being used as a statement of moral principles rather than as a necessity for social control. Governance through hypocrisy can sometimes have the extremely useful social effect of allowing us to proclaim certain moral values while actually dealing with life in its particular contexts. Being earnest may not always be so important.

Much of the literature on China interprets the sorts of behavior we have been describing as either resistance against the state (e.g., house churches) or collusion.[27] That is, most scholars see contextual hypocrisy purely as refracted through the lens of notation: either as the conscious challenge to a rule, or as a competition between two different sets of rules. Instead, we are suggesting that it might be more fruitfully understood through the pragmatic lens of shared experience. This is not a story about justice or rule of law, but instead about Aristotle's "equity" and his leaden rule.

The kinds of context-bound compromises that we have been discussing are inherently unofficial, ad hoc, and informal. They rely on winks and nudges in a way that cannot function if they are formalized into the notational realm. That is why "don't ask, don't tell" has been such a problematic policy for dealing with homosexuality in the U.S. military: as soon as you announce it as formal policy, you have "told." Because these arrangements are ad hoc, they will not necessarily generalize across a country as large and varied as China. We know of situations where one township might turn a blind eye to house churches, while the one right next door might repress them according to the letter of the law.

Such situations thus have an inherent instability over time and space. A change from the top leadership could lead to sudden enforcement of the law, or a local official could simply decide to make an example of a particular group by arresting its leaders or cracking down in other ways. For the official, this might send a message to other groups about how far they can push, or it could simply be a way of harassing an enemy. As a form of governance, turning a blind eye has the advantages of offering enormous flexibility in context, in a system otherwise known for its rigidity. Yet it also creates tensions of its own, and thus has its own modes of repression.

Turning a blind eye is another form of bracketing out some aspects of the situation. In this case, obvious bits of behavior are set aside (like big

unregistered congregations meeting openly) or weakly claimed to be
something else (like an athletic or agricultural competition). All bracketing like this is subject to accusations of hypocrisy. We can see this most
clearly in religious reactions against ritualization, like the Calvinist critique of Catholicism, or Mozi's early critique of Confucian ritual as a point-
less waste of money and time. In the cases under discussion here, the
tension with hypocrisy is especially powerful because the bracketing is so
open and so improvised. We are not dealing with rituals, after all, but with
recent, ad hoc, and constantly changing adaptations to particular contexts.

As with the subjunctive worlds that rituals create, however, the artificial conventionality—in these cases, something close to a simple lie—is
not really a problem. As Roy Rappaport argued for ritual, the point of subjunctive artifice is not to express facts (or lies) about the world, but to
express one's acceptance of the convention.[28] Unlike ordinary acts of
resistance, calling the ghost ritual an athletic contest goes on the public
record as full acceptance of government policy. This use of shared experience to cross the boundary between state and society allows people to live
with a great deal of ambiguity in practice, even as they claim obedience to
the rules.

On the other hand, such solutions are also inherently unstable. Because
the hypocrisy is so close to the surface and because occasional repression
is so much a part of the system, there is a lot of pressure against ritualizing them very much. Unlike ritual proper, the techniques of governing
with a blind eye cannot recur forever. They exist less in the endless repetitions of rhythmic time than in the pulse of history, always subject to
changing constraints and renegotiations. Their inherent instability is not
necessarily a problem, however, because it is also the key to their use as a
positive mode of governance, a way for people and officials to find ways to
work together.

Conclusion

At the beginning of the twentieth century, Clemenceau famously declared
that *la révolution est un bloc*. By this he meant that one could not disaggre-
gate the values of human rights, secularism, democracy, and republi-
canism, which together represented the unified and coherent inheritance
of the revolution of 1789. All were part and parcel of the same general and
generalizable system of abstract ideals. Today, we know better. We know
that democratic elections can bring to power militant and repressive

theocratic regimes. It is also clear that religious elites and parties are not necessarily anti-democratic or opposed to human rights. We know, too, that secularism per se is no guarantee of peaceful relations between nations or the enactment of human rights. In short, it is evident that modernity can mean many things in different places and at different times, so that it seldom resembles an integrally woven skein of meanings, commitments, and value orientations. Again and again, local historical contexts have given the lie to more abstract systems of meaning.

This reality, together with the effects of globalization, the enmeshing of worldwide economies, the massive movements of population across the world (including the growth in Europe of its non-Christian populace), and the intermixing of various ideologies of post-modernism, have all led to a questioning of conventional understandings in the social and historical sciences, political thought, religious studies, literature, and law. Scholars of law have expressed this in the growing recognition that the centrism characterizing the legal order of the state was much more problematic than it was once thought to be. We see this in different ways in both the Jewish and Chinese examples we have discussed in this interlude.

With the growth of the nation-state during the nineteenth century, and with the extension of its power and hegemony over ever more arenas of human action and interaction, the law of the state came to be seen as the only source of legally valid normative orders. The legal system of the state attained its apogee in positivistic legal thought, procedural in nature, which made nary a claim to transcendent, revelatory, or otherwise otherworldly or ultimate sources of authority. In very dissimilar ways and in accordance with widely different political imperatives, both Carl Schmitt and Hans Kelsen have been major theorists of this approach.[29]

This picture began to change about a quarter of a century ago. The publication of Robert Cover's "Nomos and Narrative" made clear the existence of very different "interpretive communities" within the boundaries of the nation-state that did not necessarily share the same "narrative" of meaning-giving order that was represented in and through the legal codes of the state.[30] At roughly the same time, the idea of legal pluralism began to take root. It argued for the existence within one country of multiple legal orders and normative frameworks—of communities that regulated their lives according to different (often hierarchically ordered) sets of legal criteria, not all of which could be subsumed within the logic of the law of the state. This was, of course, the state of affairs before the emergence of the modern nation-state and recalls the examples we presented above of Jewish law dealing with and at times accepting Gentile jurisdiction.

Debates abound within the literature devoted to legal pluralism over the existence of weak and strong forms of pluralism. Weak legal pluralism here indicates the delegation by the state of a particular area of legal adjudication to a system of law that is autonomous of state principles and codes. The existence of Rabbinic courts or Muslim Sharia courts in Europe and North America are examples of this type of legal pluralism in which the state, while granting a certain degree of legal autonomy to an alternative system, ultimately maintains its hegemony. Thus, one can marry according to Jewish ritual law, but what makes the marriage legally valid is the signing of a certificate issued by the secular authorities. Strong legal pluralism implies the de facto existence of alternative legal orders, which are responsible for compliance by a certain populace and which exist independent of the state's legitimizing mechanisms (if not, of course, of its coercive force). The debates over strong and weak forms of legal pluralism, their social correlates, and especially their prescriptive dimensions have only intensified following the events of September 11, 2001, and the increased argument over Islam in Europe, Sharia courts, the veiling of women, polygamy, and so on. The arguments presented here and in the previous chapter suggest that these debates have much to gain from looking more seriously at context and experience, rather than only at shared notation.

Consider, for example, the case for the Islamic presence in Europe, which has evoked serious debate concerning the legal orders of EU member states. How current European law can or cannot accommodate Islam and Islamic practices (from family law, to dietary restrictions, to personal codes of behavior) has already generated a vast and important literature. This issue has become one of the major challenges facing legal theorists, policy makers, and religious leaders in today's world in the form of the problem of legal pluralism, that is, the coexistence within distinct nation-states of vastly different interpretations and understandings of what were once viewed as a unified and coherent frame of worldviews and normative orders. In some cases in Europe, a pragmatic and ground-up approach, flexible and context-rich, emerging from the experiences of a shared life, is coming to replace reliance on notational absolutes as we come to mediate the boundaries between increasingly ritualized communities in worlds once assumed to be secular and sincere. Thus, for example, Dutch law now recognizes *kafala* "parentage," a Moroccan form of family living that is not formal adoption, but is currently sufficient to allow family subsidies under the Child Benefit Act. Similarly, the increasing legitimacy of the "cultural defense" argument in courts throughout Europe and the Americas points to a growing awareness to the importance of local particularities, and to the experience of difference in adjudicating wide varieties of cases, even within criminal law.[31]

Such an approach focuses knowledge on particularities and hence on what is, in essence, experience. In this, it calls to mind John Dewey's strictures on experience, which he taught is the central component in thinking. "To learn from experience" he tells us, "is to make a backward and forward connection between what we do to things and what we enjoy and suffer from things in consequence. Under such conditions, doing becomes a trying; an experiment with the world to find out what it is like."[32] In this process, we cannot separate the intellect from experience. Indeed, the attempt to force such separation leaves us with disembodied, abstract knowledge that all too often emphasizes things rather than the relations or connections between them.[33] Such knowledge, however, offers little help in our attempt to connect the multitude of disconnected data that the world presents into a framework of meaning. Meaning rests not on the knowledge of "things" but on the relations between them, that is, between us. We can assess these relations, as Dewey argued, only through experience, because only through experience do we bring the relevant relations between things into any sensible sort of juxtaposition.

In the construction of a shared social world, which includes those who are different, challenging, unknown and even threatening, we benefit from being open to experience, rather than falling back on preconceived ideas and abstract forms of knowledge. We must enter a process that can only be realized through a slow, cumulative and not always conscious process of straddling the boundaries of our existing and developing modes of thought through the challenges of shared action—of embodied experience. In so doing, we may come to recognize the only partial, fragile, mutable, and heavily freighted nature of the interpretive and notational frames that we bring to our experiences, even as we overcome them in our newly shared human encounters.

Conclusion

CONSTRUCTING CATEGORIES IS one of the fundamental skills that make up our human capacity for culture. We cannot speak without a language that divides the world into categories, just as we cannot function socially without some concepts of role and personhood. Some scholars describe this as a way of making order out of the underlying ambiguities of experience, just as stories from many peoples around the world describe creation as an act of ordering a primordial chaos. It may be just as useful to turn this around, however. Ambiguity is possible only because categories exist, and it cannot be conceptualized except through and in contrast to categories. In other words, ambiguity and order are permanently intertwined. Because our categories, rules, and orders are all constructed—always too abstract and too concrete at the same time, as we argued in chapter 1—ambiguities threaten to undermine them, and we can never fully avoid this danger. Yet we cannot live without putting some order on the world. The problem that we have been exploring is how to live with ambiguity while still retaining order.

This issue pervades human life, but we have been especially interested in one crucial aspect of it: How can we live with people who differ from us in some fundamental ways? At an individual level, the process of distinguishing self from other has seen a great deal of attention from psychologists. The social version of the question, however, seems increasingly pressing in the current world. How can social groups live together peacefully, even though they may not share even traits that they see as basic to human nature or national character (eating rice, bathing every day, speaking English, wearing clothes that button, accepting Jesus)? The line between social self and other nearly always worries people because the difference threatens to undermine so much that we can otherwise take for granted as normal. At the same time, however, we always share a great deal with any human other. The boundary is ambiguous.

For many people in the contemporary world, the first resort to resolve problematic ambiguity seems to be the creation of new categories and new rules. We see this in self-improvement manuals, like how to cure dependence in 12 steps, or become a better manager by following 10 (or 100, or 365) simple rules. It appears again in pop psychological advice to parents that they just have to set clear boundaries in order to raise good children. And again in the attempt to legislate solutions to inevitable ambiguities that arise as technologies and social habits change, for instance in privacy rights after electronic communications became common. One need only glance at the gargantuan Federal Register to see this in action. The constant push to litigate, especially in the United States, is part of this as well. Litigation works to create legal precedents to disambiguate issues of law, to solve the inherent ambiguities of all rules by making more rules in the form of legal precedents.

This job of making new rules and new categories to occupy the ambiguous spaces never ends because it cannot ultimately succeed. This is not simply because every new category has a new ambiguity at its edges. It is also because rules and categories—what we have been calling notation—tend toward the universal, toward a claim of validity in all times and places. They are written in stone, sometimes literally. The world, however, is not. Everything varies across space and time. That is, true and total repetition is impossible, as we discussed in chapter 3. Systems of rules and categories decontextualize by their nature. We need them exactly because they allow us to generalize across times and contexts. And yet, history happens anyway. Notation can never be complete, and we thus constantly have to inscribe new stones. Notation's escape from the fetters of space and time is both its advantage and its weakness. Categories and rules give us the crucial ability to generalize, but they are never adequate for any particular context.

We frequently use notational mechanisms to address problems of social difference. People sometimes use it to forbid any kind of difference, as with ethnic cleansing. Sometimes difference is allowed in private but forbidden in public behavior, as in current European movements to ban the Muslim head scarf. Sometimes it is allowed in public, too, for instance where alternative legal systems are allowed to exist in some countries. Every single one of these mechanisms, however, also absolutizes difference. At its most horrific, notation has purified the boundary through mass murder. At its most generous, it guarantees certain rights to be different. Either way, however, creates a rock-hard boundary around the group, a brick wall with no room for ambiguity or variation. We can see this at its most ludicrous, perhaps, in an earlier American attempt to titrate "race" into ever finer ranges—dividing people into quadroons and octoroons, or dividing new European immigrants into Slavic, Baltic, Hungarian, Irish, Hebrew, and a host of other races.

One of our most important goals in writing this book has been to highlight alternative ways of thinking about boundaries and ambiguity. There may be many of these, but we have concentrated on two that seem both important and revealing about the range of possibilities: ritual and shared experience. Each of them deals in a different way with boundaries and with the closely related problem of time and history.

Ritual, we have argued, is like notation in the sense that it both creates and accepts boundaries. Notation as an ideal type tells us how to live within those boundaries, but in this sense ritual is completely different: it always takes us across boundaries. Rituals are alternative moments that bring us temporarily into another state. This includes the liminal period often discussed for rites of passage, but is true just as much for calendrical rites, like the example of the Chinese lunar New Year, mentioned in chapter 3, in which families gather to present themselves as an imagined whole that may not exist on any other occasion. Even the moment of shaking hands or saying "please" marks the imagination of a special state that may not exist in other contexts. If notation is parallel to simple indicative statements of fact, then rituals are like metaphors in their ability to make difference productive.

Scholarly analysis usually concentrates on the processes and symbols within particular rituals, but the inevitable boundary crossing becomes clear only when we see rituals in the broader flow of life. There is a tick for every tock, an absence for every presence. That is, in addition to all the other possible ways in which rituals may involve negotiation across boundaries, we must cross into and out of every performance of a ritual subjunctive.

Ritual, in other words, impels a flow of time in a way that notation need not. Any boundary crossing implies movement over time, from point A now to point B later. Ritual regularizes this through conventionalized repetitions—the constructed and shared rhythms that we have been calling "meter." Ritual creates time, in the sense that its shared meters allow people to feel that the world is not total chaos, that what happened before can reliably happen again, that we share a past and potentially a future. This is a critical prerequisite for any sense of trust, without which the prospect of crossing the boundary to accept the Other seems doomed. Ritual requires and creates that past and future in a way that notation does not. The regular flow of time, with its rhythmic ritual interludes, itself carries us across boundaries of all kinds. Notation can define boundaries that exist without time, but we cannot cross them without the passage of time. Ritual supplies this and thus allows for the negotiation across difference. It opens the door for a pluralism that allows us to penetrate boundaries, even as we accept them. In that sense, ritualization creates the potential for an openness that is far more difficult to achieve under notation alone.

Even though ritual accomplishes this, in part, through its shaping of time, it still does not offer a truly historical time. That is, ritual's meter resembles notation in its relative inflexibility in the face of the inevitable drifts, conflicts, and transformations of real time. This is one reason that nearly every strong ritual tradition has been met by criticism that its repetitions are meaningless hypocrisy, out of touch with personal and social reality. Such critiques are sometimes met with reworked rituals to make them more fitting (as with Zhu Xi's neo-Confucianism), and sometimes with anti-ritual reactions (as with Buddhism's critique of Hinduism, Christianity's of Judaism, Protestantism's of Catholicism, and so on).

Of the three ways of ordering ambiguity that we have discussed, only the third—shared experience—dwells in the unpredictable variations of life in their full historical complexity. We are thinking especially of those occasions in which people lay aside their differences for a moment in order to accomplish some task at hand. All of those boundaries of notation and ritual are temporarily bracketed out, or perhaps it is more accurate to say that each person brings the full complexity of her many identities and selves and allows them to interact freely with others, rather than reducing everyone to one side or another of a simple boundary. Thus, rather than the hard barriers of notation or the permeable boundaries of ritual, we have intricate interactions between many possible boundaries. This is less a wall than the infinitely complex edge of a fractal whose convolutions never simplify into a simple line at any scale. Another image might be the sorts of boundaries that cross-cut a mosaic, perhaps even the ever-changing mosaic patterns of a kaleidoscope. This last image may be especially useful because its patterns evolve over time without ever exactly repeating; they are truly historical. Their rhythms are the pulse that grows out of the nature of the activity, but not the strict repetitions of meter, which create time but not historical change.

Our emphasis on experience draws on the writings of John Dewey, who taught us to pay greater heed to experience than to our preexisting perceptions, which could include both notational and ritual concepts. He tried to teach us to think in new ways, to think "reflectively," as he termed it—with a constant openness to the challenges of experience and change. Yet, he also cautioned:

> Reflective thinking is always more or less troublesome because it involves overcoming the inertia that inclines one to accept suggestions at their face value; it involves the willingness to endure a condition of mental unrest and disturbance. *Reflective thinking, in short, means judgment suspended during further inquiry, and suspense is likely to be somewhat painful.* . . . To maintain a state of doubt and to carry on a systematic and protracted inquiry—these are the essentials of thinking.[1]

At the end of this study of ambiguity and the different ways in which we confront it, we want to stress that such thinking through experience, suspending judgment even as one forms new conjectures, can potentially lead us to new forms of action.

Our encounter with the other, with the partially unknown, with the ambiguous, has the potential to open up new possibilities for understanding, self-reflection, and ultimately, for action. To realize this potential, however, we must be willing to recognize and accept the ambiguity that adheres to all forms of otherness. We must thus be open to the other, to the challenges to our boundaries, and to the difficulties of the dialogue that may ensue. Dialogue—genuine dialogue—exists only where, as Martin Buber taught us, "each of the participants really has in mind the other or others in their present and particular beings and turns to them with the intention of establishing a living mutual relation between himself and them."[2] Such mutuality implies as well our willingness to relinquish control of the developing encounter, creating an open-endedness that does not exist with either notation or ritual. While not negating ourselves, we must nevertheless abandon our inherent desire to control the situation and to order it according to our own dictates—we must be willing to live with ambiguity. This is not easily achieved. But it is not impossible, either.

The art of the encounter with the other, the openness to the transformative potential that this contains, actually constitutes experience itself.

Such experience differs greatly from the type of rational control and descriptive acumen that we identify with notational knowledge. We end with a presentation of a small "tool-kit" of possible ways to further such reflective thinking and openings to shared experience. These include:

- Holding all claims to absolute truth in abeyance. Many such claims, especially those that center on issues of morality and society, are irrelevant and often counterproductive for concrete action.
- Recognizing the partial nature of all understandings. David Hume's famous dictum "Explanation is where the mind rests" is never the place of full knowledge, but only of a purpose well served.
- Allowing experience to precede judgment. Bring in the minimum assumptions needed to get the job done, rather than a checklist of principles against which the experience itself is to be verified.
- Understanding knowledge to be *for* the achievement of some goal, rather than *of* any set of essential characteristics of the other, her dreams and desires. We should be careful to define this knowledge *for* in non-ideological terms, without reference to our own fantasies and fears.
- Distancing our own commitments (to our own well-being or the well-being of our group, for example) from our idea formations and explanations of the concrete other with whom we are in contact.

If we can keep these principles in mind and so maintain the importance of shared experience alongside both abstract thought and more communally bounded forms of ritual, we may well find the way for accepting and working with that ambiguity that inheres to all forms of order.

We are not claiming that humans can live without notation and its boundary-etching strategy for negating ambiguity. Speaking itself, that most human of activities, is impossible without the categories (semantics) and rules (syntax) of notation. Rather, we hope to have drawn attention to ritual and shared experience as alternative, non-notational mechanisms that allow us to accept ambiguity without succumbing to it completely. Even though ritual and shared experience differ in important ways, both share a commitment to action in the world. If notation serves to order knowledge *of* the world, ritual and shared experience instead offer knowledge *for* the world. We would like to suggest that in the arena of society and public policy, we might stand to gain by moving away from an idea *of* the other, and toward ideas *for* certain joint purposes.

When we try to explain a certain given reality only in terms of knowledge of the other, and that other is in so many ways different from us or threatening to us, the result often heightens social exclusion. That other person's difference appears so great, her world so monumentally unlike our own, that the default position can easily be to construct an almost impregnable cognitive and emotional barrier behind which the mind can rest in relative peace and security. The real experience of a transformative encounter, however, and of accepting the ambiguity that resides in the other, allows our goals to become knowledge for, which sidesteps these pitfalls to allow the construction of a shared world through shared action and experience.

Ritual and shared experience accomplish this in quite different ways. Ritual allows us to move regularly over a border, decreasing ambiguities in a way similar to notation, but forcing us to realize that boundaries are crossed, rather than letting us rest comfortably inside them. Like shared experience, ritual is oriented toward action more than toward defined knowledge. A ritual is successful because it has been performed properly in a particular time and space, not because people have understood it in a particular way. One can, of course, accrete notational information onto rituals (by learning catechisms, for instance), but many rituals around the world make no such demands. Instead, they demand performance—an acceptance of their social conventions. These ritualized features, we have argued, create the possibility for empathy and trust. Both empathy and trust require us to cross a boundary to the other, and in that sense differ greatly from the notational exercise of differentiating us from them.

Shared experience goes beyond the empathetic crossing of boundaries by putting those simple demarcations aside in favor of highly contextualized action toward an end. By itself, such a mechanism may not suffice to create a full society. Genuinely historical in the full sense of the word, it creates neither ritual's shared past and future through metrical repetition, nor notation's timeless unities. It takes place instead in the here and now, with all of the potential rewards and instabilities that implies.

Neither ritual nor notation is possible without shared experience. Periodic ritual renewals come precisely from the pressures of historical change, where shared experience leads to a revision of the ritual corpus. Notational systems often deal with change through more notation, that is, they give rules about how to change the rules. Yet the actual content of the new rules can never be foreseen by the old rules. The substance of notational change has to come from outside the system, from the struggles and hopes of shared experience and from the joint attempt to accomplish an end.

We cannot avoid the ambiguities that are inherent to the socially necessary process of drawing the boundaries between categories. In this book, our goal has been to imagine those boundaries in more than one way: the solid line of notation, the permeable membrane of ritualization, and the fractal complexity of shared experience. Each of those approaches moves us in quite different directions, and in ways that we did not entirely foresee as we began this book. The form of the boundary, for example, turns out to have intimate connections to the way in which time is structured, and that in turn plays back on how, if at all, we can cooperate or empathize across boundaries.

In the back of our minds at all times has been the pressing problem of pluralism, where the dominance of notational boundaries limits the ways that we think about how to live together with difference, and where the more unorthodox conceptions of ritualization and shared experience may offer us important resources. Ordering ambiguity is a crucial task, and these alternate ways of understanding boundaries may be key to living together with difference.

Notes

INTRODUCTION

1. Auguste Escoffier, *Le guide culinaire*, 4th ed., trans. H. L. Cracknell and R. J. Kaufmann (New York: Mayflower Books, 1921), 397.
2. Julia Child, Louisette Bertholle, and Simone Beck, *Mastering the Art of French Cooking*, vol. 1 (New York: Knopf, 1981), 258–261.

CHAPTER 1

1. A great deal has been written about this, with some argument about what the root note of the chord "really" is in this musical context. Wikipedia has a convenient summary, *Tristan Chord*, accessed August 17, 2009, http://en.wikipedia.org/wiki/Tristan_chord.
2. On constructivism in philosophy, see Nelson Goodman, *Of Mind and Other Matters, Ways of World Making* (Cambridge, MA: Harvard University Press, 1984) and *Languages of Art* (Indianapolis: Hackett Publishing, 1976).
3. Émile Durkheim and Marcel Mauss, *Primitive Classification* (Chicago: University of Chicago Press, 1963 [1903]), 4.
4. Émile Durkheim, *The Elementary Forms of Religious Life* (New York: Free Press, 1995 [1912]), 52, 62.
5. Claude Lévi-Strauss, *Introduction to a Science of Mythology*, vol. 1, *The Raw and the Cooked* (New York: Harper and Row, 1970), 279.
6. Lévi-Strauss, *The Raw and the Cooked*, 281.
7. Edmund Leach, "Anthropological Aspects of Language: Animal Categories and Verbal Abuse," in *New Directions in the Study of Language*, ed. Eric H. Lenneberg (Cambridge, MA: MIT Press, 1964), 23–63.
8. Mary Douglas, *Purity and Danger: An Analysis of Concepts of Pollution and Taboo* (London: Routledge, 1986), 41–57, 167–173.
9. Ibid., 130.

10. Paul Ricoeur, *The Symbolism of Evil* (New York: Harper and Row, 1967), 35.

11. Donald N. Levine, *The Flight from Ambiguity: Essays in Social and Cultural Theory* (Chicago: University of Chicago Press, 1985).

12. A. R. Radcliffe-Brown, "On Joking Relationships," in *Structure and Function in Primitive Society* (New York: Free Press, 1952), 90–104.

13. Keith H. Basso, "'To Give up on Words': Silence in Western Apache Culture," in *Language and Social Context*, ed. Pier Paolo Giglioli (New York: Penguin, 1972), 67–86.

14. See, e.g., Victor Turner, *The Ritual Process: Structure and Anti-Structure*, Symbol, Myth, and Ritual Series (Ithaca, NY: Cornell University Press, 1969).

15. Victor Turner, *Dramas, Fields, and Metaphors: Symbolic Action in Human Society* (Ithaca, NY: Cornell University Press, 1974), 243.

16. As recently as 1998, Mary Douglas reaffirmed the essential validity of this model, though questioning its validity for biblical rules of animal classification in the Book of Leviticus; *Leviticus as Literature* (Oxford: Oxford University Press, 1999), vii.

17. Cf. Else Frenkel-Brunswik, "Intolerance of Ambiguity as an Emotional and Perceptual Personality Variable," *Journal of Personality* XVIII (1949), 108–143.

18. Robert Merton, Sociological Ambivalence" in *Sociological Ambivalence and Other Essays* (New York: Free Press, 1976), 7. See also Ihor Zielyk, "On Ambiguity and Ambivalence," *Pacific Sociological Review* 9, no. 1 (Spring 1966), 57–64; Edgar Mills Jr. "Sociological Ambivalence and Social Order: The Constructive Uses of Normative Dissonance," *Sociology and Social Research* 67, no. 3 (1983), 279–287.

19. Merton, ibid., 6.

20. Ibid., 17.

21. Levine, *The Flight from Ambiguity: Essays in Social and Cultural Theory*, 12.

22. Theodor W. Adorno, E. Frenkel-Brunswik, and D. J. Levinson, *The Authoritarian Personality* (New York: Harper, 1950).

23. Turner did recognize an affiliation with post-modernism late in his career, e.g., Victor Turner, "The Anthropology of Performance," in *The Anthropology of Performance*, ed. Victor Turner (Baltimore, MD: PAJ Publications, 1988), 72–99.

24. Jacques Derrida, *Of Grammatology*, trans. Gayatri Chakravorty Spivak (Baltimore, MD: Johns Hopkins University Press, 1976 [1974]). For a very useful summary, see Terry Eagleton, *Literary Theory: An Introduction* (Minneapolis: University of Minnesota Press, 1983), 127–132.

25. See, for instance, Fish's discussion of "structures of interpretation." Stanley Fish, *Is There a Text in This Class? The Authority of Interpretative Communities* (Cambridge, MA: Harvard University Press, 1980).

26. One might relate this to Needham's analysis of Robert Knox's report on kings and beggars in seventeenth-century Ceylon. Both kings and beggars stood outside a finely honed hierarchy of social boundaries—kings because their power was absolute, and beggars because they were utterly cast out. Beyond boundaries, both could reportedly commit incest, which was completely abhorrent to the rest of society. See Rodney Needham, "Robert Knox and the Structure of

Absolutism." In Rodney Needham, *Exemplars* (Berkeley: University of California Press, 1985), 44–56.

27. D. W. Winnicott, *Playing and Reality* (New York: Routledge, 1971).

28. Sigmund Freud, *Civilization and Its Discontents*, vol. XXI, in *The Complete Psychological Works of Sigmund Freud* (London: Hogarth Press, 1961), 114.

29. Norbert Elias, *The Civilizing Process*, trans. Edmund Jephcott (New York: Urizen, 1978).

30. See, on this, M. Lichbach and A. Seligman, *Market and Community: The Basis of Social Order, Revolution and Relegitimation* (University Park: Pennsylvania State University Press, 2000).

31. *Oxford English Dictionary*, compact edition (Oxford: Oxford University Press, 1971), 68.

32. John Dewey, *The Quest for Certainty: A Study of the Relation of Knowledge and Action* (New York: Milton Balach, 1930), 17.

33. Ibid., 8.

34. Ibid., 21.

35. William Empson, *Seven Types of Ambiguity* (New York: New Directions, 1966), 5–6.

36. Ibid., 155.

37. Owen Barfield, *Poetic Diction: A Study in Meaning* (Middletown, CT: Wesleyan University Press, 1984), 115.

38. Ibid., 85–86.

39. George Lakoff and Mark Johnson, *Metaphors We Live By* (Chicago: University of Chicago Press, 1980), 3.

40. Roy A. Rappaport, *Ritual and Religion in the Making of Humanity* (Cambridge, UK: Cambridge University Press, 1999).

41. Ernst Cassirer, *The Philosophy of Symbolic Forms*: vol. 1, *On Language* (New Haven, CT: Yale University Press, 1965), 76.

42. Aspects of this renunciation correlate with what Victor Turner described in his concept of *communitas* (Turner, *The Ritual Process: Structure and AntiStructure*, Hawthorne, NY: Aldine de Gruyter, 1995), and Max Weber attempted to grasp in his idea of pure charisma (Weber, *Economy and Society*, vol. II, Berkeley, University of California Press, 1975, 1111–1145).

43. Heinz Hartmann, *Essays on Ego Psychology: Selected Problems in Psychoanalytic Theory* (New York: International Universities Press, 1965).

44. Marion Milner, "Acts of Symbolism in Comprehension of the Not-Self" *International Journal of Psychoanalysis* 33 (1952), 182.

45. Jones, "Theory of Symbolism" in his *Papers in Psychoanalysis* (London: Maresfield Reprints, 1948).

46. Milner, op cit., 189.

47. Roman Jakobson, "Linguistics and Poetics" in *Style in Language*, ed. Thomas Sebeok (Cambridge, MA: MIT Press, 1961), 350–377; Roland Barthes, *S/Z* (New York: Hill and Wang, 1974).

48. Joseph Kess and Ronald Hoppe, *Ambiguity in Psycholinguistics* (Amsterdam: J. Benjamins B.V., 1981), 14, 15.

49. Max Gluckman "Les Rites de Passage," in *Essays on the Ritual of Social Relations*, ed. Max Gluckman (Manchester: Manchester University Press, 1962), 1–52.

50. Dewey, op cit., 6.

51. Ibid.

52. Edgar Levenson, The *Ambiguity of Change* (New York: Basic Books, 1963), 122.

INTERLUDE: AMBIGUITY, ORDER, AND DEITY

1. Th. C. W. Oudemans and A. P. Lardinois, *Tragic Ambiguity: Anthropology, Philosophy and Sophocles' Antigone* (Leiden: Brill, 1987), 87.

2. Ibid., 58.

3. Jon Levinson, *Creation and the Persistence of Evil* (Princeton: Princeton University Press, 1988), 133.

4. Ibid., 14.

5. Benjamin Foster, *Before the Muses: An Anthology of Akkadian Literature.* (Bethesda, MD: CDL Press, 1996).

6. The translation of Job is that of Robert Gordis, one of the foremost students of the text, who published numerous studies of it. The translation of *The Bacchae* is that of G. S. Kirk (Cambridge, UK: Cambridge University Press, 1970).

7. On date of redaction, see R. Gordis, *The Book of God and Man.* (Chicago: University of Chicago Press, 1965), 20, 216–218.

8. On Job, see Louis Ginzburg, *Legends of the Jews*, vol. II (Philadelphia: Jewish Publication Society of America, 1913). On *The Bacchae*, see Charles Segal, *Dionysiac Poetics and Euripides' Bacchae* (Princeton: Princeton University Press, 1982); as well as the older R. P. Winnington-Ingram, *Euripides and Dionysus* (Cambridge, UK: Cambridge University Press, 1948).

9. Gordis, *The Book of God and Man*, 7, 55–64.

10. Horace Kallen wrote an interesting book in 1918, titled *The Book of Job as a Greek Tragedy* (New York: Hill and Wang, 1959). He raises the interesting, though generally discredited, hypothesis that the book of Job was, in fact, inspired by Euripidean tragedy. The thesis, however, has ancient provenance, as pointed out by George F. Moore; it was articulated by Theodore of Mopsuestia in the 5th century c.e. (Kallen, xxii). Our comparison is, of course, not trying to revive his hypothesis, but rather to point to similarities in *problematique* between the two works.

11. Winnington-Ingram, 1.

12. Segal, *Dionysiac Poetics and Euripides' Bacchae*, 4

13. Ibid., 48.

14. Walter Burkett, *Ancient Mystery Cults* (Cambridge, MA: Harvard University Press, 1987), 35.

15. Ibid., 22.

16. Segal, 213, 214.

17. Goodman, "Themes of Theodicy in the Exegesis of the Book of Job: Situating Saadiah's Reading in Its Historic and Philosophical Setting," 28–92, in his translated edition of *The Book of Theodicy—Translation and Commentary on the Book of Job by Saadiah Ben Joseph Al-Fayyumi* (New Haven, CT: Yale University Press, 1988), 33.

18. Ibid.

19. Maimonides, *The Guide of the Perplexed*, vol. 2 (Chicago: University of Chicago Press, 1963), 486–497.

20. See Nahum Glatzer (ed.), *The Dimensions of Job* (New York: Schocken Books, 1969); Ralphe Hone (ed.), *The Voice of the Whirlwind: The Book of Job* (San Francisco: Chandler Publishing, 1960); Horace Kallen, *The Book of Job as a Greek Tragedy* (New York: Hill and Wang, 1959); Gustavo Gutierrez, *On Job God-talk and the Suffering of the Innocent* (New York: Orbis Books, 1987).

21. Maimonides, *Guide*, 489.

22. *The Bacchae of Euripides*, op. cit., lines 699–712.

23. Ibid., lines 733–764.

24. Job 38:4–11.

25. Job 38:12–33.

26. Job 39:13–18.

27. Job 10:10–11.

28. Ginzburg, *Legends*, vol. 2, 225.

29. Glatzer, *Dimensions*. Already in the third century C.E., the story was understood as parable.

30. Maimonides, *Guide*, 487–490.

31. Otto Rank, *Myth of the Birth of the Hero* (Baltimore, MD: Johns Hopkins University Press, 2004).

32. Walter Burkett, *Savage Energies, Lessons of Myth and Ritual in Ancient Greece* (Chicago: University of Chicago Press, 2000), 9.

33. Ibid, 16.

34. Aristotle, *Poetics*, 6:22–29.

35. *Poetics*, 9:4.

36. On this notion, see Owen Barfield, *Poetic Diction: A Study in Meaning* (Middletown, CT: Wesleyan University Press, 1984).

CHAPTER 2

1. Herodotus, *The History*, trans. David Grene (Chicago: University of Chicago Press, 1987), 37–38.

2. Francois Hartog, *The Mirror of Herodotus: The Representation of the Other in the Writing of History* (Berkeley: University of California Press, 1988), 331.

3. Rahel Wasserfall, "Gender Encounters in America: An Outsider's View of Continuity and Ambivalence" in P. DeVita and J. Armstrong, eds. *Distant Mirrors: America as a Foreign Culture* (Belmont, CA: Wadsworth, 1993), 106.

4. Ibid.

5. Wilma Vollebergh, *The Limits of Tolerance*. PhD dissertation, Rijksuniversiteit te Utrecht, 1991.

6. Ibid., 138, 139.

7. Sigmund Freud, *Jokes and Their Relation to the Unconscious*, vol. 8 of *The Complete Psychological Works of Sigmund Freud* (New York: W. W. Norton, 1960 [1905]), 110–111.

8. Ibid., 110.

9. Ibid.

10. Umberto Eco, "The Frames of Comic 'Freedom'," in *Carnivale!*, ed. Thomas A. Sebeok (Berlin: Mouton, 1984), 1–10.

11. Umberto Eco, "Frames of Comic Freedom," 2.

12. Ibid., 8.

13. Ibid.

14. Brent Berlin and Paul Kay, *Basic Color Terms* (Berkeley: University of California Press, 1969).

15. John Henry Newman, *An Essay in Aid of a Grammar of Assent* (London: Longmans, Green, 1903), 52. Newman actually uses the term "notional," but means something very similar to our concept of notation.

16. Translated in Wing-tsit Chan, *A Source Book in Chinese Philosophy* (Princeton: Princeton University Press, 1963), 140.

17. Jalal al-Din Rumi, *The Essential Rumi*, trans. Coleman Barks and John Moyne (New York: HarperOne, 1997), 20.

18. Stephen Toulmin, *Cosmopolis: The Hidden Agenda of Modernity* (New York: Free Press, 1990), 24.

19. Ibid., 44.

20. Alain Besançon, *The Rise of the Gulag: Intellectual Origins of Leninism* (New York: Continuum, 1981), 29–30.

21. Lynn Hunt, *Politics, Culture, and Class in the French Revolution* (Berkeley: University of California Press, 1984), 75–77.

22. Hunt, *Politics, Culture, and Class in the French Revolution*, 106.

23. Mao Zedong, "Talks on the Yenan Forum on Literature and Art," in *Selected Readings from the Works of Mao Tse-tung* (Beijing: Foreign Languages Press, 1971 [1942]), 77.

24. Piero Weiss and Richard Taruskin, *Music in the Western World: A History in Documents* (Belmont, CA: Wadsworth, 1984), 212–219.

25. Gregory Bateson, *Communication: The Social Matrix of Psychiatry* (New York: W. W. Norton, 1951), 23.

26. Alfred Korzybski, *Science and Sanity: An Introduction to Non-Aristotelian Systems and General Semantics*, 3d ed. (Lakeville, CT: Institute of General Semantics, 1948 [1933]), 749.

27. Ibid., 751, emphasis in the original.

28. Ibid., 750, emphasis in the original.

29. Gregory Bateson, "Form, Substance and Difference," in *Steps to an Ecology of Mind* (New York: Ballantine, 1972), 448–465.

30. Laurence Schneider, *A Madman of Chu* (Berkeley: University of California Press, 1980). The authenticity of Qu's authorship of at least some of these poems has been questioned for 2,000 years, but the image of his poetic output in exile remains strong.

31. Larry Levine, *Highbrow/Lowbrow: The Emergence of Cultural Hierarchy in America* (Cambridge, MA: Harvard University Press, 1988).

32. Neil Sheehan, *A Bright Shining Lie: John Paul Vann and America in Vietnam* (New York: Vintage, 1989).

33. Michel Foucault, *The History of Sexuality*, vol. 1: *The Will to Knowledge* (London: Penguin, 1998 [1976]), 10–24.

34. Judith Butler, *Excitable Speech: A Politics of the Performative* (New York: Routledge, 1997).

35. Basil Bernstein, *Class, Codes and Control: Theoretical Studies Towards a Sociology of Language* (London: Routledge and Kegan Paul, 1971).

36. James Laver, *Costume and Fashion* (London: Thames and Hudson, 1982); L. De Hegermann-Linderncrone, *In the Courts of Memory 1858–1875; from Contemporary Letters* (Project Guttenberg e-book number 7044, 1912, released 2004, retrieved June 9, 2011).

37. Koerner, J. *The Reformation of the Image* (Chicago: University of Chicago Press, 2004).

38. Eisenstadt, S. N. "Ritualized Personal Relationships," *Man* 96 (1956), 90–95.

39. Paine, R. "Anthropological Approaches to Friendship" *Humanitas* 6 no. 2 (1970), 139–159.

40. D'Arcy, M. C., *The Mind and Heart of Love* (New York: Meridian, 1956).

41. Evans-Pritchard, E. E. "Zande Blood Brotherhood" *Africa* 6 (1933), 369–401.

42. Maine, Henry Sumner, *Ancient Law* (London: John Murray, 1861), 23, 24.

43. Ibid., 25, 26.

44. Jan Assman, *Moses the Egyptian: The Memory of Egypt in Western Monotheism.* (Cambridge, MA: Harvard University Press, 1997), 44–54.

45. This contrast between trust and confidence is taken from Adam Seligman, *The Problem of Trust* (Princeton: University Press, 1997).

46. Annette Baier, "Trust and AntiTrust," *Ethics* 96, no. 2 (1986), 231, 250.

47. See Adam Seligman, "Role Complexity, Risk and the Emergence of Trust," *Boston University Law Review* 81, no. 3 (June 2001), 619–634.

48. Adam Seligman, *The Problem of Trust* (Princeton: Princeton University Press, 1997), 44.

49. Levenson, *The Ambiguity of Change*, 81.

50. Seligman, *The Problem of Trust.*

51. Milner, "Acts of Symbolism in Comprehension," 182.

52. Donald A. Schön, *The Reflective Practitioner: How Professionals Think in Action* (New York: Basic Books, 1983).

53. Adam B. Seligman, Robert P. Weller, Michael Puett and Bennett Simon, *Ritual and Its Consequences: An Essay on the Limits of Sincerity* (Oxford: Oxford University Press, 2008).

INTERLUDE: THE ISRAELITE RED HEIFER AND THE EDGE OF POWER
IN CHINA

1. See, e.g., Mary Douglas, *Purity and Danger: An Analysis of Concepts of Pollution and Taboo* (London: Routledge, 1986), 130.

2. Jacob Milgrom, *Numbers: Ba-Midbar: The Traditional Hebrew Text with the New JPS Translation* (Philadelphia: Jewish Publication Society of America, 1990), 158–161.

3. See Baruch Levine, *Numbers 1–20: A New Translation with Introduction and Commentary* (New York: Anchor Bible, 1993), 468–478, on parallels with the ancient Near East cult of the dead. We should note that the ancient Israelites were not the only ones to observe such rituals. Herodotus recounts something similar in *The History*, Book II, par. 38.

4. This material on the dedicatory act of sprinkling the ashes in the direction of the Sanctuary and the role of the ritual in acknowledging death—and in a sense incorporating it within the parameters of the theodic system—was developed together with Nehemia Polen a number of years ago in the context of joint work on the ritual of the Red Heifer. It owes much to his cogent insights into the dynamics of priestly ritual in the Bible and we are grateful to him for sharing it.

5. See Jacob Neusner, *The Idea of Purity in Ancient Judaism* (Leiden: E. J. Brill, 1973); A. Buchler, *Studies in Sin and Atonement in the Rabbinic Literature of the First Century* (New York: Ktav, 1967); Jonathan Klawans, *Impurity and Sin in Ancient Judaism* (Oxford: Oxford University Press, 2000).

6. Horovitz, H. S., ed. *Siphre D'Be Rav (Siphre ad Numeros Adjecto Siphre Zutta)* (Jerusalem: Shalem Books, 1992), 300–306.

7. On sin offering and its relation to Temple sanctity, see Milgrom, *Numbers* (Philadelphia: Jewish Publication Society, 1990), Excursus #49, "The Effects of the Sinner upon the Sanctuary," 444–447.

8. G. William Skinner, "Marketing and Social Structure in Rural China," Parts 1–3, *Journal of Asian Studies* 24 (1964–1965), 3–43, 195–228, 363–399.

9. Clifford Geertz, *Negara: The Theatre State in Nineteenth-Century Bali* (Princeton: Princeton University Press, 1980), 11–15.

10. Emma Jinhua Teng, *Taiwan's Imagined Geography: Chinese Colonial Travel Writing and Pictures, 1683–1895* (Cambridge, MA: Harvard University Press, 2004), 41–42.

11. K. C. Chang traces this distinction between grain and complementary "dishes" all the way back to the Zhou, see K. C. Chang, *Early Chinese Civilization: Anthropological Perspectives* (Cambridge, MA: Harvard-Yenching Institute, 1976), 135.

12. Stuart E. Thompson, "Death, Food, and Fertility," *Death Ritual in Late Imperial and Modern China*, ed. James L. Watson and Evelyn S. Rawski (Berkeley: University of California Press, 1988), 71–108.

13. The nails, *ding*, are a pun on a word for sons.

14. James C. Scott, "Why Civilizations Can't Climb Hills: State and Non-State Spaces in Southeast Asian History," presentation at seminar series on Authoritarian Power (Boston University, April 2003).

15. Even the Hakka, who are universally classified as Han now but who often lived in mountain environments, were known for women who did not bind their feet and who worked in the fields.

16. Robert P. Weller, *Resistance, Chaos and Control in China: Taiping Rebels, Taiwanese Ghosts and Tiananmen* (London: Macmillan, 1994), 56–60.

17. Teng, *Taiwan's Imagined Geography: Chinese Colonial Travel Writing and Pictures, 1683–1895.*

18. Thompson, "Death, Food, and Fertility," 97.

CHAPTER 3

1. Roy A. Rappaport, *Ritual and Religion in the Making of Humanity* (Cambridge, UK: Cambridge University Press, 1999), 24.

2. Adam B. Seligman et al., *Ritual and Its Consequences: An Essay on the Limits of Sincerity* (Oxford: Oxford University Press, 2008), ch. 1.

3. Needless to add, shared empathy also invokes the limits of empathy and of those beyond the boundaries of empathy—who are often recalled at the same moment of ritual enactment (as in Jewish Passover and Christian Easter).

4. Wing-Tsit Chan, *A Source Book of Chinese Philosophy* (Princeton: Princeton University Press, 1963), 25.

5. Maimonides, *Mishneh Torah, Hilchot Tephila* (Jerusalem: n.p., 1986), 4.

6. Durkheim, Emile, *The Elementary Forms of Religious Life* (New York: The Free Press, 1995 [1912]).

7. Immanuel Kant, *Foundations of the Metaphysics of Morals*, trans. L. White Beck (Saddle River, NJ: Prentice Hall, 1989).

8. Thomas Nagel, *Moral Questions* (Cambridge, UK: Cambridge University Press, 1979), 25.

9. Funk & Wagnalls, *Standard Dictionary of the English Language* (New York, 1937).

10. We are grateful to Shlomo Fischer for this insight.

11. Henri Focillon, *The Life of Forms in Art* (New York: Wittenborn, 1948), 3.

12. Thomas Ogden, *The Matrix of the Mind* (Northvale, NJ: Aronson, 1986), 225.

13. Rosemary Dinnage, "A Bit of Light," in *Between Reality and Fantasy: Winnicott's Concepts of Transitional Objects and Phenomena*, eds. S. Grolnick et al. (London: Jason Aronson, 1978), 370.

14. Durkheim, *The Elementary Forms of Religious Life* (New York: The Free Press, 1995).

15. Ogden, op cit., 227–228.

16. Gilbert Rose, "The Creativity of Everyday Life," in *Between Reality and Fantasy: Winnicott's Concepts of Transitional Objects and Phenomena*, eds. S. Grolnick et al. (London: Jason Aronson, 1978), 355.

17. Rodney Needham, "Percussion and Transition." *Man* n.s. 2, no. 4 (1967), 606–614.

18. Abraham Joshua Heschel, *The Sabbath: Its Meaning for Modern Man* (New York: Farrar Straus and Young, 1951).

19. David Epstein, *Beyond Orpheus: Studies in Musical Structure* (Cambridge, MA: MIT Press, 1979), 55–65.

20. Note also the work of the sociologist Alfred Schutz on music, where he makes a similar point. "Making Music Together" in *Collected Papers*, vol. 2 (The Hague: Nijhoff, 1964), 159–178.

21. Maurice Bloch, "Symbols, Song, Dance and Features of Articulation," *European Journal of Sociology* 15, no. 1 (1974), 55–81.

22. M. Granet, *La pensée chinoise* (Paris: Michel, 1934).

23. George Kubler, *The Shape of Time* (New Haven, CT: Yale University Press, 1962), 100; M. L. von Franz, *Time: Rhythm and Repose* (London: Thames and Hudson, 1978), 11.

24. *Genesis* 8:21, 22. We use the translation and commentary in *JPS Torah Commentary: Genesis*, commentary by Nahum Sarna (Philadelphia: Jewish Publication Society of America, 1985).

25. Jean Piaget, *The Child's Conception of Time* (New York: Basic Books, 1970).

26. "Religious Rejections of the World and Their Direction," in *From Max Weber*, eds. H. H. Gerth and C. W. Mills (New York: Oxford University Press, 1946), 323–362; "The Social Psychology of World Religions," *From Max Weber*, 267–302.

27. E. Troeltsch, *The Social Teaching of the Christian Churches*, vol. 1. (Chicago: University of Chicago Press, 1981).

28. E. Voegelin, *The New Science of Politics* (Chicago: University of Chicago Press, 1952)

29. Gilles Deleuze, *Difference & Repetition* (New York: Columbia University Press, 1995), 70–74.

30. Freud, *Beyond the Pleasure Principle*, in the Standard Edition of the *Complete Psychological Works of Sigmund Freud*, vol. 18 (New York: W. W. Norton, 1955 [1920]), 15.

31. Charles Keil, "Motion and Feeling Through Music," in Charles Keil and Steven Feld, *Music Grooves* (Chicago: University of Chicago Press, 1994).

32. Søren Kierkegaard, *Repetition*, trans. E. H. Hong and H. V. Hong (Princeton: Princeton University Press, 1983), 170.

33. Ibid, 171.

34. Ibid, 149.

35. Ibid, 149.

36. Roy A. Rappaport, *Ritual and Religion in the Making of Humanity* (Cambridge, UK: Cambridge University Press, 1999), 24.

37. Ibid., 69–107.

38. Jacques Lacan, *The Four Fundamental Concepts of Psycho-Analysis* (London: Penguin, 1994), 60–61.

39. Ibid., 60.

40. Adam B. Seligman, Robert P. Weller, Michael Puett, and Bennett Simon, *Ritual and its Consequences: An Essay on the Limits of Sincerity* (New York: Oxford University Press, 2008).

41. Ibid., 93–97.

42. Umberto Eco, "The Frames of Comic Freedom," 2.
43. Moses Maimonides, *The Guide of the Perplexed*, vol. 2 (Chicago: University of Chicago Press, 1963), 526.
44. Seligman et al., ch. 2.

INTERLUDE: CROSSING THE BOUNDARY OF EMPATHY

1. Nick Thorpe, *'89: The Unfinished Revolution* (London: Reportage Press, 2009), 166.
2. Eliot Horowitz, *Reckless Rites: Purim and the Legacy of Jewish Violence* (Princeton: Princeton University Press, 2006).
3. As cited in H. N. Bialik and Y. H. Ravnitzky, *The Book of Legends*, trans. William Braude (New York: Schocken Books, 1992), 639.
4. H. S. Horovitz, ed., *Siphre D'Be Rav (Siphre ad Numeros Adjecto Siphre Zutta).* (Jerusalem: Shalem Books, 1992), 301.
5. Cited in Bialik and Ravnitzky, op. cit., 188.
6. Cited in Bialik and Ravnitzky, op. cit., 459–460.
7. E.g., Horovitz, *Siphre D'Be Rav*, op. cit., 305:13.
8. On the debate over how much Rabbinic sources actually reflect social conditions and concerns, see Jacob Neusner and Alan Avery-Peck, *Judaism in Late Antiquity Pt. III* (Leiden: E. J. Brill, 1995). On the view that the Babylonian Talmud reflects the view of Rabbinic elites rather than the masses, see Seth Schwartz, *Imperialism and Jewish Society 200 BCE to 640 CE* (Princeton: Princeton University Press, 2001).
9. See Aharon Lichtenstein, "Does Jewish Tradition Recognize an Ethic Independent of Halakha?" in *Modern Jewish Ethics: Theory and Practice*, ed. Marvin Fox (Columbus: Ohio State University Press, 1975), 62–87. See also Louis Newman, *Past Imperatives: Studies in the History and Theory of Jewish Ethics* (Albany: State University of New York Press, 1975).
10. Jehuda Halevi, *The Kuzari*, Pt. III, par. 53 (New York: Schocken, 1987).
11. We are grateful to Nehemia Polen for this insight on the relation of Rabbinic culture to Biblical text.
12. On the ritualized nature of Rabbinic writings, see Ishay Rosen-Zvi, *The Rite That Was Not: Temple, Midrash and Gender in Tractate Sotah* (Jerusalem: Magnes Press, 2008). Hebrew.
13. Arthur Waley, *The Analects of Confucius* (New York: Random House, 1938).
14. Robert M. Gimello, "Chang Shang-Ying on Wu-T'ai Shan," in *Pilgrims and Sacred Sites in China*, eds. Susan Naquin and Chün-fang Yü (Berkeley: University of California Press, 1992), 89–149; Pei-yi Wu, "An Ambivalent Pilgrim to T'ai Shan in the Seventeenth Century," in *Pilgrims and Sacred Sites in China*, eds. Susan Naquin and Yü Chün-fang (Berkeley: University of California Press, 1992), 65–88.

15. See, for instance, the classic works of Arthur Wolf, "Gods, Ghosts, and Ancestors," in *Religion and Ritual in Chinese Society*, ed. Arthur P. Wolf (Stanford: Stanford University Press, 1974), 131–182; and David K. Jordan, *Gods, Ghosts, and Ancestors: The Folk Religion of a Taiwanese Village* (Berkeley: University of California Press, 1972).

16. Meir Shahar and Robert P. Weller, "Introduction: Gods and Society in China," in *Unruly Gods: Divinity and Society in China*, eds. Meir Shahar and Robert P. Weller (Honolulu: University of Hawai'i Press, 1996), 1–36.

17. Note that even an ordinary meal of rice and side dishes combines the ideas of the center and the edge, if only in a small way, at most meals. Marrying also requires the center to risk something of the power of the edge, as it forces the lineage to accept an outsider.

18. For a further elaboration of this argument, see Adam B. Seligman et al., *Ritual and Its Social Consequences: An Essay on the Limits of Sincerity* (New York: Oxford University Press, 2008).

19. John Shepherd, *Statecraft and Political Economy on the Taiwan Frontier, 1600–1800* (Stanford: Stanford University Press, 1993), 190.

20. For more on these groups, see Donald S. Sutton, *Steps of Perfection: Exorcistic Performers and Chinese Religion in Twentieth-Century Taiwan* (Cambridge, MA: Harvard University Asia Center, 2003). For another case, including ties to local gangsters, see Avron Boretz, "Righteous Brothers and Demon Slayers: Subjectivities and Collective Identities in Taiwanese Temple Processions," in *Religion and the Formation of Taiwanese Identities*, eds. Paul R. Katz and Murray A. Rubenstein (New York: Palgrave Macmillan, 2003), 219–251.

21. See, for one of many possible examples, Thomas L. Friedman, *The World Is Flat: A Brief History of the Twenty-first Century* (New York: Farrar, Strauss and Giroux, 2005).

CHAPTER 4

1. Basil Bernstein, "A Sociolinguistic Approach to Socialization; with Some Reference to Educability," in *Directions in Sociolinguistics: The Ethnography of Communication*, eds. John L Gumpertz and Dell Hymes (New York: Holt, Rinehart and Winston, 1972), 474.

2. William Labov, "The Logic of Nonstandard English," in *Language and Social Context*, ed. Pier Paolo Giglioli (Harmondsworth, Middlesex, UK: Penguin, 1972), 192.

3. For a classic statement of this position, see Dell Hymes, "Toward Ethnographies of Communication: The Analysis of Communicative Events," in *Language and Social Context*, ed. Pier Paolo Giglioli (Harmondsworth, Middlesex, UK: Penguin, 1972), 21–44.

4. Mary Douglas, *Natural Symbols: Explorations in Cosmology* (New York: Random House, 1973), 50.

5. M. Sandel, *Liberalism and the Limits of Justice* (Cambridge: Cambridge University Press, 1998).

6. James C. Scott, *Seeing like a State: How Certain Schemes to Improve the Human Condition Have Failed* (New Haven, CT: Yale University Press, 1998).

7. For more detail on this, see Robert P. Weller, *Resistance, Chaos and Control in China: Taiping Rebels, Taiwanese Ghosts and Tiananmen* (London: Macmillan, 1994).

8. We should distinguish clearly between spirit possession and what we have been calling ritual. Ritualization, as we have been discussing it, involves a high degree of repetitive formalization and an acceptance of external convention, which is not the case with spirit possession.

9. Hans-Georg Gadamer, *Truth and Method* (New York: Continuum, 1975 [1960]), 311.

10. Roy A. Rappaport, *Ritual and Religion in the Making of Humanity* (Cambridge, UK: Cambridge University Press, 1999), 52–54.

11. Based on the field experiences of Tulasi Srinivas, personal communication.

12. They managed this, at least, for those Jews who did not follow another path that began at nearly the same time, which reworked the tradition into Christianity. See for example, Jonathan Boyarin, *Borderlines: The Partition of Judeo-Christianity.* (Philadelphia: University of Pennsylvania Press, 2004).

13. Chu Hsi, *Chu Hsi's Family Rituals: A Twelfth-Century Chinese Manual for the Performance of Cappings, Weddings, Funerals, and Ancestral Rites,* trans. Patricia Buckley Ebrey (Princeton: Princeton University Press, 1991), 3.

14. Marshall McLuhan, *Understanding Media: The Extensions of Man* (New York: Mentor, 1964).

15. Walter J. Ong, *The Presence of the Word: Some Prolegomena for Cultural and Religious History* (New Haven, CT: Yale University Press, 1967), 111.

16. Haym Soloveitchik, "Rupture and Reconstruction: The Transformation of Contemporary Orthodoxy," *Tradition* 28, no. 4 (Summer 1994), 2.

17. Ibid., 19

18. David Montgomery, *The Transmission of Religious and Cultural Knowledge and Potentiality in Practice: An Anthropology of Social Navigation in the Kyrgyz Republic.* Ph.D. dissertation, Boston University, 2007.

19. On center, see Edward Shils, *Center and Periphery: Essays in Macro Sociology* (Chicago: University of Chicago Press, 1975); Rudolph Arnheim, *The Power of the Center* (Berkeley: University of California Press, 1982).

20. Donald A. Schön, *The Reflective Practitioner: How Professionals Think in Action* (New York: Basic Books, 1983), 300.

21. Ibid., 43.

22. Ibid., 49–54.

23. Benoît Mandelbrot, "How Long Is the Coast of Britain? Statistical Self-Similarity and Fractional Dimension," *Science,* New Series, 156 (May 5, 1967), 636–638.

24. Donald A. Schön and Martin Rein, *Frame Reflection: Toward the Resolution of Intractable Policy Controversies* (New York: Basic Books, 1994).

25. Ibid., 176.
26. Ibid., 174.
27. Richard White, *The Middle Ground: Indians, Empires and Republics in the Great Lakes Region, 1650–1815* (Cambridge, UK: Cambridge University Press, 1991).
28. Ibid, 80.
29. Ibid.
30. Ibid.
31. Maurice Merleau-Ponty, "Indirect Language and the Voices of Silence," in M. Merleau-Ponty, *Signs* (Chicago: Northwestern University Press, 1964), 45–46.
32. Op cit.
33. Personal communication from a local Jordanian Army officer, who resided in Irbid (February 2003).

INTERLUDE: EXPERIENCE AND MULTIPLICITY

1. Aristotle, *Nicomachean Ethics*, Book V, x #7, lines 331–332 (New York: Oxford University Press, 2009).
2. See Albert R. Jonsen and Stephen Toulmin, *The Abuse of Casuistry* (Berkeley: University of California Press, 1990), 26–27; for a detailed comparison of different modes of knowledge in Aristotle, see Joseph Dunne, *Back to the Rough Ground: Practical Judgment and the Lure of Technique* (Notre Dame: University of Notre Dame Press, 1997).
3. Aristotle, *Nichomachean Ethics*, Book VI, ix, lines 8–9.
4. Joseph Dunne, *Back to the Rough Ground*, 305.
5. Or, as Dunne claims, virtue itself! Dunne, 264–267.
6. On the use of the term of work of ritual, see Jonathan Z. Smith, *To Take Place: Towards a Theory of Ritual* (Chicago: University of Chicago Press, 1987), 110.
7. Book VI, xiii, line 6.
8. Robert Cover, *Narrative, Violence and the Law: The Essays of Robert Cover* (Ann Arbor: University of Michigan Press, 1992), 95–96.
9. Ibid., 96.
10. Ibid.,101.
11. Ibid., 108.
12. *Tosephta Sanhedrin.*, M. S. Zuckermandel edition (Jerusalem: n.p., 1937 [1884]), 415.
13. Isadore Twersky, "The Shulkan Aruk: Enduring Code of Jewish Law," *Judaism*, 16, no. 2 (Spring 1967), 149.
14. See Moshe Halbertal, *People of the Book: Canon, Meaning and Authority* (Cambridge, MA: Harvard University Press, 1997), 100–119.
15. Ibid, 156.
16. See Gregg Stern, *Philosophy and Rabbinic Culture: Jewish Interpretation and Controversy in Medieval Languedoc* (London: Routledge, 2009).

17. This is shown in the monumental work by Shmuel Shilo, *Dina De-Malkhuta Dina [The Law of the State is the Law]* (Jerusalem: Academic Press, 1974).

18. Tur (Jacob ben Asher), *Hoshen Mishpat, Laws of Testimony* (Jerusalem: H. Vagshel, 1990), § 28.

19. According to Tur (Jacob ben Asher), *Hoshen Mishpat, Laws of Testimony* (Jerusalem: H. Vagshel, 1990), § 28.

20. See Jay Berkovitz, *Protocols of Justice: The Metz Rabbinic Court, 1771–1789* (Boston and Leiden: E. J. Brill, forthcoming).

21. George L. Mackay, *From Far Formosa: The Island, Its People and Missions* (New York: Fleming H. Revell, 1895), 129–131.

22. Robert P. Weller, "The Politics of Ritual Disguise: Repression and Response in Taiwanese Religion," *Modern China* 13 (1987), 17–39.

23. Weller, "The Politics of Ritual Disguise," op. cit.

24. They finally relented on this, trusting the researcher to maintain confidentiality.

25. Tik-sang Liu, "Associating Local Traditions with the State Apparatus: A Way of Revitalizing Popular Religion in South China," paper presented at the Workshop on "Religion" in China: Rethinking Indigenous and Imported Categories of Thought, Harvard University, 2005. Information also comes from discussion at that workshop.

26. Bingzhong Gao, "An Ethnography of a Building Both as Museum and Temple: On the Double-Naming Method as an Art of Politics," paper presented at the Annual Meeting of the American Anthropological Association, Washington, DC, December 2005; Liu, "Associating Local Traditions with the State Apparatus: A Way of Revitalizing Popular Religion in South China."

27. For a summary of this literature, and an approach more similar to ours, see Hans Steinmüller, "Communities of Complicity: Notes on State Formation and Local Sociality in Rural China," *American Ethnologist* 37, no. 3 (2010), 539–549. On collusion, see Zhou Xuegang, "The Institutional Logic of Collusion among Local Governments in China, *Modern China* 36 (2010), 47–78, and Kevin O'Brien's comment, "How Authoritarian Rule Works," *Modern China* 36 (2010), 79–86.

28. Rappaport, *Ritual and the Making of Humanity*.

29. E.g., Carl Schmitt, *The Concept of the Political* (Chicago: University of Chicago Press, 2006 [1927]); Hans Kelsen, *Pure Theory of Law* (Berkeley: University of California Press, 1978 [1934]).

30. Cover, *Narrative, Violence and the Law*, 255.

31. See Marie-Claire Foblets and Alison Dundes Renteln, *Multicultural Jurisprudence: Comparative Perspectives on the Cultural Defence* (Oxford: Hart Publishing, 2009), and Andre Hoekema and Wibo M. Van Rossum, "Empirical Conflict Rules in Dutch Legal Cases of Cultural Diversity," in *Cultural Diversity and the Law: State Responses from Around the World*, eds. M. C. Foblets, J.-F. Gaudreault-DesBiens, and A. Renteln (Bruxelles: Bruylant, 2010), 851–888.

32. John Dewey, *Democracy and Education* (New York: Dover Publications, 2004), 134.

33. Ibid., 137.

CONCLUSION

1. Dewey, John. *How We Think* (Boston: D. C. Heath, 1910), 13.

2. Martin Buber, *Between Man and Man* (Boston: Beacon Press, 1955), 19.

References

Adorno, Theodor W., E. Frenkel-Brunswik, and D. J. Levinson. *The Authoritarian Personality*. New York: Harper, 1950.

Aristotle. *Nicomachean Ethics*. New York: Oxford University Press, 2009.

———. *Poetics*. Ann Arbor: University of Michigan Press, 1967.

Arnheim, Rudolph. *The Power of the Center*. Berkeley: University of California Press, 1982.

Assman, Jan. *Moses the Egyptian: The Memory of Egypt in Western Monotheism*. Cambridge, MA: Harvard University Press, 1997.

Baier, Annette. "Trust and AntiTrust." *Ethics* 96, no. 2 (1986): 231, 250.

Barfield, Owen. *Poetic Diction: A Study in Meaning*. Middletown, CT: Wesleyan University Press, 1984.

Barthes, Roland. *S/Z*. New York: Hill and Wang, 1974.

Basso, Keith H. "'To Give up on Words': Silence in Western Apache Culture." In *Language and Social Context*, edited by Pier Paolo Giglioli, 67–86. New York: Penguin, 1972.

Bateson, Gregory. *Communication: The Social Matrix of Psychiatry*. New York: Norton, 1951.

———. "Form, Substance and Difference." In *Steps to an Ecology of Mind*. New York: Ballantine, 1972.

Berkovitz, Jay. *Protocols of Justice: The Metz Rabbinic Court, 1771–1789*. Boston: E. J. Brill, forthcoming.

Berlin, Brent, and Paul Kay. *Basic Color Terms*. Berkeley: University of California Press, 1969.

Bernstein, Basil. *Class, Codes and Control: Theoretical Studies Towards a Sociology of Language*. London: Routledge and Kegan Paul, 1971.

———. "A Sociolinguistic Approach to Socialization; with Some Reference to Educability." In *Directions in Sociolinguistics: The Ethnography of Communication*, edited by John L Gumpertz and Dell Hymes, 474. New York: Holt, Rinehart and Winston, 1972.

Besançon, Alain. *The Rise of the Gulag: Intellectual Origins of Leninism*. New York: Continuum, 1981.

Bialik, H. N., and Y.H. Ravnitzky, *The Book of Legends*. Translated by William Braude. New York: Schocken Books, 1992.

Bloch, Maurice. "Symbols, Song, Dance and Features of Articulation." *European Journal of Sociology* 15, no. 1 (1974): 55–81.

Boretz, Avron. "Righteous Brothers and Demon Slayers: Subjectivities and Collective Identities in Taiwanese Temple Processions." In *Religion and the Formation of Taiwanese Identities*, edited by Paul R. Katz and Murray A. Rubenstein, 219–251. New York: Palgrave Macmillan, 2003.

Boyarin, Jonathan. *Borderlines: The Partition of Judeo-Christianity*. Philadelphia: University of Pennsylvania Press, 2004.

Buber, Martin. *Between Man and Man*. Boston: Beacon Press, 1955.

Buchler, A. *Studies in Sin and Atonement in the Rabbinic Literature of the First Century*. New York: Ktav, 1967.

Burkett, Walter. *Ancient Mystery Cults*. Cambridge, MA: Harvard University Press, 1987.

———. *Savage Energies, Lessons of Myth and Ritual in Ancient Greece*. Chicago: University of Chicago Press, 2000.

Butler, Judith. *Excitable Speech: A Politics of the Performative*. New York: Routledge, 1997.

Cassirer, Ernst. *The Philosophy of Symbolic Forms*. Vol. 1 of *On Language*. New Haven, CT: Yale University Press, 1965.

Chan, Wing-tsit. *A Source Book in Chinese Philosophy*. Princeton, NJ: Princeton University Press, 1963.

Chang, K. C. *Early Chinese Civilization: Anthropological Perspectives*. Cambridge, MA: Harvard-Yenching Institute, 1976.

Child, Julia, Louisette Bertholle, and Simone Beck. *Mastering the Art of French Cooking*. Vol. 1. New York: Knopf, 1981.

Chu, Hsi. *Chu Hsi's Family Rituals: A Twelfth-Century Chinese Manual for the Performance of Cappings, Weddings, Funerals, and Ancestral Rites*. Translated by Patricia Buckley Ebrey. Princeton, NJ: Princeton University Press, 1991.

Cover, Robert. *Narrative, Violence and the Law: The Essays of Robert Cover*. Ann Arbor: University of Michigan Press, 1992.

D'Arcy, M.C. *The Mind and Heart of Love*. New York: Meridian, 1956.

De Hegermann-Linderncrone, L. "In the Courts of Memory 1858–1875." In *Contemporary Letters*. Project Guttenberg e-book 7044, 1912, released 2004 (retrieved June 9, 2011).

Deleuze, Gilles. *Difference and Repetition*. New York: Columbia University Press, 1995.

Derrida, Jacques. *Of Grammatology*. Translated by Gayatri Chakravorty Spivak. Baltimore, MD: Johns Hopkins University Press, 1976[1974].

Dewey, John. *How We Think*. Boston: D. C. Heath, 1910.

———. *The Quest for Certainty: A Study of the Relation of Knowledge and Action*. New York: Milton Balach, 1930.

————. *Democracy and Education.* New York: Dover Publications, 2004.

Dinnage, Rosemary. "A Bit of Light." In *Between Reality and Fantasy: Winnicott's Concepts of Transitional Objects and Phenomena,* edited by S. Grolnick and L. Barkin, 365–377. London: Jason Aronson, 1978.

Douglas, Mary. *Natural Symbols: Explorations in Cosmology.* New York: Random House, 1973.

————. *Purity and Danger: An Analysis of Concepts of Pollution and Taboo.* London: Routledge, 1986.

————. *Leviticus as Literature.* Oxford: Oxford University Press, 1999.

Dunne, Joseph. *Back to the Rough Ground: Practical Judgment and the Lure of Technique.* Notre Dame: University of Notre Dame Press, 1997.

Durkheim, Emile. *The Elementary Forms of Religious Life.* New York: The Free Press, 1995 [1912].

Durkheim, Emile, and Marcel Mauss. *Primitive Classification.* Chicago: University of Chicago Press, 1963 [1903].

Eagleton, Terry. *Literary Theory: An Introduction.* Minneapolis: University of Minnesota Press, 1983.

Eco, Umberto. "The Frames of Comic 'Freedom.'" In *Carnivale!,* edited by Thomas A. Sebeok, 1–10. Berlin: Mouton, 1984.

Eisenstadt, S. N. "Ritualized Personal Relationships." *Man* 96 (1956): 90–95.

Elias, Norbert. *The Civilizing Process.* Translated by Edmund Jephcott. New York: Urizen, 1978.

Empson, William. *Seven Types of Ambiguity.* New York: New Directions, 1966.

Epstein, David. *Beyond Orpheus: Studies in Musical Structure.* Cambridge, MA: MIT Press, 1979.

Escoffier, Auguste. *Le guide culinaire.* 4th ed. Translated by H. L. Cracknell and R. J. Kaufmann. New York: Mayflower Books, 1921.

Euripides. *The Bacchae.* Translated by G. S. Kirk. Cambridge, UK: Cambridge University Press, 1970.

Evans-Pritchard, E. E. "Zande Blood Brotherhood." *Africa* 6 (1933): 369–401.

Fish, Stanley. *Is There a Text in This Class? The Authority of Interpretative Communities.* Cambridge, MA: Harvard University Press, 1980.

Foblets, Marie-Claire, and Alison Dundes Renteln. *Multicultural Jurisprudence: Comparative Perspectives on the Cultural Defence.* Oxford: Hart Publishing, 2009.

Focillon, Henri. *The Life of Forms in Art.* New York: Wittenborn, 1948.

Foster, Benjamin. *Before the Muses: An Anthology of Akkadian Literature.* Bethesda, MD: CDL Press, 1996.

Foucault, Michel. *The History of Sexuality.* Vol. 1 of *The Will to Knowledge.* London: Penguin, 1998 [1976].

Frenkel-Brunswik, Else. "Intolerance of Ambiguity as an Emotional and Perceptual Personality Variable." *Journal of Personality* 18 (1949): 108–143.

Freud, Sigmund. *Civilization and Its Discontents.* Vol. 21 of *The Complete Psychological Works of Sigmund Freud.* London: Hogarth Press, 1961.

——. *Jokes and Their Relation to the Unconscious*. Vol. 8 of *The Complete Psychological Works of Sigmund Freud*. New York: W. W. Norton, 1960 [1905].

——. *Beyond the Pleasure Principle*. Vol. 18 of *The Complete Psychological Works of Sigmund Freud*. New York: W. W. Norton, 1955 [1920].

Friedman, Thomas L. *The World Is Flat: A Brief History of the Twenty-First Century*. New York: Farrar, Strauss and Giroux, 2005.

Gadamer, Hans-Georg. *Truth and Method*. New York: Continuum, 1975 [1960].

Gao, Bingzhong. "An Ethnography of a Building Both as Museum and Temple: On the Double-Naming Method as an Art of Politics." Paper presented at the Annual Meeting of the American Anthropological Association. Washington, DC, December 2005.

Geertz, Clifford. *Negara: The Theatre State in Nineteenth-Century Bali*. Princeton, NJ: Princeton University Press, 1980.

Gimello, Robert M. "Chang Shang-Ying on Wu-T'ai Shan." In *Pilgrims and Sacred Sites in China*, edited by Susan Naquin and Chün-fang Yü, 89–149. Berkeley: University of California Press, 1992.

Ginzburg, Louis. *Legends of the Jews*. Vol. 2. Philadelphia: Jewish Publication Society of America, 1913.

Glatzer, Nahum, ed. *The Dimensions of Job*. New York: Schocken Books, 1969.

Gluckman, Max. "Les Rites de Passage." In *Essays on the Ritual of Social Relations*, edited by Max Gluckman, 1–52. Manchester: Manchester University Press, 1962.

Goodman, Nelson. *Languages of Art*. Indianapolis, IN: Hackett Publishing, 1976.

——. *Of Mind and Other Matters, Ways of World Making*. Cambridge, MA: Harvard University Press, 1984.

Gordis, R. *The Book of God and Man*. Chicago: University of Chicago Press, 1965.

Granet, M. *La pensée chinoise*. Paris: Michel, 1934.

Gutierrez, Gustavo. *On Job God-talk and the Suffering of the Innocent*. New York: Orbis Books, 1987.

Halbertal, Moshe. *People of the Book: Canon, Meaning and Authority*. Cambridge, MA: Harvard University Press, 1997.

Halevi, Jehuda. *The Kuzari*. Part 3. New York: Schocken, 1987.

Hartmann, Heinz. *Essays on Ego Psychology: Selected Problems in Psychoanalytic Theory*. New York: International Universities Press, 1965.

Hartog, François. *The Mirror of Herodotus: The Representation of the Other in the Writing of History*. Berkeley: University of California Press, 1988.

Heschel, Abraham Joshua. *The Sabbath: Its Meaning for Modern Man*. New York: Farrar, Straus and Young, 1951.

Herodotus. *The History*. Translated by David Grene. Chicago: University of Chicago Press, 1987.

Hoekema, Andre, and Wibo M. Van Rossum. "Empirical Conflict Rules in Dutch Legal Cases of Cultural Diversity." In *Cultural Diversity and the Law: State Responses from Around the World*, edited by M. C. Foblets, J.-F. Gaudreault-DesBiens, and A. Renteln, 851–888. Brussels: Bruylant, 2010.

Hone, Ralph E., ed. *The Voice Out of the Whirlwind: The Book of Job.* San Francisco: Chandler, 1960.

Horovitz, H. S., ed. *Siphre D'Be Rav (Siphre ad Numeros Adjecto Siphre Zutta).* Jerusalem: Shalem Books, 1992.

Horowitz, Eliot. *Reckless Rites: Purim and the Legacy of Jewish Violence.* Princeton, NJ: Princeton University Press, 2006.

Hunt, Lynn. *Politics, Culture, and Class in the French Revolution.* Berkeley: University of California Press, 1984.

Hymes, Dell. "Toward Ethnographies of Communication: The Analysis of Communicative Events." In *Language and Social Context,* edited by Pier Paolo Giglioli, 21–44. Harmondsworth, UK: Penguin, 1972.

Jakobson, Roman. "Linguistics and Poetics." In *Style in Language,* edited by Thomas Sebeok, 350–377. Cambridge, MA: MIT Press, 1961.

Jones, Ernst. *Papers in Psychoanalysis.* London: Maresfield Reprints, 1948.

Jonsen, Albert R., and Stephen Toulmin. *The Abuse of Casuistry.* Berkeley: University of California Press, 1990.

Jordan, David K. *Gods, Ghosts, and Ancestors: The Folk Religion of a Taiwanese Village.* Berkeley: University of California Press, 1972.

JPS Torah Commentary: Genesis. Commentary by Nahum Sarna. Philadelphia: Jewish Publication Society of America, 1985.

Kallen, Horace. *The Book of Job as a Greek Tragedy.* New York: Hill and Wang, 1959 [1918].

Kant, Immanuel. *Foundations of the Metaphysics of Morals.* Translated by L. White Beck. Saddle River, NJ: Prentice Hall, 1989.

Keil, Charles. "Motion and Feeling Through Music." In *Music Grooves,* edited by Charles Keil and Steven Feld, 53–76. Chicago: University of Chicago Press, 1994.

Kelsen, Hans. *Pure Theory of Law.* Berkeley: University of California Press, 1978 [1934].

Kess, Joseph, and Ronald Hoppe. *Ambiguity in Psycholinguistics.* Amsterdam: J. Benjamins B.V., 1981.

Kierkegaard, Søren. *Repetition.* Translated by Edna H. Hong and Howard V. Hong. Princeton, NJ: Princeton University Press, 1983.

Klawans, Jonathan. *Impurity and Sin in Ancient Judaism.* Oxford: Oxford University Press, 2000.

Koerner, J. *The Reformation of the Image.* Chicago: University of Chicago Press, 2004.

Korzybski, Alfred. *Science and Sanity: An Introduction to Non-Aristotelian Systems and General Semantics.* 3rd ed. Lakeville, CT: Institute of General Semantics, 1948 [1933].

Kubler, George. *The Shape of Time.* New Haven, CT: Yale University Press, 1962.

Labov, William. "The Logic of Nonstandard English." In *Language and Social Context,* edited by Pier Paolo Giglioli, 192. Harmondsworth, UK: Penguin, 1972.

Lacan, Jacques. *The Four Fundamental Concepts of Psycho-Analysis.* London: Penguin, 1994.

Lakoff, George, and Mark Johnson. *Metaphors We Live By*. Chicago: University of Chicago Press, 1980.

Laver, James. *Costume and Fashion*. London: Thames and Hudson, 1982.

Leach, Edmund. "Anthropological Aspects of Language: Animal Categories and Verbal Abuse." In *New Directions in the Study of Language*, edited by Eric H. Lenneberg, 23–63. Cambridge, MA: MIT Press, 1964.

———. *Culture and Communication: The Logic by Which Symbols Are Connected: An Introduction to the Use of Structuralist Analysis in Social Anthropology, Themes in the Social Sciences*. Cambridge: Cambridge University Press, 1976.

Levenson, Edgar. *The Ambiguity of Change*. New York: Basic Books, 1963.

Levine, Baruch. *Numbers 1–20: A New Translation with Introduction and Commentary*. New York: Anchor Bible, 1993.

Levine, Donald N. *The Flight from Ambiguity: Essays in Social and Cultural Theory*. Chicago: University of Chicago Press, 1985.

Levine, Larry. *Highbrow/Lowbrow: The Emergence of Cultural Hierarchy in America*. Cambridge, MA: Harvard University Press, 1988.

Levinson, Jon. *Creation and the Persistence of Evil*. Princeton, NJ: Princeton University Press, 1988.

Lévi-Strauss, Claude. *Introduction to a Science of Mythology*. Vol. 1 of *The Raw and the Cooked*. New York: Harper and Row, 1970.

Lichbach. M., and A. Seligman. *Market and Community: The Basis of Social Order, Revolution and Relegitimation*. University Park: Pennsylvania State University Press, 2000.

Lichtenstein, Aharon. "Does Jewish Tradition Recognize an Ethic Independent of Halakha?" In *Modern Jewish Ethics: Theory and Practice*, edited by Marvin Fox, 62–87. Columbus: Ohio State University Press, 1975.

Liu, Tik-sang. "Associating Local Traditions with the State Apparatus: A Way of Revitalizing Popular Religion in South China." Paper presented at the Workshop on "Religion" in China: Rethinking Indigenous and Imported Categories of Thought. Harvard University, 2005.

Mackay, George L. *From Far Formosa: The Island, Its People and Missions*. New York: Fleming H. Revell, 1895.

Maimonides, Moses. *Mishneh Torah, Hilchot Tephila*. Jerusalem: n.p., 1986 (Hebrew).

———. *The Guide of the Perplexed*. Vol. 2. Chicago: University of Chicago Press, 1963.

Maine, Henry Sumner. *Ancient Law*. London: John Murray, 1861.

Mandelbrot, Benoît. "How Long Is the Coast of Britain? Statistical Self-Similarity and Fractional Dimension." *Science, New Series* 156 (May 5, 1967): 636–638.

Mao, Zedong. "Talks on the Yenan Forum on Literature and Art." In *Selected Readings from the Works of Mao Tse-tung*. Beijing: Foreign Languages Press, 1971 [1942].

McLuhan, Marshall. *Understanding Media: The Extensions of Man*. New York: Mentor, 1964.

Merleau-Ponty, Maurice. "Indirect Language and the Voices of Silence." In M. Merleau-Ponty, *Signs*, 45–46. Chicago: Northwestern University Press, 1964.

Merton, Robert. *Sociological Ambivalence and Other Essays.* New York: Free Press, 1976.

Milgrom, Jacob. *Numbers: Ba-Midbar: The Traditional Hebrew Text with the New JPS Translation.* Philadelphia: Jewish Publication Society of America, 1990.

Mills, Edgar W., Jr. "Sociological Ambivalence and Social Order: The Constructive Uses of Normative Dissonance." *Sociology and Social Research* 67, no. 3 (1983): 279–287.

Milner, Marion. "Acts of Symbolism in Comprehension of the Not-Self." *International Journal of Psychoanalysis* 33 (1952): 182.

Montgomery, David. "The Transmission of Religious and Cultural Knowledge and Potentiality in Practice: An Anthropology of Social Navigation in the Kyrgyz Republic." Ph.D. dissertation, Boston University, 2007.

Nagel, Thomas. *Moral Questions.* Cambridge, UK: Cambridge University Press, 1979.

Needham, Rodney. "Percussion and Transition." *Man* 2, no. 4 (1967): 606–14.

———. *Exemplars.* Berkeley: University of California Press, 1985.

Neusner, Jacob. *The Idea of Purity in Ancient Judaism.* Leiden: E. J. Brill, 1973.

Neusner, Jacob, and Alan Avery-Peck. *Judaism in Late Antiquity.* Part 3. Leiden: E. J. Brill, 1995.

Newman, John Henry. *An Essay in Aid of a Grammar of Assent.* London: Longmans, Green, 1903.

Newman, Louis. *Past Imperatives: Studies in the History and Theory of Jewish Ethics.* Albany: State University of New York Press, 1975.

O'Brien, Kevin. "How Authoritarian Rule Works." Comment. *Modern China* 36 (2010): 79–86.

Ogden, Thomas. *The Matrix of the Mind.* Northvale, NJ: Aronson, 1986.

Ong, Walter J. *The Presence of the Word: Some Prolegomena for Cultural and Religious History.* New Haven, CT: Yale University Press, 1967.

Oudemans, Th. C.W., and A.P. Lardinois. *Tragic Ambiguity: Anthropology, Philosophy and Sophocles' Antigone.* Leiden: E. J. Brill, 1987.

Oxford English Dictionary. Compact edition. Oxford: Oxford University Press, 1971.

Paine, R. "Anthropological Approaches to Friendship." *Humanitas* 6, no. 2 (1970): 139–159.

Piaget, Jean. *The Child's Conception of Time.* New York: Basic Books, 1970.

Qian, Yiben. "Xiangchao, juan 1." Reprinted in *Si Ku Quan Shu Cun Mu Cong Shu, Jing Bu.* Vol. 14. Jinan: Qi Lu Shu She Chubanshe, 1997.

Radcliffe-Brown, A. R., *Structure and Function in Primitive Society.* New York: Free Press, 1952.

Rank, Otto. *Myth of the Birth of the Hero.* Baltimore, MD: Johns Hopkins University Press, 2004.

Rappaport, Roy A. *Ritual and Religion in the Making of Humanity.* Cambridge, UK: Cambridge University Press, 1999.

Ricoeur, Paul. *The Symbolism of Evil.* New York: Harper and Row, 1967.

Rose, Gilbert. "The Creativity of Everyday Life." In *Between Reality and Fantasy: Winnicott's Concepts of Transitional Objects and Phenomena*, edited by S. Grolnick and L. Barkin, 347–361. London: Jason Aronson, 1978.

Rosen-Zvi, Ishay. *The Rite That Was Not: Temple, Midrash and Gender in Tractate Sotah.* In Hebrew. Jerusalem: Magnes Press, 2008.

Rumi, Jalal al-Din. *The Essential Rumi.* Translated by Coleman Barks and John Moyne. New York: HarperOne, 1997.

Saadiah, Ben Joseph Al-Fayyumi. *The Book of Theodicy: Translation and Commentary on the Book of Job by Saadiah Ben Joseph Al-Fayyumi.* Translated by L. E. Goodman. New Haven, CT: Yale University Press, 1988.

Sandel, M. *Liberalism and the Limits of Justice.* Cambridge, UK: Cambridge University Press, 1998.

Schmitt, Carl. *The Concept of the Political.* Chicago: University of Chicago Press, 2006[1927].

Schneider, Laurence. *A Madman of Chu.* Berkeley: University of California Press, 1980.

Schön, Donald A. *The Reflective Practitioner: How Professionals Think in Action.* New York: Basic Books, 1983.

Schön, Donald A., and Martin Rein. *Frame Reflection: Toward the Resolution of Intractable Policy Controversies.* New York: Basic Books, 1994.

Schutz, Alfred. "Making Music Together." Vol. 2 of *Collected Papers.* The Hague: Nijhoff, 1964.

Schwartz, Seth. *Imperialism and Jewish Society, 200 BCE to 640 CE.* Princeton, NJ: Princeton University Press, 2001.

Scott, James C. *Seeing like a State: How Certain Schemes to Improve the Human Condition Have Failed.* New Haven, CT: Yale University Press, 1998.

———. "Why Civilizations Can't Climb Hills: State and Non-State Spaces in Southeast Asian History." Presentation at seminar series on Authoritarian Power, Boston University, April 2003.

Segal, Charles. *Dionysiac Poetics and Euripides' Bacchae.* Princeton, NJ: Princeton University Press, 1982.

Seligman, Adam B. *The Problem of Trust.* Princeton, NJ: Princeton University Press, 1997.

———. "Role Complexity, Risk and the Emergence of Trust." *Boston University Law Review* 81, no. 3 (June 2001): 619–634.

Seligman, Adam B., Robert P. Weller, Michael Puett, and Bennett Simon. *Ritual and Its Consequences: An Essay on the Limits of Sincerity.* New York: Oxford University Press, 2008.

Shahar, Meir, and Robert P. Weller. "Introduction: Gods and Society in China." In *Unruly Gods: Divinity and Society in China*, edited by Meir Shahar and Robert P. Weller, 1–36. Honolulu: University of Hawai'i Press, 1996.

Sheehan, Neil. *A Bright Shining Lie: John Paul Vann and America in Vietnam.* New York: Vintage, 1989.

Shepherd, John. *Statecraft and Political Economy on the Taiwan Frontier, 1600–1800.* Stanford: Stanford University Press, 1993.

Shilo, Shmuel. *Dina De-Malkhuta Dina [The Law of the State Is the Law]*. Jerusalem: Academic Press, 1974 (Hebrew).

Shils, Edward. *Center and Periphery: Essays in Macro Sociology*. Chicago: University of Chicago Press, 1975.

Skinner, G. William. "Marketing and Social Structure in Rural China." *Journal of Asian Studies* 24 (1964–1965): 3–43, 195–228, 363–399.

Smith, Jonathan Z. *To Take Place: Towards a Theory of Ritual*. Chicago: University of Chicago Press, 1987.

Soloveitchik, Haym. "Rupture and Reconstruction: The Transformation of Contemporary Orthodoxy." *Tradition* 28, no. 4 (Summer 1994): 2.

Standard Dictionary of the English Language. New York: Funk and Wagnalls, 1937.

Steinmüller, Hans. "Communities of Complicity: Notes on State Formation and Local Sociality in Rural China." *American Ethnologist* 37, no. 3 (2010): 539–549.

Stern, Gregg. *Philosophy and Rabbinic Culture: Jewish Interpretation and Controversy in Medieval Languedoc*. London: Routledge, 2009.

Sutton, Donald S. *Steps of Perfection: Exorcistic Performers and Chinese Religion in Twentieth-Century Taiwan*. Cambridge, MA: Harvard University Asia Center, 2003.

Teng, Emma Jinhua. *Taiwan's Imagined Geography: Chinese Colonial Travel Writing and Pictures, 1683–1895*. Cambridge, MA: Harvard University Press, 2004.

Thompson, Stuart E. "Death, Food, and Fertility." In *Death Ritual in Late Imperial and Modern China*, edited by James L. Watson and Evelyn S. Rawski, 71–108. Berkeley: University of California Press, 1988.

Thorpe, Nick. *'89: The Unfinished Revolution*. London: Reportage Press, 2009.

Tosephta Sanhedrin. M.S. Zuckermandel edition. Jerusalem: n.p., 1937 [1884].

Toulmin, Stephen. *Cosmopolis: The Hidden Agenda of Modernity*. New York: Free Press, 1990.

Tristan Chord. Wikipedia, accessed 17 August 2009, http://en.wikipedia.org/wiki/Tristan_chord.

Troeltsch, E. *The Social Teaching of the Christian Churches*. Vol. 1. Chicago: University of Chicago Press, 1981.

Tur (Jacob ben Asher). *Hoshen Mishpat, Laws of Testimony*. Jerusalem: H. Vagshel, 1990.

Turner, Victor. *The Ritual Process: Structure and Anti-Structure, Symbol, Myth, and Ritual Series*. Ithaca, NY: Cornell University Press, 1969.

———. *Dramas, Fields, and Metaphors: Symbolic Action in Human Society*. Ithaca, NY: Cornell University Press, 1974.

———. *The Anthropology of Performance*. Baltimore: PAJ Publications, 1988.

———. *The Ritual Process: Structure and Anti-Structure*. Hawthorne, NY: Aldine de Gruyter, 1995.

Twersky, Isadore. "The Shulkan Aruk: Enduring Code of Jewish Law." *Judaism* 16, no. 2 (Spring 1967): 149.

Voegelin, E. *The New Science of Politics*. Chicago: University of Chicago Press, 1952.

Vollebergh, Wilma. "The Limits of Tolerance." Ph.D. dissertation. Utrecht: Rijksuniversiteit te Utrecht, 1991.

von Franz, M.L. *Time: Rhythm and Repose*. London: Thames and Hudson, 1978.

Waley, Arthur. *The Analects of Confucius*. New York: Random House, 1938.

Wasserfall, Rahel. "Gender Encounters in America: An Outsider's View of Continuity and Ambivalence." In *Distant Mirrors: America as a Foreign Culture*, edited by P. DeVita and J. Armstrong, 106. Belmont, CA: Wadsworth, 1993.

Weber, Max. *Economy and Society*. Vol. 2. Berkeley: University of California Press, 1975.

———. "Religious Rejections of the World and their Direction." In *From Max Weber*, edited by H. H. Gerth and C. Wright Mills, 323–362. New York: Oxford University Press, 1946.

———. "The Social Psychology of World Religions." In *From Max Weber*, edited by H. H. Gerth and C. Wright Mills, 267–301. New York: Oxford University Press, 1946.

Weiss, Piero, and Richard Taruskin. *Music in the Western World: A History in Documents*. Belmont, CA: Wadsworth, 1984.

Weller, Robert P. "The Politics of Ritual Disguise: Repression and Response in Taiwanese Religion." *Modern China* 13 (1987): 17–39.

———. *Resistance, Chaos and Control in China: Taiping Rebels, Taiwanese Ghosts and Tiananmen*. London: Macmillan, 1994.

White, Richard. *The Middle Ground: Indians, Empires and Republics in the Great Lakes Region, 1650–1815*. Cambridge, UK: Cambridge University Press, 1991.

Winnicott, D. W. *Playing and Reality*. New York: Routledge, 1971.

Winnington-Ingram, R. P. *Euripides and Dionysus*. Cambridge, UK: Cambridge University Press, 1948.

Wolf, Arthur. "Gods, Ghosts, and Ancestors." In *Religion and Ritual in Chinese Society*, edited by Arthur P. Wolf, 131–182. Stanford: Stanford University Press, 1974.

Wu, Pei-yi. "An Ambivalent Pilgrim to T'ai Shan in the Seventeenth Century." In *Pilgrims and Sacred Sites in China*, edited by Susan Naquin and Chün-fang Yü, 65–88. Berkeley: University of California Press, 1992.

Zhou, Xuegang. "The Institutional Logic of Collusion among Local Governments in China." *Modern China* 36 (2010): 47–78.

Zielyk, Ihor. "On Ambiguity and Ambivalence." *Pacific Sociological Review* 9, no. 1 (Spring 1966): 57–64.

Index

Note: Page numbers in *italics* refer to illustrations.

CPSIA information can be obtained at www.ICGtesting.com
Printed in the USA
BVOW02s2111130415

395984BV00001B/3/P